Warrior of Oulart Hill

MICK JACOB

WITH ALAN AHERNE

www.**HERO**BOOKS.digital

HEROBOOKS

PUBLISHED BY HERO BOOKS
1 WOODVILLE GREEN
LUCAN
CO. DUBLIN
IRELAND

Hero Books is an imprint of Umbrella Publishing
First Published 2021
Copyright © Mick Jacob and Alan Aherne 2021
All rights reserved

ISBN 9781910827307

Cover design and formatting: jessica@viitaladesign.com
Ebook formatting: www.ebooklaunch.com
Photographs: The Jacob family collection, Sportsfile, Ed Rowsome,
Wexford Photos
and People Newspapers Wexford

Dedication

To the memory of my loving
parents George and Ellen,
and my ever-supportive uncles
Mikie and Owen Kinsella

Contents

« ACKNOWLEDGEMENTS »

MY FIRST WORDS of deepest gratitude must go to my loving parents George and Ellen, who created a happy home for me and my siblings. Thank you also to my brothers Robbie and Christy, and my sister Bridie, who were always there for me and to my uncles Mikie and Owen Kinsella, who provided practical love and care following the untimely death of our father, and later throughout my life. A special word of appreciation to Robbie, who sat with us during the interviews for this book and provided lots of forgotten details.

Hurling has been a huge part of my life and has brought great joy and satisfaction, coupled with tough challenges and disappointments. To those who helped and accompanied me on my hurling journey, I am forever grateful. Thank you to the many club officials, mentors, coaches, trainers and players, who have served Oulart-The Ballagh so faithfully. And thanks also to the Wexford GAA players and officials who did likewise during my county career.

Thank you to Liam Hayes of Hero Books, who considered my life story and my hurling career worthy of publication, and to Alan Aherne for his endless patience and professionalism in researching and writing this story. We had known Alan from his sports journalism with *The People Group* and from his long involvement with Wexford GAA and camogie, but with this project we came to know and admire him as a friend, while his skill in presenting the story of an ordinary life leads me to believe that it will not be his last venture into biography.

My wife and best friend Breda has been by my side for the best part of half a century. She knows I love her dearly and I really appreciate the care, support and affection she has always provided. She is a fantastic wife, mother and grandmother, and she wasn't 'a bad little camogie player' either (her words!). Her support, encouragement and co-operation enabled me to prolong my involvement with my club and county. We have created great memories together and look forward to many more years of shared happiness.

Our children Michael, Helena, Rory and Ursula have brought nothing but joy to our lives and we are proud of the good people they've grown to be. Our daughters-in-law Judy and Joanne, and soon to be son-in-law Brendan are wonderful people that we are so proud to welcome into our family, while our grandchildren Seán, MJ and Ella delight us every day.

Thank you to all our friends and especially to the people of Oulart-The Ballagh, who it was a privilege to grow up with and grow old with.

To my club Oulart-The Ballagh, thanks for the life long memories, the joyful moments and the opportunity to live out my dreams. You mean everything to me, always and forever.

Mick Jacob
April 2021

◄◄◆►►

I REMEMBER HAVING my first big conversation about Mick Jacob on Wexford senior hurling final day in 1982. I had just turned 10 years old.

On the short walk from our home to Wexford Park, my father explained that every neutral would be hoping Oulart-The Ballagh's star centre-back would finally win a coveted county medal. He advised me to keep a close eye on Mick and his approach to the game; how he never took his gaze off the sliotar, and how he was always brilliantly prepared for the contest at hand.

And how Mick Jacob was an out-and-out sportsman.

My father arrived in the county from his native Cork in 1966, and he told me the best individual display he had seen was the one Mick produced in the 1974 county final.

I had already watched Mick in various matches, notably the Leinster final of

1981, but I paid him closer attention than ever before on that particular day.

Sadly, it was like 1974 all over again, with Mick's Man of the Match heroics not enough to give him the medal he desired more than any other.

My interest in newspapers and the written word was also developing at that time, and later in the week I was fascinated by the coverage of the game. While the exploits of Buffers Alley in capturing the title were rightly lauded, several column inches were also devoted to the greatness of Mick Jacob and his forlorn quest for a county senior medal.

Fast forward almost six years and, at the tender age of 15, I was on my first summer work placement with *The People*. One of the earliest senior matches I covered was a clash in Enniscorthy between Cloughbawn and an Oulart-The Ballagh side with a midfield pairing of 42-year-old Mick and a 20-year-old protégé named Liam Dunne.

That was a real master and pupil moment in Mick's first year back playing senior after his recovery from the serious eye injury that ended his county career in 1984.

In the time since, I have marvelled at his hurling ability with Oulart-The Ballagh juniors and the Wexford Masters, his shrewdness as a coach and mentor with various teams, and the equally outstanding contributions made by his four children with club and county.

As a result, I deemed it an honour in October 2019 when Liam Hayes of Hero Books asked me to collaborate with Mick in writing his life story for the 'Legends Series'. Of course, none of us could possibly have foreseen what was coming next, with numerous best-laid plans cut to ribbons as Covid-19 took over our lives from the following March onwards.

I had luck on my side at the outset; in order to do justice to the project and ensure nothing was missed, I decided to go back to the start and fully research Mick's career from the very beginning.

I joked with him that he hadn't made it easy for me, as he was still going strong almost 40 years after playing his first adult hurling game with Oulart-The Ballagh in 1962.

That research lasted from late-October 2019 until Thursday, March 5, 2020 – the first restrictions would be imposed by the end of the following week, so I got the work done just in time.

Gráinne Doran, Wexford's county archivist, made all the original newspaper files at their HQ in Ardcavan available to me. I am very grateful to Gráinne and her staff, with a special mention for Ger Browne, who took a personal interest in the project given his father's close links to Oulart.

By the time the interviewing process arrived, improvisation was necessary. We developed a smooth routine – chatting for between 90 minutes and two hours every Tuesday and Wednesday evening from May 19 all the way through to August 25.

Those trips down memory lane started on Zoom, but we quickly switched to speakerphone after I realised the internet connection in Oulart isn't nearly as reliable as the super hurlers it has produced!

My deepest thanks to Mick for talking me through his life and times, and to Breda and Robbie who were by his side and contributed in such rich measure to the project – it wouldn't have been possible without them.

We were joined by Michael and Rory in the last few weeks, and I'm equally grateful to them, and to Helena and Ursula in more recent times, for ensuring no stone was left unturned.

My deep appreciation also to Dave Bernie, Jim Breen, Tom Dempsey, Liam Dunne and Ed Rowsome for their contributions, and to Liam Hayes – a footballer I admired so much in my teens – for his trust, guidance and patience.

Finally, thanks to my family for their interest and support – my parents Tom and Mary; my sister Aisling and brother-in-law Pádhraic; my brother Brian and his partner Donna, and my sister Louise.

A special word is reserved for my nephews Darragh, Adam and Conor, and my niece Ella. On the days when I needed to step away from this project to recharge the batteries, they were always on hand to provide much-needed light relief and laughter.

Whatever paths they take in life, I hope they all find something that fills them with the same joy I have derived from watching and writing about hurling heroes like Mick Jacob.

Alan Aherne
April 2021

« PROLOGUE »

Wexford Park, Sunday, October 27, 2019

IT'S COUNTY HURLING final day in Wexford, and for once Mick Jacob can sit back, relax and enjoy every aspect of this landmark occasion.

Sitting in the centre of the stand with Breda, his wife since 1978, he's there as a special guest of the Wexford County Board. Their long-standing policy of honouring the silver jubilee champions dates back to the mid-80s, but this is the first opportunity for Mick's beloved Oulart-The Ballagh to be presented to the crowd at half-time.

Their breakthrough victory in 1994 came after endless years of heartbreak and near misses, a joyful release and undoubtedly the most emotional occasion in the club's long history. Before pipping St Martin's by one point on that fateful day, Oulart-The Ballagh's name had never appeared on the championship roll of honour.

'Winning that first one was the hardest part,' Mick explains. 'I always felt that once we finally got over the line, more would follow because of the belief it instilled in the players.'

Even in his wildest dreams, though, he couldn't possibly have envisaged the golden era it unleashed.

ON OCTOBER 16, 1994, the Oulart-The Ballagh troops entered Wexford Park without a senior title to their name. And now, 25 years and 11 days later, incredibly they are positioned second on the roll of honour with 13 championships as Mick prepares to re-unite with those who got the ball rolling.

It wasn't always such a happy experience, as county final day brought nothing but pain in his own playing career, particularly in 1974 and '82. He was lauded in the local newspapers for his Man of the Match displays in those years, in spite of figuring on the losing side to the big two stumbling blocks in his quest for a medal – Rathnure and Buffers Alley.

There was bitter disappointment, too, in 1975, and again in '89 when Mick would switch from player to trainer. The Alley had the edge in those finals also, as well as in 1992 when he was a 46-year-old substitute, but he never, ever lost hope.

'My generation didn't get over the line on the big day, but I think we passed down a lesson to the crew that came after us. No matter how disappointed we were, we never threw in the towel.

'We always talked things through over the winter, and resolved to have another crack. I think that helped the lads in '94; they had grown up watching us, and we kept coming back for more.

'That rubbed off on them. After their own disappointments in 1989 and '92, they stuck at it and got there in the end.'

Mick Jacob's fingerprints were all over that first success. Even at the height of his own long tenure in the Wexford colours, he somehow managed to combine playing at the highest level, working on the farm, and starting a family, in addition to his role as chief trainer with the school and Bord na nÓg teams in the parish.

Practically all of the heroes of 1994 – Martin Storey, Liam Dunne and their colleagues – had been guided through the rudimentary aspects of the game as youngsters by the county's first-ever All Star, a man once dubbed 'The Prince of Centre-Backs'.

They couldn't have wished for a better role model, and they will be forever in his debt.

WEXFORD PARK HAS changed considerably in the 25 years of Oulart-The Ballagh dominance. Mick and Breda are sitting in a new stand, officially opened in 2001, for starters, and as they watch St Martin's pipping St Anne's to the 2019 title, there is considerably less traffic on the sideline than there was on that special occasion for their club.

The day isn't without its sad aspects either.

The previous two Octobers were marred by the deaths of two of Mick's fellow selectors from 1994 – Willie Sunderland in 2017, and Tom Neville 12 months later. The end of Tom's Wexford career coincided with Mick's early years, and they would battle for a common goal both on and off the field.

Only Mick and 'Pender' – Jimmy Prendergast, another long-time companion with club and county – are left to fly the flag for the backroom team of 1994, but their departed friends will never be forgotten.

To know Mick Jacob is to appreciate that, for all he achieved in the Wexford jersey, his total devotion to the Oulart-The Ballagh club is what really and truly defines him.

This is a man who played his first county final in the junior grade as a 16-year-old goalkeeper, and who didn't finally hang up his boots until the age of 54 – in spite of a serious eye injury that ended his county career and kept him out of the game for three years.

And then there's his incredible contribution to preparing the under-age teams in the parish. At the height of it, in a period from 1992 to '97, he trained every single Oulart-The Ballagh club side in the minor, juvenile, under-14 and under-12 grades across both codes… eight teams in total.

A supreme stylist on the field, he's also a devoted family man… Breda's husband; father to Michael Jnr, Helena, Ursula and Rory; grandfather to Seán, MJ and Ella; and brother to Robbie, Christy and Bridie.

A successful farmer, a hunting and shooting enthusiast, and a humble, modest man with a ready smile and time for everyone, Mick Jacob is one of Oulart-The Ballagh's most famous sons.

IT'S NO COINCIDENCE that this celebration of the 1994 breakthrough victory happens to fall on the same day that he has chosen to start sharing his story. Mention his club anywhere in Wexford or further afield, and the name of this hurling great is certain to crop up.

He was, indeed, a class act.

And his graceful play on the county scene at various levels from 1963 to '84 was matched only by his thorough decency off the field.

« CHAPTER 1 »

MICHAEL JACOB CAME into the world on January 14, 1946, the third surviving son of George and Ellen, and a younger brother to Robert and Christopher.

The family was completed one year later with the birth of Bridget, and in the years that followed the shortened versions of their names would become very familiar to keen followers of hurling and camogie.

Robbie, Christy and Mick led the charge as the Oulart-The Ballagh club rose from relative obscurity to become a formidable force. In the process, they earned selection with various Wexford teams and put the Jacob name on the map in the sporting world.

Not to be outdone, Bridie was a late starter but ended up being every bit as talented as the boys, gaining All-Ireland honours with the county camogie team in 1975.

The GAA has played an immense role in the lives of the four Jacob children since their arrival in a five-year spell from 1942 to '47.

And yet, the family background of their forefathers offered no hint of this lifetime involvement to come.

WHEN THE ASSOCIATION was founded in 1884, the Jacobs' great-grandfather George was a 34-year-old member of the Church of Ireland community.

A farmer by profession, he lived with his wife Jane in the townland of Ballaman near Kilrush in the north-west of County Wexford, not far from the Wicklow border and in the district electoral division of Tombrack.

The census returns for 1901 show that their household occupants included a 23-year-old son named Robert, and he was about to make a decision that would have a profound impact on the lives of every Jacob that succeeded him.

Robert fell in love with Bridget Kinsella, a Roman Catholic from nearby Curraduff, who was 11 years his senior. This was in an era when mixed marriages were extremely rare, and something of a taboo subject on both sides of the religious divide. Indeed, the Catholic Church's Ne Temere decree came into force on Easter Sunday in 1908, meaning it would not recognise a marriage between a Protestant and a Catholic unless it took place in a Catholic church.

Robert was left with a dilemma, but the solution was obvious in his eyes. He made a selfless sacrifice by converting to the Catholic faith, and the couple were duly married.

Bridget was the daughter of Moses and Margaret Kinsella, the middle child of three living with them in the family home at Curraduff in 1901, along with her older brother Edward and a younger sister named Catherine. She is buried in the old graveyard in Oulart along with Robert, who died in 1943.

Mick's father George was born in 1910, and he had one sister Jane, who spent most of her life in England. 'I remember meeting her daughter, our first cousin, at a wedding in Arklow in 1963,' Mick recalls.

The Jacob family maintained strong connections with their Protestant relations and friends through the years, especially in their childhood days when visits to Clough, Courtown and Kilmuckridge were commonplace to visit the Rigley, Bailey and Fitzsimons clans.

In George's early childhood, the Jacobs were one of three families who had adjoining farms in Ballaman, along with the Rigleys and the Nolans.

Owen Nolan was a very successful farmer, and he looked to expand by purchasing a larger holding in Knockshemolin in the parish of Oulart. Part of that deal, the Jacobs believe, involved buying the smaller farm in Ballaman, owned by their grandfather Robert.

A lasting connection had already formed between the Kinsellas of Curraduff and the Nolans, and this was reflected when Bridget and Robert Jacob moved to Oulart with their good friends after those business dealings were conducted.

This move occurred around 1926, at a time when George was about 16 years of age. He had already acquired a love for Gaelic football at that stage, inspired by his early days in Ballyroebuck National School and the deeds of famed Brideswell, the first known club to be formed in the parish of Kilrush and Askamore.

He was nine years old when they won the delayed county junior football final of 1918 in October of the following year, beating Gusserane by two points in Wexford Park.

And he maintained that interest after arriving in Oulart, with hurling added to the mix at that stage. Football was very much the number one sport in Wexford during George's formative years, with the county falling off the hurling radar after losing the All-Ireland final of 1918 to Limerick.

They wouldn't contest two championship games in the same year from then until 1939, and it wasn't until the emergence of the great team of the 50s that hurling clubs started to develop in places like Kilrush and Askamore, that would have been football-only beforehand.

George's finest hour on a football field arrived in 1935, at the age of 25, when he helped Oulart to capture the Gorey District Junior Championship title.

And although they subsequently lost the county semi-final to Starlights in Ferns by 3-2 to 2-2, it wasn't for the want of trying on George's part as he scored both goals and was a real livewire that the Enniscorthy town men struggled to deal with.

One year later, they retained that District title and went one step further, only to lose the county final to a Volunteers side from Wexford town that featured Brendan Corish, the future leader of the Labour Party. The game wasn't played until April 18, 1937, and it was a one-sided affair in Bellefield as the Vols romped home by 4-9 to no score.

The biggest influence on George's playing career was a teammate in that county final, Pat Hernan, captain of the Gorey District winners one year earlier. A local garda in Oulart at the time, he hailed from Donegal and is largely credited with developing Gaelic football after his arrival in the parish.

The pair became firm friends, and it wasn't long before a family connection was added to the mix. George had a first cousin in Kilrush named Margaret O'Hanlon, and she met and married Pat Hernan.

MICK AND HIS siblings retain childhood memories of their father talking about the great games he played in during the 1930s. Although aligned to the Enniscorthy District for games purposes when Mick started playing, in those days Oulart was attached to Gorey District and came up against some tough customers.

Willie Doran and his Buffers Alley team had the same fighting qualities as his sons and their colleagues of the 70s and 80s, while Ballycanew could always be relied upon to produce a strong side. And then there was Ballinglen, featuring many players destined to appear in latter years with the Castletown club on their gradual rise to the top.

Anything won in those days was hard earned, and George cherished those two Gorey District junior football medals from 1935 and '36.

Pace was his biggest asset on the playing fields, a talent honed through his regular participation in athletics after moving to Oulart. Sprints over 100 and 200 yards were his speciality, travelling to sports meetings all over the region with two great friends, the Doyle brothers from Dranagh, Aidan and John – granduncles of Adam Nolan, the 2012 Olympian boxer from The Ballagh.

And as anyone who watched Mick in his prime will readily agree, he also possessed that speed off the mark that gave him a head start over opponents. Clearly, it was in the genes.

◄◄◆►►

MICK'S PATERNAL GRANDPARENTS died before his birth in 1946, but he was fortunate enough to establish a close bond with his grandmother and grandfather on his mother's side of the family.

Michael Kinsella married Elizabeth Mythen around the 1917 or 1918 mark, and their farm and home was in the townland of Ballinerode, within a stone's throw of Oulart Hill.

The place is steeped in history, the scene of one of the key incidents during the United Irishmen rebellion of 1798. On Whit Sunday, May 27, pike-wielding rebels led by Fr John Murphy of Boolavogue annihilated a detachment of 110 men, the dreaded and notorious North Cork Militia.

Almost all of north county Wexford joined the rebellion after news of the

Battle of Oulart Hill spread, with crown forces and loyalist civilians ceding control of the countryside, seeking shelter and safety instead in the towns of Enniscorthy, Gorey and Wexford.

The Kinsellas' land was connected to that historic spot by a Mass path, and with every step taken it was impossible not to feel a close bond to those brave rebels of 1798.

MICK'S GRANDFATHER MICHAEL was born in 1879, the eldest son of Owen and Ellen, a brother to William and Timothy.

His grandmother Elizabeth was a Mythen from Monavullen, daughter of James and Margaret, and one of seven children in all, along with Jim, Ellen, Mary, Hannah, Patrick and Kate.

She had a striking physical appearance, as Mick vividly recalls.

'She was the biggest woman I ever saw. She must have been nearly six feet tall, very broad… with a powerful physical frame.'

It was a daunting look to those who didn't know her, but it belied a heart of gold and a friendly demeanour. 'She was very good with children and when nobody else was around, the sweets would be pulled out and shared.

'She was probably never at a match in her life. When the radio was on in the 50s, and Michael O'Hehir was going strong, sometimes the tension would get too much for her when Wexford were playing. She'd get up and head out… go for a walk up Oulart Hill.'

The Kinsellas' farm at Ballinerode was of the smaller variety, no more than 30 acres. Michael tended to it with devotion and was always in good form, even though it wasn't easy to make ends meet.

'He was a very quiet man, very good humoured. He always had a moustache, and he used to go down to the village in his horse and cart. He'd be singing away to himself on his way to the shop.'

Elizabeth's homeplace in Monavullen was across the fields from Ballinerode, roughly one mile away, and the family farm of the Mythens was even smaller than that of the Kinsellas.

Her brother Jim, better known to his peers as 'Big Jem', was something of a local legend in Oulart, carrying a permanent air of mystery that stayed with him right up to his death at the age of 80 in 1960.

He was a hurling hero for starters, having played on the All-Ireland winning Wexford senior team of 1910. His heavy involvement in the War of Independence ensured he was often absent from the family home, being forced to go on the run at different times.

A powerful man with a physique similar to Elizabeth, local legend has it that his strength knew no bounds. Indeed, when a monument to the heroes of 1798 was being erected on Oulart Hill to mark the 150th anniversary in 1948, 'Big Jem' is said to have carried bags of cement on his shoulders all the way up from Cooney's store in the village – no mean feat for a man who was 68 years of age at the time.

After Michael Kinsella married Elizabeth Mythen, the Jacobs' mother Ellen was their first born in 1919. She was followed by Margaret (Maggie), Agnes, Tim (who died as an infant), Owen, Hannah, Michael (Mikie) and Statia.

And it was a major struggle for this rapidly-growing family, living off the land and endeavouring to put food on the table for the hungry youngsters. 'It was very tough trying to make ends meet. In fact, it wasn't far off a famine situation at times, with food so hard to come by.'

Happily, Ellen lived to the grand old age of 92 before her death in 2011. And while she was reluctant to talk to her own children in any great depth about those difficult times, she was more forthcoming as she grew older.

By that stage of her life, she was a contented woman, happy in the knowledge that her children and grandchildren had all made their way successfully in the world.

They didn't need protecting or minding at that stage; Ellen could afford to be more open with her memories, now that Mick, Robbie, Christy and Bridie were well able to look after themselves.

Robbie's son Jim was fascinated by his grandmother's recall of her childhood years, constantly probing her with questions. The more she answered, the more information Jim sought. It was during one such fireside chat that she vividly depicted a particularly tough period for the family, when she went for three full days without getting any food.

Often times, her visit to the neighbouring Nolan clan a few hundred yards away would be more than just a social call. Deep down, a famished Ellen would be hoping against hope that she might be offered a bite to eat; anything at all, even a morsel of bread, would do for a young girl who knew what it meant to go hungry.

She walked to school every day across Oulart Hill, and down into the village. And on many occasions it was on an empty stomach, or perhaps, if she was lucky, one slice of homemade brown bread with no butter.

The situation Ellen found herself in was of the make-or-break variety. A weaker-willed person might have thrown in the towel and succumbed to the constant struggle for food. Thankfully, she reacted in the opposite way, and her children will never forget the lengths she would go to for her family.

'Our mother was a massive woman for work. They started with just 30 acres on that farm but, because of the work ethic of the Kinsella family, they gradually built it up.

'Owen and Mikie farmed the land all their lives after leaving school, and our aunt Agnes was there too. Our mother, being the eldest, would have been a great help to our grandmother in keeping the rest of them on their toes and making sure they mucked in.

'She got married at 20 or 21, which was quite common at the time, and you wouldn't get any better than her when it came to sheer hard work.'

That application and constant desire to better themselves led to much brighter days for the Kinsellas and, by extension, the Jacobs. 'They would buy four or five farms in the locality, and ended up with a couple of hundred acres of the best land. That all came from raw, hard work. A lot of it was very physical in nature, involving the horse and plough, and Owen was a savage man in that regard. He never married, and really devoted himself to his family and the land.

'Mikie made the commercial decisions, and he was a great judge of cattle. He had a real eye for it… the buying, the finishing on the farm… then the selling on.'

The situation her family faced, and ultimately overcame, steeled Ellen Kinsella for some really tough days to follow. She fell in love with George Jacob and married a loyal, hard working man. He was the best possible father to their four surviving children, but the dreams they harboured of sharing a long life together would be shattered in the most harrowing of circumstances.

◄◄◆►►

GEORGE AND ELLEN Jacob were less than two years married when their first-born son Robert (Robbie) arrived and made them proud parents in 1942.

The couple's next child Michael sadly died as an infant before Christopher (Christy) came along in 1944.

And when the Jacobs were looking forward to the arrival of their fourth-born, they agreed that if God was good and another healthy boy was delivered, then they would also name him Michael to honour the memory of the little angel they had lost. That happy event occurred on a Monday in early 1946, January 14 to be precise.

The Jacobs were living in Ballincash, Oulart, when their sons were born, but they were on the move just a few months afterwards to a new abode. By the time their only daughter Bridget (Bridie) completed the family in 1947, their base was at Coolnahinch, on the main road between Ballycanew and Gorey.

A house filled with fun and laughter, it was two miles outside the town. And when the time came for the children to start their education, their first port of call was the Loreto National School in Gorey.

'In those days everyone started there with the nuns, but after first class the boys would move across the road to the Christian Brothers,' Mick recalls.

'I remember cycling in to school from home, and my mother had Bridie on a carrier.'

Robbie, the first of the clan to sample school life, was often brought in to town by a neighbour Mrs Hall on an ass and cart.

He was very protective of his brothers when they joined him, letting it be known around the yard that nobody was to lay a hand on young Michael.

'I didn't do much hurling in Gorey if I'm honest,' Mick says. He can recall a Brother Histon, a native of Cork who spoke of some connection with the great Christy Ring as a youngster.

And then there was Master McGrath, or 'The Duck' to his pupils. He was a very good footballer with the Gorey Blues, and knew Mick's father well from coming up against George's final club Tara Rocks in hotly-contested local derby matches.

TARA ROCKS WAS founded in 1947, selecting from small rural areas dotted around the outskirts of Gorey. And they met with near-instant success, winning the county junior football title of 1948.

Mick was too young at the time to remember anything about that achievement, but it was a proud moment for his father.

The final didn't take place until May 5 of the following year, with Tara Rocks pipping a double-seeking St Martin's in Enniscorthy's Bellefield by 0-5 to 0-4. It was the only county medal George Jacob ever won, and it meant a great deal to him as he was very much in the veteran ranks at the time.

'I remember him leaving the house before that game,' Robbie says. 'He wasn't on the starting 15 but he would have been brought on and was heavily involved in most of the matches.'

One of the main men on that team was Mick Carty, father of the star Wexford footballer of the same name – who captained UCD to the All-Ireland club title in 1975. Other players were Mike and Pat Carroll, a grandfather and a granduncle of Wexford star hurler Garrett Sinnott.

The final was delayed until 1949 because of the twin involvement of St Martin's, who were also seeking the junior hurling title. That particular showdown took place three weeks earlier at the same venue, and their victims were the Oulart Father Murphys, beaten on a 3-4 to 1-3 scoreline.

IN YEARS TO come, Michael morphed into Mick Jacob in the hurling world, but that change was forcibly resisted as a child. 'I resented anyone calling me Mick rather than Michael. My mother was very serious about the difference. As far as she was concerned, I was Michael… and she didn't want me to be called Mick at all.'

Robbie reckons any scrapes his generally mild-mannered youngest brother got into had their roots in this issue. Children being children, they would repeat the 'Mick' mantra if they thought it was upsetting him. And whenever young Jacob would rise to the bait, he could always rely on Robbie and Christy to weigh in with back-up.

This is confirmed by Jim Breen, a future secretary of Coiste na nÓg Loch Garman, who sat side-by-side in the same desk as Robbie in third class. However, the Jacobs weren't as innocent as the driven snow either!

'I remember Mick and Christy too when they were in the CBS. They got away with murder, and I will give you just one example,' Jim says. 'You might be standing in the yard and talking to another lad when Mick would get down on his hands and knees behind you, and Christy would come along and give you a push. Of course, you ended up on the concrete, and your first reaction would be to kill that little so and so.

'However, by the time you got to your feet, the two boys would be standing beside big brother Robbie, so that eliminated any chance of taking retribution straight away.

'Mick and Christy were forever up to something or other, getting into mischief.'

Even then, it was clear that the Jacobs came as a package; if you messed with one of them, you had three to contend with, and they were great believers in the concept of strength in numbers!

Nowadays, Wexford's first-ever All Star is more than happy for people to refer to him as Mick. He had precious little choice in the matter really, given that the shortened version was used from the earliest stage of his career by the majority of journalists.

One notable exception was Enniscorthy scribe Billy Quirke, who always referred to him as Michael. I imagine he took his cue in that regard from Ellen Jacob, as she never wavered from using the full version of her youngest boy's name.

Likewise, he is Michael to Breda, his wife since 1978. The family naming conventions were complicated slightly with the birth of their first child, also Michael, in 1980.

Michael Senior and Michael Junior might have been a bit of a mouthful, so it was certainly more convenient from that point onwards to refer to father and son as Mick and Michael.

COOLNAHINCH, THE FIRST townland inside the Gorey parish boundary for GAA purposes, was nearer in distance to the village of Ballycanew, and the Jacobs had firm connections and good friends in both places.

With the children so close in age, it made for a home full of joy. And while Ellen busied herself with the household tasks, with Bridie by her side, George and the boys would repair to the garden at every opportunity where fun was guaranteed.

'We used to have these football games against each other,' Mick recalls. 'It was usually Robbie with Christy, and I'd be playing against them with daddy because I was the youngest.

'Sure, it was like playing in an All-Ireland final, and it wouldn't be unusual to get a bad belt on the shin. We used to love those games, and we were learning all the time.

'And unknown to us in many ways, our father was developing that competitive instinct we always had in our hurling careers. He created so much fun for us, and a real love for sport.

'Daddy never needed persuading to come out and play with us. Usually he was the one getting us out of the house, any time he wasn't working. He always loved a bit of craic too… I must say it was a very happy childhood for as long as it lasted.'

One thing that Mick Jacob also picked up from his father was an enduring passion for the land.

After grandfather Robert sold his small holding in Ballaman, and the family moved to Oulart, it meant George had to almost start from scratch in terms of progressing his own career in farming.

He did this by working for several land owners, and he harboured a massive passion to get into a position of greater responsibility.

He became the modern-day equivalent of a farm manager, with a particularly keen eye for cattle. His judgement in bovine matters was trusted and respected. When it came to cattle and everything relating to them, people were well aware that George Jacob really knew his stuff.

At the time of Mick's birth in 1946, his father was managing a farm in Ballincash for one of the local priests Fr Doyle.

Late that year, it was sold to the O'Grady family, who arrived in the parish from Urlingford, Co Kilkenny. Agnes Kinsella, an aunt of Mick's, went on to marry Pat O'Grady and they moved further south to Rathangan where they ran one of the best dairy farms in the county, a regular recipient of awards for the quality of milk produced.

The change of ownership in Ballincash meant the Jacobs were on the move when Mick was an infant, but their first port of call was only part of a temporary arrangement.

George briefly managed a farm in Courtclough for the grandfather of Mary and Una Leacy, both four-time All-Ireland senior camogie medal winners with Wexford from 2007 to '12. Of course, Mick's two girls Ursula and Helena also shared in those successes, more than 60 years after their family paths crossed for the first time.

That was a short-lived posting, a brief stepping stone on the way to a new life away from Oulart, and the house in Coolnahinch.

The George Warren auctioneering firm was founded in Gorey in 1871, and George Jacob never looked back after joining the agricultural wing of this thriving business. His ultimate ambition was to save enough money to buy his own farm, and he worked hard to provide for his family and give them the best life possible.

Warrens had a lot of prime agricultural land on their books around Gorey, and Mick's father became the main man in the operation.

'He was responsible for buying and looking after cattle on their farms. And as time went on, he started to buy and trade himself, all geared towards getting his own farm.'

One of Mick's most vivid childhood memories is of the fair day in Gorey, a once-a-month occurrence from April to September.

'My father and uncle Mikie were working closely together that time with the cattle. They'd be buying, finishing and selling them on to make money, and it was all part of my father's ambition to get back to farming and having his own place.

'The tradition that time was to sell the cattle by bringing them in to town in Gorey. You'd put them out on the street every month, and dealers would come from Dublin and other places to negotiate.

'Those fair days were a great way of toughening us up as young fellas. You'd have to get up at 4.0 or 4.30am, and collect the cattle from the field. Then you'd walk them in the road from Ballycanew into Gorey, stand on the street and mind them for the day.

'Farmers would come from all over to trade, and you'd need to have your wits about you as some of them would try to buy and sell you.

'I remember doing that with Robbie and Christy from the age of eight or nine. We'd be starving by nine or ten in the morning, but there was a long way to go before we'd be fed. There would be a beef dinner at the end of it, and sure it would be wolfed down… we'd be famished.

'And then of course, if you didn't sell some of the cattle, you'd have to walk them back out the road home in the evening. You'd sleep soundly after a day like that!'

George Jacob was a central figure in a business move that saw the traditional fair days come to an end in Gorey in the mid-50s.

In late 1954, George Warren expanded when he built a livestock mart, establishing a sales ring and giving buying and selling farmers alike a considerably more civilised way of doing business.

When he wasn't working or helping Ellen with the children, George liked to go back into Gorey town for a few jars, with a bottle of Guinness his preferred tipple. 'People used to call to the house to play cards too. Our father is supposed to have been a very good pontoon player.

'And he loved music as well, there would often be singing and dancing in Coolnahinch. Our grandfather Robert was a very good traditional fiddle player, so that was carried on.'

THE FIRST MAJOR sign of a Wexford hurling revival occurred when Mick was five years of age. The Leinster senior title of 1951 bridged a 33-year gap, and it created an incredible buzz in a county starved of any meaningful success since the footballers won their last provincial title in 1945.

George had a keen interest in the fortunes of that exciting hurling team, and naturally enough he made sure the children knew all about their exploits which only got better as the 50s continued.

Another Leinster title would follow in 1954, only for the legendary Christy Ring and his Cork crew to ensure the gap wasn't bridged back to Mick's granduncle Jim Mythen and his All-Ireland winning colleagues of 1910.

There wasn't long to wait, though, as 1955 was the year when it all fell perfectly into place. Beating Galway, and bringing the Liam MacCarthy Cup home, created a frenzy of excitement. It led to a new-found passion for hurling in areas of Wexford where football had previously been number one, and the main beneficiaries were Mick's generation as the game really thrived beyond all recognition throughout the 60s.

Living at Coolnahinch, close to Corriganeagh Rock, also carried one major advantage. The Jacob house was on the main Wexford-Gorey road, and that left them with a ringside seat in that memorable summer of 1955.

They mightn't have attended any of the matches, but they were engrossed by the next best thing.

'At that time, the Wexford players would all travel to Croke Park in hackney cars, and some of them would pass directly by our house,' Mick says. 'We'd all be outside, hoping to catch a quick glimpse of Ned Wheeler, Jim Morrissey, Seamus Hearne or Billy Rackard. It was such a thrill for us as children.

'And then, a few hours later, we'd all huddle around the radio and listen to

Michael O'Hehir as he talked about the men we had seen passing our own front door.

'That brought an unbelievable energy into our house. We got a real feeling for what hurling is all about, and it never left us.'

A natural connection to Oulart, in the valley directly to the rear of their dwelling, provided a link with early childhood.

The Owenavarragh River flowed serenely behind the Jacob homestead, on the final leg of its journey. From its source near Oulart Hill, it meandered on an 18-mile trip in a north-easterly direction across flat pasture, surrounded by some of the finest farmland in the county.

The river entered the Irish Sea at Courtown Harbour, but when tragedy struck the family in early 1956, it must have felt like it was pulling them back in the opposite direction, into the comforting arms of loved ones.

◄◄◆▷►

LIFE WAS AS rewarding as it could possibly be for the Jacobs as autumn turned to winter in 1955.

It was a happy, loving home in Coolnahinch, and all was well in the world.

The children, ranging in age from 13 to 8, made for a close-knit quartet, and they had every possible support they could wish for from their adoring parents.

School life was going well, they had plenty of friends, and all of their spare time was spent in the back lawn where they dreamed of emulating their hurling heroes, now officially crowned the best team in the land.

They were well fed and watered, with Ellen determined to ensure the poverty she had endured herself as a young girl would never visit their front door. The three boys and Bridie – her mother's right-hand woman around the home – were always impeccably turned out, and a mannerly and welcoming quartet whenever visitors called.

As for George, that goal of doing well enough to purchase his own farm was very much on track. He was an essential cog in the wheel of his employer, with George Warren valuing the immense contribution he was making to such a smooth-running operation.

The man of the house was willing to put in the hours, and his appetite for hard work would rub off on his children when they moved into adulthood. Sadly, they would do so without the guiding hand of their beloved father.

All they were left with were those pleasant memories of fun-filled, carefree days in Coolnahinch, with George the centre of their innocent world as they competed for his attention with laughter filling the air.

Mick and the rest of the Jacobs were shattered by the events of Sunday, January 8, 1956.

MICK WAS NINE years of age at the time, all set to hit double digits on his birthday just six days later. It should have been another one of those happy family occasions that were part and parcel of life in Coolnahinch, but nobody was in the mood for celebrating this time.

On January 8, Mick and his siblings were given the devastating news that no young child should have to hear; the man they loved with all their hearts was dead. George had succumbed to pneumonia after a short illness at the age of 46.

Life would never be the same again.

The days that followed were a complete blur, with Mick and his brothers and sister struggling to make sense of it all. Raw grief was mixed with a child's confusion over this unexpected turn of events. Mick knew his father was sick, and had been admitted to hospital, but he was invincible in his eyes. *Why wasn't he coming home?*

'I remember going in to see him one last time in Gorey after he died,' Mick says. 'He'd only been out of the house for a short while, but I couldn't believe how old he looked in the coffin.'

His voice trails away as he recalls this shocking sight like it happened only yesterday. Some things will remain forever lodged in one's memory, and that image is as upsetting to Mick now as it was all those years ago. George's perfect health prior to his sudden demise made it even more difficult for the boys and Bridie to comprehend.

'He was very healthy all the way up, there was never a complaint or a problem… or indeed a history of anything lurking in the background.

'Jack Horan was a prominent member of the Church of Ireland community in the locality, and a successful farmer. He told us our father was renowned for his physical strength.

'Whenever cattle had to be dosed or dehorned, it was never a bother to him. He'd grab them by the horns if he had to; it came so naturally to him and he made what was sometimes a difficult task look easy. He was fierce strong.'

In years to come, Mick and the Jacobs would piece together the cause of their father's demise.

The last month of 1955 was one of the wettest on record. 'It was unbelievable, with floods everywhere. The main road outside our own house was like a small river.

'Our father was looking after the cattle for Warrens, and he got soaked on a regular basis. He was out in the open all the time. He couldn't avoid it really, it was essential to his job, but it took a huge toll.

'We noticed it first in the evenings when he'd come home. He'd be coughing a lot, and this lasted for a week or maybe 10 days. He stayed going against the odds really, and probably pushed himself too far. That all boiled down to the work ethic he had, it would take an awful lot to halt him.

'Eventually he had to stop, and he ended up in bed at home. It was expected he'd be okay, but then he got another turn, and he was even worse. He was sick for the best part of a month, and the next thing we knew was that he was on his way into the hospital in Gorey.

'We didn't see him alive any more after that.'

The children knew the situation was serious, but they had to rely on their own intuition for the most part to make that call. At the time the natural instinct of adults was to shield youngsters from bad news. Certainly, nobody ever sat down with Mick and his siblings either before or after George's death to explain the full gravity of the situation.

And the children harbour no criticism of the grown-ups for that; it was simply the ways things were, and nobody knew any different. 'There was tension around the house, that was fairly obvious. Aunts and uncles were down from Oulart, and people were coming and going into Gorey all the time.'

Nobody was in the mood to celebrate the onset of 1956, with a dark cloud looming over the house in Coolnahinch.

George had been perhaps 10 days in hospital at that stage, and he never came home.

It was especially tough on the children that they didn't get to hold a conversation with their father one last time, or to say their goodbyes.

Robbie, the eldest at 13, remembers when the sad news of his father's demise was confirmed. 'I took it on board, and it registered with me, but I have to say it was a serious shock at the same time.'

And the subsequent trip into the hospital morgue will stay with Mick and his siblings for the rest of their days.

'I remember having a conversation with Bridie about it, a long time afterwards,' Robbie adds. 'She was eight at the time, a year younger than Mick. She told me that after going through the trauma involved, she knew that there was nothing – and I mean nothing – else in life that could possibly upset her to the same extent. We would all concur with that.'

'I certainly do,' Mick agrees. 'I have the exact same attitude, and I always will. I was a few days away from turning 10, and all of a sudden my father wasn't there any more. That was an awful shock to the system… the worst kind.

'Because of what happened to our father, all of us really appreciate the lives we have had, and our health. We've been so lucky.

'It's just a shame that he wasn't around to share it with us. He was a tremendous loss, and we'll never forget him.'

◄◄◆►►

THE DAYS DIRECTLY before and after Mick's tenth birthday – Saturday, January 14, 1956 – were surreal, completely beyond the comprehension of any child of that age. On the previous Sunday, the children were gathered together in Coolnahinch to be given the harrowing news that their father was dead.

His funeral and burial took place on the Tuesday. And on the very next day, their mother packed up their belongings and the family moved out of that once-happy home, never to return.

Oulart was their destination and, while they would grow to love their new abode, it didn't appear to be such a welcoming place on that bleak winter's day. 'We came from flat land close to Courtown Harbour, and arrived at the house looking up at Oulart Hill beside it in very bad weather.

'I can remember driving into the laneway, and both sides were packed up with snow.'

Fate played such a huge part in the life path of the Jacob children, and the subsequent rise to prominence of Oulart-The Ballagh GAA club. 'We never really wanted to come back from Coolnahinch, we were so happy there. Only for our father dying, I'd say we would never have come back.'

They will forever remain eternally grateful for the kindness of their neighbours around that trying time.

Mike D'Arcy came from Ballywalter, across the river from their home, and he was very supportive.

And more than half a century later, during a golden era for Wexford camogie, Mike's grand-daughter Mags D'Arcy and Mick's daughter Helena would spend hours training together as the two goalkeepers on the squad.

Pat Fanning from Ballycanew, another granduncle of Garrett Sinnott of Oulart-The Ballagh and Wexford hurling fame, was a great friend of George Jacob through their shared interest in football and farming.

He did all he could to assist Ellen too, along with Michael O'Brien who ran a pub in the village.

Jack Horan, one of George's closest contacts in the buying and selling of cattle, was another to step up when the family was at its lowest ebb.

There was no discussion with the children before that swift move, it simply happened.

'Our mother didn't want to hang around the house for a second longer. She was in unbelievable shock, to be fair.' She sought comfort in the bosom of her family down in Oulart, and that was understandable in the circumstances.

'She was under incredible pressure to do right by us. And she was probably haunted by her own childhood, and how times can be so tough.'

Her main motive for returning to Oulart was clear.

The closer she was to her brothers in Ballinerode and her extended family, the more support would be on hand to help her look after Robbie, Christy, Mick and Bridie. And amidst all the trauma, the familiar faces of uncles Mikie and Owen, and grandparents Michael and Elizabeth, did help the Jacob children to adjust to this stark new reality: a life without their father, and in a new parish.

One of the first ports of call for Mick was the national school in Oulart, which he attended along with Christy and Bridie.

Robbie embarked on a different path. As a sixth class pupil in Gorey CBS, he only had a few months to go before moving on to secondary school.

Pat Hernan, the former garda in Oulart and one of George's best friends, was by now running the Cotton Tree pub in the heart of Enniscorthy town, directly across from the bridge over the River Slaney.

It was decided that Robbie would transfer to the nearby CBS, at the far end of Mill Park Road, and he moved in with the Hernans in another act of kindness that underlined the widespread respect people had for the Jacobs. In the meantime, Mick and the other siblings were trying to adjust to their new surrounds, and that didn't happen overnight.

On school days they wheeled their small bikes across Oulart Hill, before completing the short journey into the village.

'I was in third class first, and Miss Hall was my teacher,' Mick recalls. 'Jimmy Hallahan, a Corkman, was the principal, and his wife was teaching there as well. Settling in was a big thing, and it wasn't one bit easy. It was a new environment, and we didn't know anybody of our own age at first.

'I would say it took a full year or two to get fully settled after the shock of our father dying. It was tough without having him there. And then our mother had to look after the three of us still under her roof. I did worry about her and how she had the job of rearing us on her own.'

THE HAND OF fate had also intervened when it came to securing a new home for the Jacobs in Oulart.

During the Coolnahinch days, part of the rhythm of the summer was to take holidays in Ballinerode.

The boys would all head down to their mother's homeplace, and work on the farm with their uncles.

And Robbie has a clear recollection of the events of August 1955.

'A farm came up for sale in Monavullen, three or four fields away from our place in Ballinerode.

'I remember a big discussion taking place in the kitchen over dinner. During a feed of potatoes, bacon and cabbage, my grandfather and uncles talked about this farm, and whether they should put in a bid for it.'

The Kinsellas had prospered over the years since Ellen married George and left the family home. Their unrelenting work ethic meant that, by 1955, it was no longer a fanciful notion to be considering buying more land. And it was very close to their base, only separated from Ballinerode by one farm, owned by the O'Brien family.

'Eventually, my grandfather said to go ahead, he had the final decision of course. On the day of the auction, I headed across the fields along with Mikie and Owen, over to this farm that the Hayden family were offering for sale,' Robbie says.

A representative of Warren's office in Enniscorthy was on hand to conduct proceedings, and at first it looked like the Kinsellas would be returning home empty-handed.

'My uncles weren't number one in the countdown for the purchase. I can't recall exactly, but I'd say a figure of around £730 was probably the final amount. And in those days, maybe one more bid of even a fiver could make all the difference.'

Robbie, at 13 years of age, was engrossed in proceedings, witnessing the 'ins and outs' of an auction up close and personal for the first time. That fierce competitive instinct of the Jacobs was already part of the children's make-up, handed down by their elders.

And when it looked like disappointment was in store, it really kicked in. 'I said to Mikie, "Go on, have one more go… one more bid". So, his hand shot up again and this time the other man decided to pack it in.'

Robbie, Mikie and Owen didn't hang about on their way back across the fields to share the news of their good fortune with the rest of the Kinsellas. They say everything happens for a reason, and Robbie lays out the magnitude of this purchase in stark terms.

'That happened in August of 1955. And on January 11 of the next year, our mother left our home near Gorey along with the four of us. And we headed for Monavullen, to that house bought from the Haydens. It was a freak situation, part of our destiny… hard to get your head around really.

'You see, our father didn't own any property, but when he died we had this new place to move into.

'Christy is still living there, in that very same house in Monavullen.' And all because Mikie Kinsella was encouraged to take that one last gamble on a fateful August day.

Carefree days in Coolnahinch... Mick, Bridie and Robbie with their mother and father, Ellen and George, and a canine companion; at the time of his premature death, George (right) was well on his way to achieving his ambition of farm ownership.

Robbie, Bridie and Mick without a care in the world in Coolnahinch (above); a young Mick, or Michael as his mother insisted, with a broad smile for the camera (right).

« CHAPTER 2 »

MICK'S PASSION FOR hurling was honed in the yard in Oulart National School.

With no organised club competition for boys under the age of 14 in Wexford until 1971, the pathway into the sport wasn't as seamless as it is nowadays. He was only nine years old when he left Coolnahinch, and has precious little recollection of any hurling activity beforehand.

'I didn't really do much at all in Gorey,' he says. 'Christy played in a school league held in the Garden City grounds, but I was too young for that. It was mainly for the 13- and 14-year-olds in the top class, with a few of the better younger lads like Christy involved too. But I was only nine so it wasn't going to happen for me.'

Wexford was gripped by a hurling fever during that trying time when Mick lost his father and the family moved to Oulart.

THE REIGNING LEINSTER and All-Ireland champions retained both titles in 1956, and school yards all over the county came alive to the clash of the ash. 'It was probably a couple of years before what I would call real hurling came to the school, but when it did it was fantastic,' Mick says.

'We played on a small parcel of ground behind the school, where the first pitch in Oulart village is still located. It was the parish field, but this area for playing in was probably only about 25 x 40 yards. It used to be completely packed.'

Johnny Parle, a future goalkeeper with Oulart-The Ballagh and Wexford, was one of the youngsters in the thick of it with Mick and their friends.

'Even then Johnny was a brilliant goalie, no matter what you did you'd struggle to get the ball beyond him. Matty Parle was there too, and Eddie O'Grady and Mick Ryan. The bell would go and we'd still be hurling… nobody wanted to go back into class.'

The passion for the game was growing, and everybody sought a part of it as that star-studded Wexford team inspired an entire generation.

On the days when Robbie didn't have school in Enniscorthy, he'd break away from working at home and cycle down to the field. 'I'd sit on the wall waiting for the boys to come out at break time or lunch time, and then we'd hurl away until they were called back in.'

It certainly helped that Jimmy Hallahan had such a keen interest in the game. His Cork roots ensured the principal was only too happy to see his pupils perfecting the skills at every possible opportunity.

'He was outstanding in that regard. He always let the young lads go out to play. Several county minors and very good club hurlers came out of that environment.

'Tom Kehoe was there at the time… he was full-forward with the club senior team later on, and so was Billy Dunne who played with us all the way up before sadly losing his life in a car accident.

'The school was built on the parish land, and this little area where we played was in a hollow behind it. Years later, the club purchased it and the surrounding land from the parish, and the first pitch was opened on it in 1980 and is still there today.'

There was no bigger hero on that All-Ireland winning Wexford team than Nickey Rackard. And in 1956 he had the foresight to lend his name to a new competition that sparked huge interest among young people all over the county. Everyone wanted to play in the Rackard League when they heard about it, and Mick was no exception.

At the outset, it was a hurling competition confined to rural primary schools, and it's still standing proudly 65 years later after several additions and modifications over time.

When it was introduced, only the really talented 12- and 13-year-olds were good enough to make their club's juvenile team for championship hurling. With no under-12 or under-14 competition, the Rackard League filled a massive void. There was only one problem – it was straight knockout, so Mick didn't get nearly as many games as he longed for.

It gave him a strong taste for competitive fare all the same, and it wouldn't be long before his life was organised around a regular diet of training and matches.

'I remember being very young and going over to Ballyfarnogue for one Rackard League game. I always thought some of the fellas playing against us were over-age.' Robbie, the memory man of the Jacob family, wasn't in Oulart school to play in the Rackard League, but that game against the Shelmaliers parish team has stayed with him.

'Young lads didn't have a lot of matches at the time, so everybody would be really hungry for hurling. I can remember the excitement before that one, and the lads coming home to tell me all about it. Mick played in the forwards that day, and Christy was with the other bigger lads in the backs.'

THE RACKARD LEAGUE also provided the backdrop for the beginning of a healthy and enduring rivalry in 1958. Mick and Christy were the two wing-forwards for a game against Monageer-Boolavogue that was played in Doran's field in Buffers Alley.

Tony and Joe Doran were among the opposition, along with Willie Walsh, who would go on to feature prominently on the club scene with Oylegate-Glenbrien, Shamrocks and Rapparees.

'It was a beautiful summer's evening, and we all rode over on our bikes to the game. The excitement created by the Rackard League, especially in those early days, was something else.'

Mick doesn't remember much about his first hurl. 'All I know is that we were just happy to have one,' he says. 'We had a neighbour called Pat Murphy, he was nicknamed "Tag" and he was Martin Storey's uncle. He was a great friend of the family always, and he made hurls.

'That meant we were never short of one. The ash would be sourced locally, and we were always delighted with whatever stick we were given.'

Ellen Jacob wasn't best pleased with her sons' growing interest in hurling at the outset.

In fact, she actively discouraged it for a while but, once she came around, she would support the boys every step of the way.

'When we started to break out of the nest to go hurling, she didn't want that at all. She said it would match us better if we minded our own business and our own farm. She always stressed that the two most important things were to look after your family and look after your land.

'I think she was afraid that hurling would distract us from those priorities.'

Having to guide four children through their teenage years without the help of her husband clearly hardened her attitude on that front. Life had to revolve around the house in Monavullen, and anything outside of that bubble – even hurling – was seen as a threat for a while.

'Our grandmother loved it a lot more than our mother in those days, she was always delighted to see us playing.

'I think our mother's attitude could be traced back to Jim Mythen too. When she was very young, and the family was struggling to make ends meet, Jim was missing from home a lot.

'Between hurling, and his involvement in the War of Independence, he wasn't always around the farm as much as the family needed. Our mother would never have forgotten that.'

Thankfully for Mick and his siblings, her attitude changed over time. Ellen was a shrewd woman, and she could see that going to the field to play hurling brought joy to her children's faces.

They had been through a very tough time after losing George, so anything that made them smile and took their mind off that crushing blow was surely a good thing.

All that Ellen Jacob ever wanted was for Robbie, Christy, Mick and Bridie to be happy. With hurling a readymade source, her initial displeasure quickly turned to approval.

◂◃◆▹▸

A DECISION TAKEN in 1954 had far-reaching implications for the hurling career of Mick Jacob.

Two years before the family's move to Monavullen, both sides of the parish united to line out together again under the Oulart-The Ballagh banner.

MICK JACOB CHAPTER 2

It had happened before during the playing days of his granduncle Jim Mythen but it was a short-lived experiment at the time, even though it resulted in two county final appearances.

Prior to that, Oulart had contested two senior hurling deciders, but neither were happy experiences.

The first-ever championship in Wexford was concluded on September 16, 1889, with an Oulart team captained by Phil Quirke losing to their near neighbours from Blackwater by 2-4 to no score in Kilthomas, Ferns.

Jim Mythen was nine years old, and he was firmly established on the team by the time Oulart next qualified for the final in 1908.

They travelled to the Showgrounds in Enniscorthy full of hope 12 days before Christmas, only for Castlebridge to shatter their dreams. The reigning champions registered an unanswered 5-11, but the only consolation was that Jim played well enough to ensure his continued selection for the Wexford team.

In those days, the county titleholders picked the players they wanted, and Mick's granduncle was the only Oulart man to make the grade for the All-Ireland winning campaign of 1910 – after Castlebridge's completion of the three-in-a-row at the expense of Red Rapparees from Enniscorthy in the 1909 final.

He was a strong presence in defence on the 17-a-side team that also featured five Castlebridge men, six from Screen, two apiece from New Ross and Wexford town, and the legendary Mike Cummins of Ballymurn.

Jim first featured with the county in championship hurling in 1903, with the last of his nine appearances coming 12 years later.

The margin of that 1908 county final defeat must have prompted the Oulart mentors to seek assistance from close to home, because they were united with The Ballagh for the 1911 campaign.

That championship spilled over into the following year, but Jim Mythen's name was notably absent from the Oulart-The Ballagh United team denied the title by Screen-Castlebridge on a 2-2 to 1-1 scoreline in Enniscorthy on St Patrick's Day in 1912.

However, he was back for the next campaign, the first to be played on a solely-league basis in a format that was continued all the way up to 1936. The decisive encounter to decide the destination of the 1912 championship took place in New Ross on January 19 of the following year, when Oulart-The Ballagh United went down to New Ross/Rathgarogue by 3-6 to 0-1.

Clearly, Mick Jacob's generation weren't the first to find winning the Wexford senior hurling crown such an elusive task.

After those successive final losses, the two sides of the parish must have gone their separate ways. Jim was invited to assist neighbouring Glenbrien and was involved with them when they won the championship in 1916.

After The Ballagh lost to Screen in the delayed 1921 senior hurling final on September 16, 1923, it would be 51 years and 13 days before the parish next featured at that stage. By then, Mick was the star performer on an emerging team, so unfortunate to come up against a four-in-a-row seeking Rathnure crew at the peak of their powers.

Following that 1923 game, a gap of 25 years ensued before the emergence of a team that would sow the seeds for the amalgamation of the mid-50s.

FOOTBALL WAS THE chief focus and brought more success during George Jacob's era in the 1930s, but there was a gradual shift in emphasis back to hurling.

And the first tangible evidence of progress was seen in 1948, when Fr Murphys from Oulart made it to the county junior final, powered by fine hurlers like Jack Devereux, Jim Sinnott and the Dempseys, Lar and Martin.

That team stayed together for another six years, without ever going close to contesting the final again. Mick remembers heading in to Gorey to watch what was probably their last match before the amalgamation.

Robbie takes up the story. 'That was in 1954. The Fr Murphys moved from Enniscorthy District to Gorey District for one year, but they gave a very disappointing performance.

'They were expecting to win, but Ballygarrett beat them fairly well. It was a bit of a shock to everyone, and there was a lot of soul-searching afterwards.'

It led to a meeting being called in the autumn of 1954, with a possible amalgamation between Oulart and The Ballagh the only item on the agenda.

Robbie Sinnott, the publican and grocer in The Ballagh, exerted a lot of influence on his side, while Martin Dempsey was Oulart's driving force.

Any sceptics were convinced that whatever chance they had of going places in hurling, it was surely more likely to happen if they were united rather than divided.

And so it was that the Oulart-The Ballagh club as we know it today came into being, although it took a few years before the proper structures were put in place.

Part of the problem from 1955 to '57 was the lack of any collective training before championship games. It was still common-place for the Raheenduff contingent to work away in one pod, while The Ballagh crew would do their own thing and the Oulart representatives would be elsewhere.

All that changed in 1958, and a man named John Doran must take the lion's share of the credit.

After three years of getting nowhere in the junior grade, it was accepted that the situation wouldn't change until the players came together to prepare on a regular basis.

Doran would make a fine field he owned in Mountdaniel available to the Oulart-The Ballagh club. John – a granduncle of Podge Doran, a Wexford full-forward of recent vintage – did it at great personal expense.

He could have used the land to sow corn and enjoy a nice turnover, but he was a loyal clubman first and foremost. John came to the rescue in their hour of need, and that well-trodden pitch in Mountdaniel was used to prepare every team that emerged from the parish until the new venue in Oulart village opened in 1980.

His farmer's field was one of two to have a profound influence on Mick's early years. Pat 'Tag' Murphy's in Tinnock was the place to be in the summer of 1959, with eager hurlers of all ages drawn to it like bees to a honeypot.

It was one of the warmest years on record, and the place was buzzing nearly every evening. Jim Mythen and 'Tag' were the best of friends, and Mick's grand-uncle would lie in the long grass around the perimeter of the field watching the action unfold.

Aged 79 at the time, he would pass away one year later, in 1960. And if he thought his grand-nephews were showing promise with stick and ball, they were destined to never know.

'He was a dour, serious-looking man, physically very big. He would go nine or 10 days without shaving, so he was a bit off-putting to approach,' Robbie recalls. 'You'd see him walking on the road on his way to visit certain houses, but he wouldn't stop to talk to anyone. He had a very close-knit circle of friends, and he kept very much to himself other than that.

'An air of mystery surrounded him after the War of Independence, and people tended to keep their distance from him unless they knew him particularly well. He wasn't the type of man you would approach for a casual chat.'

◄◄◆►►

MATTERS WERE GRADUALLY taking shape by the end of the 50s.

Mick and his fellow youngsters in the parish had hurling on the brain by that stage, and they couldn't get enough of it between the schoolyard and those albeit rare Rackard League outings.

The first rocky years after amalgamating the parish had been overcome, with a field secured for collective training that met with the approval of everyone.

And then, in 1959, another extremely significant piece of the jigsaw puzzle was put in place. Fr Frank Staples was appointed curate in The Ballagh, and the interest in hurling sky-rocketed like never before.

To Mick and most of his generation, this enthusiastic clergyman was the chief catalyst. The passion for the game was there already, but he added another essential ingredient... organisation.

And within a matter of weeks, there was a sense of purpose to everything that happened in Mountdaniel. Informal puckarounds were replaced with structured leagues for the young lads, and the participants responded with full support for Fr Staples and his efforts.

Mick refers to the field in a dialect unique to his parish and people. It's Mountdaniel on paper, but that's 'Mondaniel' in the Oulart-The Ballagh vernacular.

'When Fr Staples came, he was all about getting the chaps organised,' Mick recalls. 'He'd pick us up in Oulart to go over to the field in the evenings. The car would be overloaded with young lads, and he'd organise hurling for everyone over there... men and boys.

'I remember having leagues as chaps too, with three or four teams. It wasn't just the adults that were catered for. I used to love going over there. We only hurled on our own or on the school ground before that, but training was organised with Fr Staples.'

By the summer of 1960, it was family, farming and hurling all the way for Mick.

He finished his schooling for good once his primary education concluded, never to see the inside of a classroom again. That path was mapped out for him from an early age, and he was more than happy to follow it.

'I enjoyed myself enough at school, but even when I was very young I'd always head over to my uncles to work in the evenings.

'I'd go across the fields to the farm, and I got accustomed very quickly to the hard graft involved.

'Once I finished national school then, that was it for me. I was with my uncles then on the farm, until Mikie died in 1998 and Owen followed him in 2011.'

Mick's three siblings did pursue secondary education. Robbie was already in Enniscorthy CBS by that stage, while Christy went to the Vocational School in the town and spent some years back on the farm before setting up in business as a general building contractor in 1968.

As for Bridie, the baby of the family, when her turn came she flew the farthest of all away from the nest, attending boarding school in Arklow.

Mick's schooldays ended six years before the famous speech delivered by Minister Donogh O'Malley that delivered free secondary education to all. It wasn't taken as a given that students would automatically move up from primary level in his era.

Transport to the nearest town was also an issue, with schoolgoers left to their own devices in that regard. Breda, for example, remembers travelling eight or nine miles each way on her bike every day from her home in Knocknaskeaugh into Enniscorthy. Mick was thoroughly immersed in the land at that stage.

'My uncles Mikie and Owen were real father figures to me. They looked after me, and trained me very well. The three of us always got on great together, and that was most important of course.

'Some days we'd travel to marts and farms, buying cattle and sheep. Farming that time was all based around working with the horse, so you'd be at it hard all day, every day.

'From 9am say, going flat out until 5pm… or later, you'd be after covering a lot of miles by then. You'd have a good appetite for the dinner anyway, let me tell you. On a typical day, my uncles could be out ploughing, and I'd be tending to the cattle and sheep, or maybe cleaning the outhouses.

'There was a great spirit on that farm, and I was always very happy with Mikie and Owen. They were into hurling a lot as well, and that really helped when I was in the thick of it with Wexford.

'They never kept me away from hurling. They were delighted that I was doing well, and always very accommodating when it came to leaving work early in order to go to training or a game.

'My uncles were very like my mother in their attitude. They had a great spirit and drive in them, and a huge desire to succeed in everything they did. I learned an awful lot from all three of them that really stood to me in later life.'

MICK'S FIRST YEAR playing in the juvenile grade was at the age of 15 in 1961. Oulart-The Ballagh joined with Shelmaliers for a short-lived championship run, with the team looked after by Paddy Donohoe of Curracloe – son of Sim Donohoe, a teammate of Jim Mythen's for the 1910 All-Ireland win, and grandfather of current Wexford defender Simon Donohoe.

'I never remember playing much juvenile to tell you the truth,' Mick says, a victim of the straight knockout structures and the fact that the smaller rural amalgamations tended to be swallowed up by strong urban outfits.

Three successive Rackard League primary school final appearances for Oulart from 1961 to '63 highlighted the immediate strides made under the guidance of Fr Staples. After two losses, persistence paid off in 1963, with Mick's future long-time club and county colleague Jimmy Prendergast captaining the victorious team to victory.

It was the first county hurling title of any description to come to the parish since The Ballagh were crowned second division junior champions for 1916. And that, in itself, was a massive psychological boost – even to the grown-ups who needed that injection of confidence to drive them on in their own efforts.

The club junior team included one Mick Jacob by that juncture. The parish elders had seen something they liked in the youngest of George's three sons, and they didn't hesitate in throwing him in to the cauldron at the earliest opportunity.

◄ ◄ ◆ ► ►

THE FIRST INCLINATION that mentors were lining up Mick to play in goal at junior level arrived when he was a mere 14 years of age.

That happened in 1960, and it came completely out of the blue at an informal puck-around.

An additional team from the parish would enter the Enniscorthy District Junior Championship to cater for the large numbers not getting their game with Oulart-The Ballagh in the same competition.

The Tinnock Insurgents weren't a breakaway from the still relatively new club, rather an addition to make up for the oversight of not fielding two Oulart-The Ballagh teams in the first place. Mick's uncle Mikie was their unyielding full-back.

'The Tinnock lads were over in the field one evening getting ready for a game, and I had my hurl in my hand as usual,' Mick says. 'They asked me to stand in the goal and I must have done well that night. I remember Har Jeffs, who used to play with Oulart-The Ballagh at the time, coming over to me afterwards to compliment me on my performance.

'That started me off in the position. I think I might have played juvenile or minor against Blackwater, and I was in it then for a good while afterwards.'

Robbie would make the grade as a county minor in 1960, and he was part of that Tinnock team that fared better than many had expected. Their key man was John Darcy, a former Wexford senior hurler of the late-40s, who was a first cousin of the Nolan brothers from Oylegate-Glenbrien, Pat and John.

A county senior medal winner with the great Enniscorthy St Aidan's side in 1947, '52 and '54, he had a lot of experience and guile to impart to the younger players. 'John was living in Tinnock at the time, and farming over in Coolgarrow. He was from Monageer originally,' Robbie explains.

'The Insurgents beat St Kevin's from Tombrack in the first round, and we could have won the next match against Hollow Rangers too.

'We were only beaten by a point, but in one sense Darcy was pleased with how it all panned out. He was very friendly with Martin Dempsey, who would come to the field all the time to watch us train.

'There was a danger that if Tinnock kept winning, they would eventually meet Oulart-The Ballagh. Nobody was interested in that, it was never the intention. Darcy and Dempsey hatched a good plan to ensure the players not making the Oulart-The Ballagh team got to play with the Insurgents instead.'

That Tinnock side fulfilled its purpose for one year, with their championship win highlighting the depth of emerging young talent in the parish. It was a short-lived experiment, and from 1961 onwards it was Oulart-The Ballagh all the way as the Insurgents folded, never to return.

Blackwater were very strong in the junior grade at the time, having won the county title just four years earlier. They never tired of reminding their neighbours in Oulart-The Ballagh of their win when the parishes met in that first-ever county senior final in 1889.

And they would take the bragging rights again in 1961, eliminating Robbie and his teammates from the race for the Enniscorthy District title with a 5-12 to 4-1 replay win in Bellefield on September 10.

Mick, then 15, attended that match, never in his wildest dreams thinking he would be between the posts for the next meeting of the two clubs in the same grade.

Fr Staples had charge of the junior team for the 1962 campaign, with assistance from Bobby Walsh and Martin Dempsey. The first round was marked by a straightforward win over St Vincent's (Bunclody) in late May, leading Oulart-The Ballagh into another showdown with Blackwater.

'Har Jeffs had seen Mick in the goal that evening at training in 1960, and John Darcy would have studied him closely after that too,' Robbie says. 'He was at his ease in it, his body position was good, and he looked the part even as a 14-year-old.

'It was in people's minds then that he might be an option, but it happened purely by accident really.

'Two years later, he was 16, and we were coming up against Blackwater again. The idea of putting Mick in goal for the first time grew legs.'

FR STAPLES TOOK the teenager to one side and outlined the plan hatched by the selectors. Meanwhile, full-back Mylie Ryan was given very clear instructions… under no circumstances was any forward to be allowed near the youthful debutant goalie.

The No.1 was fair game for any attacker with the cuteness to evade the backs at the time. If an opponent sneaked in unnoticed, immense pleasure was derived from bundling the sliotar, and the man, into the net.

It wasn't a spot for the faint-hearted, but Mick had no fears in that regard given the quality of the cover directly in front of him. 'Mylie always stressed to me, from the very start, that I shouldn't worry. "Trust me, no one is going to get in here today",' he'd say. 'And you know what, he never let me down that way. "I'll watch the man… you watch the ball", that was Mylie's motto.'

The full-back was flanked by the experienced Nicky Sutton on the right, while the left corner-back was another emerging young gun in Jimmy Roche, a double Leinster medal winner in the senior and junior grades with St Peter's College in 1960, captaining the latter team.

'There was always great rivalry between Oulart-The Ballagh and Blackwater, and it really peaked around that time,' Mick continues. 'I'll never forget the crowd at that game, Bellefield was absolutely packed. I'd say it was the biggest ever attendance there for a junior match; it certainly felt like that to me.'

Oulart-The Ballagh needed to make a major statement to signify real progress on their part. Eight years after the parish amalgamation, Mick's debut was marked by their finest achievement thus far.

'The team played its best hurling in a very long time, and Mick did his job,' Robbie says.

'It was my first experience of a big time game, and I was delighted with the way things went,' Mick adds.

'I was only a very small and thin lad. I was surprised to be asked to play, because it came out of the blue. I never expected to be with the junior team when I was only a juvenile, but I was thrilled just the same.

'I had no nerves, I just went out and enjoyed it.'

'Mick had a great temperament for the goal,' Robbie explains. 'He was just thinking about stopping the ball. Anything else going on around him, none of that mattered.'

Mick puts his penchant for shot-stopping down to the endless hours spent with Christy in the yard at Monavullen. 'We'd make two goals and take shots at each other, hundreds of them at a time, and I do think whatever ability I had came from there. All we had was a sponge ball, and it could take off in any direction as the yard would be rough enough. I got my eye in from those days.

'I might take 10 shots on Christy, and then he'd take the next 10 on me. You could be hitting three or four hundred balls in an hour, and trying to stop shots with an ordinary hurl. I didn't have a goalie's hurl in those days.

'All of that really stood to me when I went in to Bellefield to play Blackwater.

'Mylie used to do the pucking out for me. With the spirit and drive that man had, sure you'd have to play well behind him. Mylie would cycle over to us in Monavullen, and then we'd all go together with him on the bikes over to Mountdaniel, five or six miles away. There would be nothing only hurling talk, over and back.

'That was really the start of our own team. If we were able to beat Blackwater, it showed everyone that we were moving in the right direction and we were capable of better things.'

THE DISTRICT SEMI-FINAL that followed was a more straightforward affair, as the Enniscorthy Shamrocks third team was dismissed with considerable ease.

On Sunday, September 9, 1962, 16-year-old Mick Jacob won his first medal in the Oulart-The Ballagh colours.

Bellefield played host to the District final against Duffry Rovers, and the men from Caim, Kiltealy and Ballindaggin stayed in contention until the final quarter. Oulart-The Ballagh led at half-time by 3-4 to 2-5, and the lead remained at two points (3-6 to 2-7) entering the last 15 minutes. The outcome hung in the balance, but the scoring power of Tommy O'Rourke (2-5) and Freddie Jeffs (2-1) ultimately powered their team home on a 6-7 to 3-8 scoreline.

And *The People* reported that the newcomer *had a wonderful game in goal.*

Sixteen years old Mick Jacob saved his side many times and following one particularly brilliant effort in the twentieth minute, Oulart swept upfield and Paddy Pender sent home a goal, to put his side four points clear again.

It was back to Bellefield a fortnight later for a handy county semi-final win over a Liam Mellows (Coolgreany) side more noted for their football prowess with Castletown. The scoreline was 5-7 to 1-3, and the game was so one-sided that nobody complained when referee Brian Dempsey from St Martin's brought proceedings to a halt five minutes early.

Youthful juvenile Mike Jacob guarded his net in splendid style, the reporter in *The Echo* wrote. *Brothers Christy and Robbie gave a delightful display in the half-forward line. Their younger brother, Mike, guarded the net well, with his courage and keen eye saving several dangerous situations.*

This was the stuff of dreams for Mick, looking forward to a county final after only a handful of appearances. Sadly, a fatal accident would mar what should have been a special day for the parish.

THE JACOB BROTHERS were raring to go on the morning of Sunday, October 7, 1962.

It was county junior hurling final day, with a 3pm throw-in for the game against Our Lady's Island in Wexford Park.

The big match was the only thing on people's minds after Mass, with the parish represented at this stage for the first time since Oulart Fr Murphys lost to St Martin's in April 1949.

Mick, Robbie and Christy couldn't wait for the ball to be thrown-in, with their anticipation growing as they piled in to the back of selector Martin Dempsey's car for the short journey into town.

Any nervous tension quickly dissipated. Their driver had played in that delayed 1948 final, so he had first-hand knowledge of the right things to say to young men counting down to the biggest game of their lives thus far.

Our Lady's Island came into the final with a strong pedigree. After pipping near neighbours and arch-rivals St Fintan's by one point, they had five to spare over St Martin's in the Wexford District decider.

The Martin's had already dethroned Shelmaliers – county championship runners-up of 1961 – so that outcome alerted everybody to the prowess of the men in blue from the deep south.

The Island had the benefit of a tougher semi-final too – edging past Cushinstown by 3-6 to 3-4 – while their games had all been played in a Wexford Park venue that was new ground for Oulart-The Ballagh.

As Martin turned the car on to the main Gorey-Wexford road, he focused on the positives rather than highlighting the obvious potential of their rivals.

They passed the pitch at Ballyfarnogue, the scene of Mick's first competitive match as a whipper-snapper in the Rackard League. A couple of miles further down the road, on the Oulart side of Castlebridge village, they could see something was amiss on their approach. It was in the townland of Kilcorral, close to the current-day turn-off that brings motorists down a narrow, winding road to the Shelmaliers club grounds in Hollymount.

Martin slowed down and, as they passed by the Neville household, they observed a car pulled across on to the other side of the road. Tommy O'Rourke, their team's top marksman and scorer of 2-5 in the District final against the Duffry, was standing on the road and appeared to be dazed and confused.

Martin didn't stop to make further enquiries. It was clear that an accident of some sort had occurred, but more than enough people were milling around to deal with it. He reasoned that his most important function at that moment was to get the Jacob boys in to Wexford Park for the county final.

Straight away, though, the mood in the car changed. 'We knew there had been an accident. There was tension all of a sudden, the three of us were in shock. We could sense that something terrible had happened,' Robbie recalls.

In those days, Wexford Park had two separate dressing-rooms, one at the Clonard end, and the other in the corner of the ground closest to St Peter's College. Oulart-The Ballagh were stationed in the latter, and slowly but surely the Jacobs' teammates started to arrive.

One man was missing, though. With every passing minute, and as each and every new face appeared through the door, the same questions were asked… 'Where's Tommy?'

'What's wrong?'

'Is he coming at all?'

The players were growing increasingly restless, and it was no way to prepare for a game of such importance.

Eventually Fr Staples arrived, the man whose word was final in their eyes. They had such immense respect for their chief mentor, and everyone turned to him for guidance. 'He said there had been an accident, although we didn't know at the time there was a fatality.

'Fr Staples tried to reassure us by adding the man involved had been at Mass and Communion that morning, but he didn't elaborate. I'll always remember those few words from him.'

Tommy O'Rourke wasn't specifically mentioned, but by that stage everyone knew he wouldn't be playing. It was a crushing blow to the hopes of Oulart-The Ballagh, already without the services of another accurate attacker in Freddie Jeffs, who had sustained injuries in a combine harvester accident during the week.

WITH TWO REGULAR members of the full-forward line missing, Oulart-The Ballagh had to re-adjust completely.

'We struggled in the first-half and didn't play well,' Mick says. 'It was definitely the shock setting in.

'We played a bit better in the second-half, but Our Lady's Island were without question the stronger team and deserved to win.'

The final score was 3-7 to 3-3, with Oulart-The Ballagh only leading for a brief period early in the second quarter. Pat Quigley goaled in the 16th minute, with that sole score of the opening half for his side giving them a 1-0 to 0-2 advantage. The Island replied with an unanswered 1-2 to take a four-point lead into the break.

Oulart-The Ballagh had the wind in their favour when the action resumed, but they were rocked by the concession of another 1-1 before eventually finding their feet.

They trailed by 3-6 to 1-1 at one stage, with Tony Byrne getting the team's first point. He later goaled from a close-in free, and Robbie also netted from 40 yards range, but there was no disputing the merits of the Island's win in a game described as... *One of the most exciting junior finals in years.*

Mick got a favourable mention, with *The People* stating he *did well and could not be blamed for any shots that beat him.*

The newspaper acknowledged the tragedy that unfolded to deny them the services of Tommy O'Rourke. *If the team did not strike the excellent form which was necessary against a tough, trying combination, its failure is pardonable.*

Disappointment after the match was placed in sharp perspective when the full extent of the accident was revealed to the players. They had lost a county final, but it was nothing compared to the grief bestowed on the Etchingham family of Ballinamona.

An account of the inquest made for harrowing reading in the local press.

Tommy O'Rourke was driving to the game with four passengers, including Patrick Etchingham who was in the back seat. At Kilcorral, they came upon two cyclists going in the same direction in front of the car. It was Patrick's father George Etchingham and James Dempsey, one of his neighbours from Ballinamona.

They were also on their way into Wexford Park, with George's teenage daughter Mary cycling some distance ahead of the pair. As they prepared to pass, Tommy sounded his horn three or four times. George Etchingham wobbled towards the centre of the road and directly into the path of the car. A collision was unavoidable.

George (66) sustained a fractured skull and his son estimated that he died, 'in about three minutes'.

It was a surreal, distressing scene for young Etchingham, coming only nine months after his mother – a first cousin of Tommy O'Rourke – passed away.

Now he knelt on a country roadside and cradled his father as he breathed his last. It was meant to be a happy day, with the Etchinghams looking on as Tommy played in the county final. The scene that unfolded instead was cruel beyond words.

Why did the match go ahead? It's a question Mick and his teammates have pondered over and over, and it has never been fully explained.

They learned that the opposition were amenable to a postponement once news of the accident reached Wexford Park. That was confirmed by Our Lady's Island official Leo Carthy, a legend of local politics and the GAA, who passed away in 2010.

For some reason that was never established, Fr Staples wanted the match to be played on the day. This was in an era when nobody questioned their local clergyman, and it never occurred to the Oulart-The Ballagh players to break ranks in that regard.

Fr Staples had already transformed hurling in his three years in the parish, and he knew best as far as they were concerned. Unfortunately, this was one call that backfired.

'It was our own fault. We didn't take the opportunity when the offer of a postponement was on the table,' Robbie says. The trouble was, none of the players were aware of this at the time, and they had absolutely no say in the matter.

They weren't consulted either when an objection was lodged by the club into the make-up of the victorious Island team.

'That would have come from Fr Staples. I think he was in shock with the result of that final. He was more than confident that we would win, over-confident really. I guess that's why he made the decision for us to go ahead and play.'

FR STAPLES HAILED from Piercestown, and his family of five siblings included three priests and a nun. He was an uncle of Vinny Staples, wing-back on the All-Ireland winning team of 1968, and was also related to George O'Connor.

'He was hot enough at times, and he could pick a row with anybody. Even in Mountdaniel, he'd be in among everyone hurling away, and he wouldn't want to get beaten. There was a strong fighting spirit in him, and he was into boxing too. He started the boxing club in The Ballagh, and they had great success.'

Fr Staples had arrived in The Ballagh after stints in Edinburgh, Kilmuckridge and Ballycanew, and he would become parish priest of Craanford in 1974. He went to live in Ballycogley after retiring, and died at the age of 86 just before Christmas 2008.

Lengthy evidence was presented to the county board to support Oulart-The Ballagh's position, and an extensive report on the meeting was carried in the local press.

However, by the end of the night a conciliatory approach was adopted by Fr Staples, and he congratulated the opposition on their success before Senator Seán Browne, chairing the meeting, declared the objection was lost.

The fall-out from that fateful day cost Mick and company a valued teammate.

Tommy O'Rourke felt extremely let down by the decision to proceed with the match, and he never played again. 'He lost all respect for the club, and carried that to the end of his days,' Robbie says. A native of Raheenduff, he farmed in Knocknaveigh, close to the parish borders with Ballymurn and Screen.

A quiet man, he never married and was regarded as a deep thinker. Sadly, the events of that day caused a rift that denied the club the services of a highly regarded player. 'We wouldn't have won the District final that year without Tommy. He scored 2-5 against the Duffry.

'He was a very cool player and made a big difference. He was an experienced man, 33 or 34 years of age at the time, and he had a great head for hurling.'

When Tommy died in late 2017, his surviving teammates of 1962 treated him the same as any of their previously fallen colleagues.

The guard of honour they formed was a final mark of respect for a man whose life changed in an instant with that freak accident. His exploits helped to put the Oulart-The Ballagh club on the map, and that's what Mick will always remember him for, first and foremost.

◄ ◄ ◆ ► ►

IT DIDN'T TAKE long for Mick's ability between the posts to attract some interest from the county selectors.

The Jacob name was already on the radar, as Robbie and Christy both made the Wexford minor panel in 1960, even though the latter was still a juvenile. By 1962, Christy was in his third and final year on the squad, and he had company for two trips to Croke Park in July.

Mick was selected as the reserve goalkeeper for both Leinster Championship outings that summer, with Peter Reck from Davidstown-Courtnacuddy between the posts.

Christy did well, lining out at left corner-forward and scoring 1-0 and 1-1 respectively in a one-point win over Offaly and a three-point final defeat to Kilkenny.

The outcome was par for the course in that era. The minor grade was established in 1928, at a time when football was king in Wexford, and the county wouldn't reach a Leinster hurling final until 1955.

Seven years later, their name still wasn't on the roll of honour, so there was no great surprise when Kilkenny ended their interest by 5-7 to 5-4.

Mick doesn't remember anything about those two games, the first of countless trips he would make to Croke Park to don a purple and gold jersey. However, he has a clear recollection of one of the journeys up that left him star-struck.

'Seeing Robbie and Christy involved definitely gave me a big incentive to get on a Wexford team. In 1962 I came in as sub-goalie on the minors, and that was the start of it. I was only 16, and I was delighted of course.

'At that time, the Wexford teams used to travel to the matches in hackney cars. The arrangement was that someone from Wexford town would collect us at our house. You'd get a note in the post, telling you that you were selected, and letting you know the time to be ready.

'Anyway, for one of those matches in 1962, and I can't remember if it was the semi-final or final, myself and Christy couldn't believe our eyes this particular morning when the car pulled up outside.

'As we hopped in to the back seat, weren't Billy Rackard and Ned Wheeler, with his head of blonde hair, sitting there too. The seniors played after us both days, beating Laois and then Kilkenny to win the Leinster title.

'It was unreal for the two of us to share a car journey to Dublin with those two men. It brought me back to our house outside Gorey as a chap in 1954 and '55, standing outside on the morning of every big game and waiting to cheer them on as they passed.

'Now, here we were in one of those very same cars with them. It was a great shot in the arm for the two of us. Billy Rackard was an idol to me. I looked up to him as an outstanding player, and Ned Wheeler was the very same.

'And they were so good to us on that trip. They talked away to us and made us feel very much at home. That created even more interest for me.

'Ned Wheeler became great friends with my mother after that. He used to drive around the county delivering home heating oil, and he'd always call in for a chat and a cup of tea. My mother was beginning to get a big interest in hurling as well around that time. She might have been dubious about us playing at first, but she had definitely converted by that stage. She was some supporter after that.'

WEXFORD HURLING HAD continued to rise after those days of innocence in the mid-50s when a flag-waving Mick cheered the players on as they passed his front door.

However, it wasn't as simple as modern times, when any youngster with even a passing interest in the game will have access to Croke Park for every big match (post-Covid, of course).

Mick and Christy didn't attend the All-Ireland final of 1955, although Robbie went to it with their uncle Mikie.

Nobody ventured to Dublin in 1956, with the appetite for attending games non-existent among the Jacobs at the time after the death of their father.

'My first Wexford match was in 1957,' Mick says. 'I didn't see them in any other game before that one. I can remember being in the Cusack Stand… but we were standing rather than in seats.'

The match in question was the Leinster final, played on August 4, and it ended in a crushing 6-9 to 1-5 loss to Kilkenny. It was a disastrous showing from a team in search of a fourth provincial title on the trot.

'Wexford were very poor that day, and I was fierce disappointed as a chap. I think they had been in New York earlier in the year, and they didn't seem to be at the races after coming back.'

Pat O'Grady, the Urlingford man who had bought the farm in Ballincash, occupied the driver's seat that day, with Mick's uncle Mikie also making the journey. Generally speaking, though, it was an occasional treat for the Jacob boys to attend Wexford matches in the late-50s.

'We were a little bit isolated where we were living at the time. We were only a short period in our new home in Oulart, and we weren't fully integrated into the community. We didn't have a car, and our uncles didn't either, so we were always relying on someone else – usually Pat O'Grady – to ask us along if he was travelling.'

Robbie was the only one to witness the Leinster final defeat of 1958 to Kilkenny, while there was no Jacob presence the next year when Wexford lost the semi-final to Dublin in Nowlan Park by one point.

However, Mick looked on as an avid spectator in 1959 as the exploits of the Oulart-The Ballagh minor team that contested the county final with Kilmore/Rathangan put his two brothers on the hurling map.

After a drawn game, a dispute arose over the replay date because, at the time, boarding students in St Peter's College weren't released for matches during school term. Both teams were affected by that situation, so a compromise saw the second meeting delayed until the summer holidays of 1960. All momentum would be lost by that stage as Oulart-The Ballagh went down by five points, but the campaign drew welcome attention to the club.

Indeed, five of the team made the Wexford minor panel for 1960, with Robbie and Christy joined by Jimmy Roche, Billy Dunne and Johnny Murray. 'Christy was the sub-goalie and he was still a juvenile. That was the start of the family goalkeeping tradition.'

Mick had an even bigger incentive to make the grade at that stage. 'When Robbie and Christy got on that minor panel, I realised it was there for me too if I really worked hard at it.'

He was in Nowlan Park on June 19, 1960, when the minors pipped Dublin by a point, with the seniors lucky to draw with them immediately afterwards.

'I got a real appreciation for what it was all about in 1960. The seniors stepped it up after that draw, and went on to win the All-Ireland. I was at those games and for the first time I was able to get a really close look at all those great players I had heard so much about.'

Mick would wear that Wexford jersey himself as a 16-year-old substitute in 1962. He had two years left as a minor, but his first brush with GAA politics was just around the corner.

◄◄◆►►

ALL THE STARS aligned for the Wexford minor hurlers in 1963, but Mick had nothing to do with it through no fault of his own.

The county set out that year in search of a first-ever Leinster title in the grade, having lost the finals of 1955 (after a replay), '56, '59, '60 and '62… all to Kilkenny.

It had taken Wexford a long time to become contenders, and the Hanrahan Cup still eluded them.

The All-Ireland senior A success enjoyed by St Peter's College in 1962 acted as a major fillip for the next year's campaign, while Enniscorthy CBS and Wexford CBS were also going well in B competitions.

And the minor breakthrough finally occurred in 1963 when Kilkenny were pipped by 6-10 to 6-8 in a high-scoring provincial final. A routine rout of Antrim followed in Belfast, before Wexford brought the All-Ireland crown home at the first attempt with a 6-12 to 5-9 success over Limerick.

It was a memorable few months for those young guns, but Mick was controversially ignored by the selectors.

AFTER BEING UNDERSTUDY to Peter Reck in 1962, both goalkeepers were still eligible for the grade and would have expected to fight it out between themselves for the No.1 jersey.

And Mick also had worthy credentials for consideration as an outfield player.

Oulart-The Ballagh united with Oylegate-Glenbrien for minor purposes in 1962, and caused a huge upset when ousting the Rathnure and Duffry Rovers combination in the District semi-final. With only a few days to recover before the decider, they were unable to repeat that performance and were hammered by Davidstown-Courtnacuddy on a 6-11 to 1-0 scoreline.

The county selectors never missed a match of any significance in those days, so Mick's displays – both at midfield, and between the posts for the juniors – would have been duly noted.

And yet, he was a startling omission when the minor squad to meet Laois in the Leinster semi-final in Croke Park on July 7, 1963, was announced.

The system at the time saw one selector chosen from each of the four Districts (Enniscorthy, Gorey, Wexford and New Ross), along with a representative of the previous year's county juvenile champions.

Liam Byrne of Rathnure caught the eye when his club beat Na Fianna from

Wexford town to win the under-16 crown in 1962, but his selection for the county minors came like a bolt out of the blue nonetheless. He was still only 15 years old for that 1963 campaign, but he got the nod in goal, with Peter Reck selected as his deputy.

Mick was left out in the cold, and it was a decision that shrewd observers struggled to understand.

Jackie Whelan, the highly-respected Gaelic games correspondent with *The Echo* newspaper in Enniscorthy, was among that cohort.

His weekly *Games of the Gael* column was required reading for all GAA followers, with his finger very much on the pulse. And in the week before that minor match with Laois, he commented on the goalkeeping issue.

Goalie Byrne (Rathnure and CBS) is undoubtedly the best juvenile net-minder in the county, but for minor purposes, where defenders have yet to learn the "keep-out-the-forwards" tactics of seniors, this year's choice should have been made from Oulart's Ml. Jacob (actually on trial Thursday for the county inter. team, no less), Shamrocks' midfield-capt. in minor, and senior sub-goalie Kevin Doyle... or last year's and CBS net-minder, Courtnacuddy's Peter Reck (sub.), with Byrne getting the job next year or the year after from an age and height point of view as apart from merit, which no one will deny he has to spare.

Jackie was at his diplomatic best in getting his point across. Nobody was disputing the quality of Byrne's goalkeeping, but he was very young and some of his elders were more than capable of doing the same job.

Mick missed out on Leinster and All-Ireland medals as a result, but there isn't a trace of bitterness as he remembers that major snub nearly 60 years later.

'It was a hard thing for Oulart players to break in to any county team at the time,' he says. 'If you went to St Peter's or one of the other strong hurling schools, you were going to at least get a chance, that was guaranteed.

'But a hurler from our club was not really recognised in the same way. We had to show we had as much talent as the rest of them, but it was that bit more difficult for us at the time.'

The fact that Mick couldn't utilise schools hurling as a 'shop window' didn't help his cause. Then again, he had performed well as a 16-year-old goalkeeper at junior level, so there was no reason to think he wouldn't be capable of handling the minor gig.

His response to the selectors' dubious call was admirable. 'It never really bothered me, if I'm honest. It just made me put the head down and go harder and stronger,' he says.

Big brother Robbie acknowledges that: 'Mick would have a great attitude in a situation like that, but it can't be denied that he got a very raw deal.

'It didn't knock him back all the same, it just put a better edge on him.

'The biggest disappointment to me was that he never even got a trial for the minors. Mick, without question, should have been in goal with them in '63.

'There was still a general attitude that there wouldn't be any hurlers in Oulart, and for some people it was convenient to ignore him.'

◄◄◆►►

THERE WAS ANOTHER twist to Mick's goalkeeping tale a mere week after failing to make the squad to meet Laois. And it's only fair to point out that, on this occasion, he had somebody to speak up for him on the selection committee, and it did him no harm at all.

Oulart-The Ballagh's District title win in 1962 led to Robbie Sinnott's appointment as a mentor with the Wexford intermediates, along with Patsy Crean (Hollow Rangers), Nick Devereux (Our Lady's Island), Seamus Redmond (Adamstown) and Tom Donohoe (Buffers Alley).

The county warmly embraced this new grade when it was introduced in 1961, winning the All-Ireland title at the first attempt.

After an opening round exit to Kilkenny one year later, they would make a good start to the 1963 campaign.

Wins over Meath and Antrim resulted in another clash with the Cats, this time in the Leinster final in New Ross on July 14. Jimmy Roche, Tony Byrne and Robbie had represented the club on the team in those opening rounds, but a problem arose when regular netminder Jimmy Crean of Hollow Rangers was unavailable for the Kilkenny game.

Robbie Sinnott spoke up, and the rest of the selectors listened... 'What about our man?'

IF A WEEK is a long time in politics, the same can surely be said with regard to

Mick's burgeoning hurling career in 1963.

Just seven days after the minors beat Laois without him, he manned the goal for the intermediates and won his first Leinster medal with a 3-8 to 3-6 success against Kilkenny.

Two late points from Eamonn Doyle got Wexford over the line in a game that could have gone either way, with Mick joined on the winning team by a club colleague Tony Byrne at left half-back.

Newspaper reports noted that he kept a *fairly good goal*, and much was made of the fact that *Jacob is still a minor who is unable to get his place between the posts for the minor team.*

The local press didn't let the issue rest as the summer progressed.

A preview of the Leinster minor final noted: *A really startling feature of the selection is that the boy who played for the full hour in Sunday week's Leinster intermediate final, M. Jacob – a minor – is not on the selection.*

The intermediate selectors obviously believed that he was worthy of deputising for regular custodian, Jimmy Crean, but the age-limit mentors think otherwise. He is not even listed as a substitute.

Fault has not been found with the chosen goalkeeper, Liam Byrne, who has had outstanding games both with his club and with Enniscorthy C.B.S., but the point is that both sets of selectors cannot be right. Incidentally, Liam Byrne is still a juvenile.

By the time the intermediates contested the All-Ireland 'Home' final against Tipperary – in Waterford on August 18 – Jimmy Crean was back from injury. Mick and Robbie were on the bench, with Tony Byrne flying the club flag on the field in a 0-17 to 2-3 defeat.

'Robbie Sinnott would have always backed me up. He'd fight his corner and stand up for the Oulart-The Ballagh players. At that time, a lot of similar type incidents would have happened with under-age teams in particular. Coming from a small club, you'd have to be an absolute star the whole time before some selectors would even look at you,' Mick says.

'I was glad to be with those intermediate lads, though. That was a good experience and it really stood to me.'

◄ ◄ ◆ ▷ ►

MICK AND HIS club colleagues still had the District junior title to defend by the end of that eventful summer of 1963.

This championship was notoriously difficult to win in the first place, let alone keep the crown for two years running. The grand total of 17 teams had their names in the hat for the competition, but Oulart-The Ballagh's path to the final was relatively straightforward.

A 6-7 to 4-5 win was recorded over St Mary's from Bunclody in early August, with their old friends from over the road in Blackwater involved in a game on the same double bill with Monageer-Boolavogue that was abandoned after a brawl.

The semi-final was a one-sided affair, with journalist Jackie Whelan trawling the records to confirm that Oulart-The Ballagh's 14-9 to 1-5 win over Shamrocks was the third highest-scoring game in the history of the championship.

Blackwater duly made it through boardroom and on-field battles to get another crack at the team that dumped them on Mick Jacob's debut in 1962. The final in Bellefield on October 13 certainly lived up to expectations, although Christy was a big loss with an injury.

There was nothing between the sides, and they were level at the interval and once again at full-time.

Oulart-The Ballagh veteran Phil Redmond, the Man of the Match, looked to have secured the winner when he tapped over a point, only for James Ormonde to equalise.

The game ended 3-5 to 2-8, and there was some confusion at the finish because a scoreboard error had Oulart-The Ballagh on 3-6. Referee John Canavan quickly confirmed it was a draw, and everybody finally got the chance to draw breath.

The Echo said *Mick proved a very cool, confident and reliable goalkeeper,* with *The People* noting that ... *both goalkeepers showed up very prominently and each in turn had some very fine saves under pressure.*

The replay was an out-and-out thriller, and it looked to be going the holders' way when a Freddie Jeffs goal with 10 minutes left gave them the lead for the first time (5-3 to 3-8). However, that man James Ormonde – who would go on to play senior championship hurling with Wexford in 1964 – rattled the net late on to give Blackwater a 4-12 to 5-4 success.

◄◄◆►►

'AH, MIKE ROWSOME... he finished me forever in the goal with Oulart!'

It's a long-standing joke between the Jacob and Rowsome families, and it relates to the clash with Monageer-Boolavogue in the Enniscorthy District Junior Hurling Championship of 1964.

Oulart-The Ballagh went into that game with their near neighbours as hot favourites, only to leave Bellefield a chastened crew after losing by 5-6 to 3-4.

And the man chiefly responsible for the surprise result was Michael Rowsome, scorer of four goals for the previously unheralded winners, who came from behind after trailing by three points at half-time. It was, indeed, Mick Jacob's last-ever club game between the posts, and his good friend gets the blame!

In the years to follow, Mick's colleagues on the Wexford senior team would include Michael's younger twin brothers Billy and Declan. Indeed, Mick and Billy were midfield partners in the Leinster final demolition of Kilkenny in 1976.

And when a 'This Is Your Life' DVD of Mick's career was compiled in 2018, it was the handiwork of Ed Rowsome, Michael's son and an absolute fanatic on all matters related to Wexford hurling.

'Mike Rowsome claims he made a hurler out of Mick that day,' Robbie jokes.

'They wanted me out the field from then on to clean up after Robbie and the lads,' is his brother's instant retort.

While that defeat came as a bitter disappointment, in hindsight it was on the cards.

After Oulart-The Ballagh's tremendous effort in 1962 and '63, the same appetite for hard work wasn't there at the third time of asking.

It didn't help that Mick and Christy were absent from a lot of the training sessions due to their growing county commitments, although that was hardly their fault; the brothers couldn't be in two places at the one time, after all.

Robbie, an ever-present at all club gatherings, branded the campaign 'a disaster'.

'We changed that year from Mountdaniel to Oulart. We got a field to use in Dempseys of The Folly, and ran a parish league similar to 1958.

'That went very well, and it looked like we could have a good year, but it all fell flat.

'The two boys used to be training in Enniscorthy with the county team, and some fellas would come to our field and wouldn't even tog out.

'The effort was nearly nil by the end, and we paid a heavy price.'

'That game against Monageer was a real wake-up call,' Mick says.

And Robbie feels the lack of any tradition for winning in the parish came to the surface in 1964.

'Deep down, too many of our players still didn't really think we could do it. After 1962 ended in disappointment, it still carried us through '63, but we collapsed in '64.

'The one thing that saved us was a tournament organised in Bunclody by a lovely man named Tony O'Loughlin, a local garda who hailed from Clare. He invited us to play in October and we were delighted to have matches. Some of our lads had gone back to their old way of thinking after the Monageer game.

'They would have felt that… *If we don't win, sure it's grand.* That was never the way we thought in our house, we had a completely different attitude.'

When Oulart-The Ballagh were drawn against Monageer-Boolavogue in the first round of that Bunclody tournament, it was a chance to re-invent themselves.

'It gave us a real thirst for hurling again, and put us back on the right path. We really needed it at the time,' Robbie recalls. Two decisions taken by the selectors before that game had a profound influence on the future direction of the club.

FIRST OF ALL, Mick was chosen at midfield, and from that day forward he never wore a No.1 jersey in the Oulart-The Ballagh colours again. In order to facilitate that, they called on his old school friend whose agility when they were children made him impossible to beat.

'Johnny Parle was living on the borders with Blackwater, and maybe he was forgotten about a little bit as a result. He was a very quiet sort, but the selectors took a chance on him for the tournament and he said he'd play,' Robbie says. 'In time, what Mick and the boys had said about him as a youngster rang true. Parle really produced the goods for us in goal.'

Indeed, he would go on to be understudy to the great Pat Nolan in the Oylegate-Glenbrien clubman's last two years as Wexford goalkeeper (1973 and '74), winning a National League medal in the process.

'Mick at midfield transformed the whole team,' Robbie adds.

'It was fairly physical, and Mick was chased around for the whole match in the Bridge Meadow by Jack O'Brien. We reversed the result of the championship match, and Jack didn't take it that well,' he adds with a laugh.

That tournament continued into 1965, and it was won outright by the new-look Oulart-The Ballagh side thanks to further wins over Davidstown-Courtnacuddy, Askamore and Duffry Rovers respectively.

'We were mad for hurling, but we had only played one championship match in 1964. Winning that tournament brought the belief back again.'

◄◄◆►►

IF THE CLUB scene didn't go as planned in 1964, a whole new adventure was only just beginning on the county front. And Mick was very much part and parcel of it, as the under-21 grade was added to the competitive mix.

It was decided that this new Wexford team would be picked by the six senior selectors, including three stars of recent vintage in Nickey Rackard, Nick O'Donnell and Mick O'Hanlon. They were joined by Art Bennett (Oylegate-Glenbrien), Peter Hayes (Enniscorthy St Aidan's) and John 'Dough' Murphy (Faythe Harriers) – and Mick was targeted as their man for the goalkeeper's jersey.

In contrast to his minor experience, he has nothing but good memories of that shrewd sextet.

'Those selectors were very fair… very good with lads. They were really organised, and they were able to deal with people in the right way. And sure, you'd be giving 100 percent all the time with a man like Nickey Rackard over the team. He was a father figure to lads like me.

'He was a great sort, always very encouraging… giving sound advice.

'He'd come up to you at training or after a game and say, "You're going well… you're doing great!"

'To hear those words from a man like Nickey, sure it was something special altogether.'

Lady luck played a part in the first game of that campaign, against Kilkenny in New Ross on April 19. Wexford crept home by 4-3 to 3-5, and it was largely down to a vital late save from Mick.

'Tom Walsh nearly scored a goal at the end alright, but I got my hurl to it,' he remembers. 'Tom went on to be a top class forward, and it was very sad what happened to him when he lost an eye in the 1967 All-Ireland final. He was a huge loss to Kilkenny.'

That late incident was described as *a narrow escape* in *The People*, with the future senior forward *racing through from far out, with Jacob just saving at the upright.* Despite that vital intervention, the reporter wasn't entirely convinced by Mick's overall display, saying he did not inspire confidence.

In fact, he even suggested that the selectors would not be wrong in choosing either Tommy Rowe (Adamstown) or Ger McWilliams (Horeswood), who had played in goal for their respective clubs in the curtain-raiser. Thankfully, Nickey Rackard and his fellow mentors had full faith in the 18-year-old from Oulart-The Ballagh, even though this particular reporter was on Mick's case again after the Leinster semi-final.

It was a runaway 8-13 to 3-6 win over Dublin, and the journalist accepted that the goalkeeper *did not get a lot to do, and saved some good shots in each half.* However, he *allowed one very harmless-looking effort from forty yards to beat him in the second-half.*

THE FIRST-EVER Leinster final in the new grade was held in Wexford Park on June 28, and it was an unremarkable contest as the home side easily accounted for Laois by 4-7 to 2-2. It left Mick with provincial intermediate and under-21 medals although he was still a minor, while Christy was an unused substitute.

Interestingly, he didn't get the nod for the intermediate squad of 1964. The fact that Robbie Sinnott was no longer the Enniscorthy District selector was probably a factor. Wexford won a second All-Ireland title in the grade in his absence, with Seamus Boggan from St Martin's between the posts, while former Leinster football full-back Andy Doyle (Camross) offered back-up.

On the weekend after winning his first Leinster under-21 medal, Mick finally got to play a little bit of minor hurling with the county.

However, even then it was by default, as initially he wasn't selected on the team to play Kilkenny in its first defence of Leinster and All-Ireland titles in Croke Park. A match preview expressed surprise to see Mick among the substitutes. *He was confidently expected to get his place at midfield. However, Pat Quigley could not be left out, while Terence Murphy, on latest form, deserves his chance,* The People added.

Mick was listed as No.17 on the programme, but 'Ternie' Murphy of Buffers Alley cried off, and he was given his chance. It passed by in the blink of an eye, so much so that he has absolutely no recollection of the game.

Mick was replaced before half-time by Pat Roche of Kilmore, and Wexford were dismissed by 3-5 to 2-3. Robbie has a theory on why that brief minor outing didn't go well for his brother.

'At that stage, most of Mick's hurling was done in goal. He was still there with the club, and he was in with the under-21 team. When he got the chance at midfield in minor, I think he lacked that little bit of sharpness needed for the position. His reactions were just slightly off, he wasn't reading the break of the ball like the others.'

And if that observation was bang on the money, it certainly couldn't be levelled at him ever again as his career flourished.

Casement Park in Belfast was the next port of call for the under-21 team in 1964, and the Jacob brothers both played big roles in a 5-8 to 2-3 victory over Antrim.

Mick had a number of fine saves to his credit, especially in the first-half, while Christy came on and scored 1-2. *His first class display will pose a very big problem for the selectors*, the match report concluded.

Christy was, indeed, chosen for the final against Tipperary in Nowlan Park on October 4, but his goal from centre-forward wasn't enough to save Wexford from an 8-9 to 3-1 hammering.

John D Hickey of the *Irish Independent* felt the game was *infinitely more entertaining than the unhealthy state of the scoreboard suggested at the call of time.*

Tipperary surged into a 4-2 to 0-1 lead after 16 minutes, largely through the brilliance of Michael 'Babs' Keating, while Mick Roche was superb at midfield. Although Dan Quigley was a powerhouse in front of Mick at full-back, the Munster lads added 2-3 without reply in the last 10 minutes.

'We got a lot of good men out of that team for the seniors,' Mick notes. 'There was Dan of course, as well as Vinny Staples, and Mick Kinsella came on. But I remember Babs and Mick Roche in particular that day, the two of them were outstanding.'

Despite that disappointment, and his treatment over two successive years by the minor mentors, Mick's stock was rising by the end of 1964. Two Leinster medals and an All-Ireland final appearance wasn't a bad return, after all, for a young lad yet to celebrate his 19th birthday.

*Mick's First Holy Communion (left), and with Bridie on their Confirmation Day (right);
given their closeness in age, the bond between brother and sister, also pictured in
Coolnahinch (centre), was always extremely strong.*

*Robbie, Mick, Bridie and Christy on a happy family occasion with their mother Ellen,
who showed courage and strength in the face of adversity after George's untimely
death in 1956.*

« CHAPTER 3 »

THE NEW UNDER-21 grade came along at the perfect time for Mick Jacob.

After a minor career comprising less than half an hour of game-time and one almighty snub, it provided him with exposure to a high standard of hurling from 1964 to '67. Of the 19 county under-21 games played by Mick over those four campaigns, only two were spent in an outfield position.

While he was freed from the goalkeeping shackles at club level from late 1964 onwards, it took a considerably longer time before he could bid a final farewell to that No.1 jersey with Wexford.

Nonetheless, the club scene showcased his prowess at midfield throughout that period, and eventually the penny dropped with the county selectors; they simply couldn't afford to do without Mick Jacob in that department.

'Bringing in the under-21 grade that time was fantastic for me,' he agrees. 'I was coming from a junior club, so it was great to get that exposure, to play in so many big games with and against the top players. There was a huge interest in it among supporters too. It was something new for starters, but also people wanted to see all these good young players in the flesh after the minors won in 1963.'

The experiment whereby the Wexford under-21 team was picked by the senior selectors ended after year one of the competition in 1964. For the following campaign, Ned Power of St Peter's College trained the squad that was chosen by Fr Paddy McDonald (Kilmore), Tom Doyle (Adamstown), John Hennessy

(Rathnure) and Tom Butler (Buffers Alley).

Mick was only substitute goalie to Pat Roche from Kilmore – the man who had replaced him outfield in the previous year's minor championship – for the first round, a ridiculously easy 17-9 to no score demolition of Wicklow in Gorey.

And a stroke of good fortune elevated him to a starting spot, as Roche cried off through illness shortly before the clash with Kilkenny in Nowlan Park on May 9.

In goal, M. Jacob brought off some magnificent saves and were it not for his brilliant display the scoreboard might have read differently at the end, the reporter in *The Echo* enthused.

The People felt… *The winners' superiority was not truly reflected in their 5-7 to 5-3 victory, but they were never in command and owe a great deal to substitute goalkeeper, Michael Jacob, who was far busier during the hour than was Kieran Purcell, his opposite number.*

In years to come, Jacob and Purcell would have some tremendous individual battles in Croke Park on Leinster final day, with their goalkeeping roles long since confined to the rear-view mirror.

One of the anomalies of the 1965 campaign was that Christy was a regular starter in the forwards with the intermediate county team at the same time, but he couldn't make the under-21 side.

He only got a chance in a 3-5 to 2-3 Leinster semi-final win over Offaly in Tullamore on June 17 because Willie Bierney – the All-Ireland winning minor captain of 1963 – was unable to get off work.

And with Christy back on the bench, Wexford's second successive provincial title arrived in a considerable degree of comfort. Dublin were dispatched by 7-9 to 1-5 in Croke Park, with Mick bringing off two excellent saves at the end of a first-half that finished with the holders in command by 6-3 to 1-3.

A quiet hour followed in the All-Ireland semi-final, with Antrim unable to match the decent challenge they had provided one year earlier. The game in Gorey was an 8-13 to 0-4 romp, and it set up a repeat meeting with holders Tipperary on the second Sunday of September.

'That was the wettest day I ever played in,' Mick remembers. 'We stripped off in a tent beside Nowlan Park. It was a great day for Wexford, but the conditions were absolutely terrible. The water was standing in the goalmouth at the two ends, but we had most of the team from the year before and played very well.

'There was Dan Quigley at full-back, with Willie O'Neill and Aidan Somers on either side. The three lads in the half-back line – Vinny Staples, Mick Kinsella and Willie Murphy – would all win senior medals with me in 1968.

'Then there was Joe Doran and Eugene Ryan in the middle of the field, and all six forwards were capable of taking a score on their good days.

'We had Con Dowdall, Pat Quigley and Seamus Barron in the half-line, and then Tony Maher, Tony Doran and Jack Berry inside. Christy came on too that day, for Seamus Barron,' Mick adds. Doran (1-2) and Berry (1-1) made key contributions in a commanding 3-7 to 1-4 success, with the big Buffers Alley man back in the fold following a truly bizarre chain of events in 1964.

After scoring six goals in the under-21 clash with Dublin, and playing in the subsequent Leinster final win over Laois, he was dropped off the panel for the All-Ireland series. Clearly, Mick Jacob wasn't the only future senior great on the receiving end of rough justice in that era.

Willie O'Neill, captain of the under-21 side in 1965, played in the All-Ireland senior final loss to Tipperary just one week earlier. On that occasion, he found the experienced Seán McLoughlin a tough customer to deal with, but he was outstanding in his own age group. Given the task of keeping tabs on 'Babs' Keating, the tenacious Kilmore man carried out his orders to perfection.

The People had high praise for the defence which was brilliant as a unit... *no star shone brighter than Michael Jacob in goal. When Tipperary did get through for shots at goal in the first-half, he proved most reliable, and when on a few occasions one was just about to shout goal for Tipperary, the Oulart youth came to the rescue with a safe and relieving clearance.*

He maintained his high standard in the second-half, although the goalmouth was a sea of mud.

◄ ◄ ◆ ► ►

THE MEETING OF great minds involved in two neighbouring clubs worked wonders in the development of Mick Jacob as a top class hurler.

When the under-21 grade was introduced in 1964, Oulart-The Ballagh only got the benefit of one game in this new knockout competition.

They were joined with Oylegate-Glenbrien, continuing an association from the previous year's minor grade, but Rathnure beat them by 5-5 to 2-3 in the Enniscorthy District semi-final. In 1965, the Oulart-The Ballagh mentors looked elsewhere. Buffers Alley were their neighbours, just a few miles up the road, but their teams operated in Gorey District. Enniscorthy was a bit of a minefield at the time, given the constant presence of Rathnure and the ability of the town itself to produce outstanding age limit teams at the drop of a hat.

It made it very difficult for a small club like Oulart-The Ballagh to advance.

On the other hand, Gorey District wasn't quite as strong overall. Ferns St Aidan's did have powerful young teams in the 60s, but the Wolfe Tones lacked consistency in the town.

At some stage in the winter months of 1964 and '65, Martin Dempsey and Robbie Sinnott met up with Willie Doran and Ger Dempsey from Buffers Alley. They agreed it would be in the best interests of both clubs to amalgamate for the next under-21 campaign.

It ensured the two younger Jacobs would be united with the Dorans and Butlers, making the prospects for success extremely bright.

THE FIRST MATCH for the new partners took place in Gorey on April 25, 1965. St Brendan's of Craanford were destroyed by 12-12 to 1-5, with Mick at centre-forward and Christy scoring 2-5 from the left wing.

The Gorey District title followed, and it paved the way for a county semi-final on a Wednesday evening in late August that produced exceptional fare.

'I'd rate that as the best club match I ever saw,' Robbie says, high praise indeed for the quality of the play produced as the Oulart-The Ballagh/Buffers Alley combination defeated a Rathnure side assisted by Duffry Rovers on a 5-5 to 2-11 scoreline. The game was played in Gorey, just three days after the county under-21s hammered Antrim in the All-Ireland semi-final at the same venue.

Several teammates were now on opposing sides, with Mick, Christy, Eugene Ryan, Tony and Joe Doran up against Dan and Pat Quigley, Aidan Somers and Seamus Barron among others.

'I was on Seamus that night in Gorey,' Mick says. 'The excitement at that game was unreal, I'll never forget it. There was no such thing as looking around and admiring yourself that night. I had to get really stuck in to Seamus and get the job done.'

Mick started alongside Tony Doran at midfield, but the threat posed by Barron soon led to his first major test as a centre-back that was passed with flying colours. 'Seamus was on a bit of a roll, and it looked like he was going to win the match for Rathnure on his own,' Robbie recalls. 'But Mick contained him, and stemmed the flow. Once he went back to face the ball, it looked like it really suited him.'

It was a match *packed with polished hurling, full blooded clashes, near misses, wonderful saves, and pulsating excitement.*

And it all happened just 18 days before nine players in that epic encounter went out together to bring home what remains the county's sole All-Ireland under-21 hurling crown.

The Oulart/Alley combination would end up taking the county title in unsatisfactory circumstances. A Kilmore/Rathangan team powered by Willie O'Neill and Jack Berry were inaugural winners in 1964, but they objected to Gorey as the choice of venue for the final and conceded a walkover.

◄◄◆►►

THE LEINSTER UNDER-21 campaign of 1966 had a low-key start. Westmeath were on the receiving end of a 15-7 to 1-2 thrashing in Portlaoise on May 22.

By the time the semi-final arrived almost two months later, Mick had played his first good game at midfield with the Wexford intermediate team. And this gave rise to a recurring theme in the local press. At every available opportunity, the case would be made that the youngest Jacob was needed outfield, and his time between the posts should be up. Even on an exceptional day for Wexford, when the under-21 team hammered Kilkenny by 6-11 to 2-0 in Enniscorthy's St Patrick's Park, one reporter addressed the issue.

Goalkeeper Michael Jacob made two very serious blunders that presented Kilkenny with their only scores. This player, who, as a minor was a brilliant custodian, is now a better midfielder, and one has only to look back on his brilliance against Kilkenny in the intermediate semi-final some weeks ago, when he partnered Oliver Cullen in that sector, to see this.

The Wexford under-21 selectors weren't entirely convinced, however, even though Mick was starting to shine outfield on a regular basis.

Oulart-The Ballagh/Buffers Alley retained their Gorey District title with two wins in the space of eight days in July. Ferns/Askamore were their victims in the final by 8-5 to 2-6, with Mick giving an *outstanding* performance at centre-back.

His versatility was noted in *The Echo* match preview prior to the Leinster under-21 final against Laois, played in Portlaoise on August 7, 1966.

An impressive nine players on that starting team had already lined out with the county seniors, and Mick was the only one of the squad representing a junior club. His third provincial medal in the grade was attained with a degree of comfort, as Laois lost out by 7-10 to 2-8.

It was back to Belfast for the All-Ireland semi-final and another handy win over Antrim by 4-13 to 1-5. However, calls for his use in an outfield role continued to grow. One match preview exaggerated by claiming he hadn't played in goal for his club *for more than three years*. Nowlan Park in Kilkenny again hosted the All-Ireland final of 1966, played on October 2 but with new opponents as Cork had come through from Munster for the first time.

The Rebels were on a high after their unexpected senior success against Kilkenny in early September, and two members of that team featured prominently along with Mick in the game's most talked-about incident.

It ended in a dramatic 5-6 to 3-12 draw, and *The People* reported Mick *could not be faulted for any of the shots that beat him.*

With five minutes left a rasping shot by Justin McCarthy was brilliantly saved by Michael Jacob, and in clearing he was called back and a free given against him. He certainly did not overcarry the ball, whatever other reason there may have been for the free. Seánie Barry took it, and it went to the net off a defender's hurley, to leave Wexford one up (5-5 to 3-10).

The game ended with a sequence of points from Barry, Seamus Barron, and Barry again, but Tipperary referee Donie Nealon came in for a hard time from supporters as he made his way off the field.

JUST ONE WEEK after that drawn final, Mick partnered 'Ternie' Murphy at midfield as Oulart-The Ballagh/Buffers Alley qualified for another county under-21 final with a five-point win over Enniscorthy St Aidan's.

He gave *an outstanding display and was in top form* in the 4-7 to 3-5 success, but still the county selectors persisted with his positioning between the posts.

They couldn't be accused of a generally conservative approach, as Mick was one of only six players from the drawn game to retain their starting positions.

The odd choice of Limerick as the replay venue didn't go down well in Wexford, but the saga would continue for another day after the teams registered 4-9 apiece.

There is a certain irony in the fact that Mick was wearing the colours of one of the two great club rivals of his career on the day that finally convinced the county selectors to remove him from goal.

Just one week after that second draw with Cork, another large crowd flocked to Bellefield for the county under-21 final. Oulart-The Ballagh/Buffers Alley were up against a St Martin's/St Mary's (Rosslare) combination featuring Liam Griffin. They wore the green jerseys with gold sash made famous by the Alley over the years, and one young man stood out above all others.

Mick was simply majestic at midfield in a 4-8 to 3-6 victory, contributing five points and giving an exhibition in all facets of play.

Finally, the Wexford mentors decided to bite the bullet.

For the second replay against Cork in Croke Park on November 13, they named Mick at midfield and took a gamble by starting minor goalkeeper Henry Butler of Buffers Alley between the posts.

Mick partnered Con Dowdall, but they were up against a formidable pair in senior duo Justin and Gerald McCarthy, determined to add to their September success.

This time around, there was no denying the superior side, as Cork won by 9-9 to 5-9.

The McCarthys dominated around the middle, and Mick moved to wing-forward during the first-half. His first goal for Wexford quickly followed, after Tony Doran blocked a lineball taken by Con Dowdall into his path, and that left the team trailing by one point. He also contributed the last point of the opening half, with Cork going in at the break ahead by 2-4 to 1-6.

The second period was a disaster as the goals flowed in, with three for the Leesiders between the 49th and 52nd minutes ending whatever slim hopes Wexford still entertained by that stage. Some of the reporters had contrasting opinions on the tactical decisions deployed by the losers.

John D Hickey in the *Irish Independent* felt that their cause was *seriously damaged by the transfer of Michael Jacob from midfield in a switch with Pat Quigley, then almost a non-combatant at left half-forward.*

Mick puts that tough day at the office in the second replay of 1966 purely down to a lack of experience. 'I was on Vinny Staples in that county final that was played before the third match with Cork. I did really well alright, so they decided to put me there on Justin McCarthy. It didn't really work out for me… I wasn't used to playing outfield.

'I hadn't the experience to leave a mark on a game like that, after they threw me in at the deep end.

'Justin McCarthy was selected as the best hurler in Ireland in 1966, so it was a big assignment to be fair.'

◄ ◄ ◆ ► ►

MICK'S LAST YEAR as an under-21 was 1967, and it's sometimes forgotten that he was re-deployed in goal just one last time.

The first round of the Leinster Championship was played in Athy on April 2, with Wexford beating Kildare by 4-11 to 2-6. They led by 2-3 to nil after 15 minutes but *were it not for the brilliance of Ml. Jacob (Oulart) in goal, Kildare might have been level.*

Two months elapsed before the semi-final against Dublin in Nowlan Park, and by that stage Mick was chosen at midfield alongside Denis Asple of Ballyhogue, already a regular on the Wexford senior football team.

His sole defeat in the province in four years as an under-21 hurler brought an otherwise very fruitful involvement in the grade to an inglorious end. A wasteful Wexford lost 4-9 to 3-10.

Mick had just two games left as an under-21, winning another Gorey District title when Ferns St Aidan's were beaten by 8-7 to 5-6. Flanked by Jimmy Prendergast and Tommy Kirwan, he was a tower of strength at centre half-back.

However, the county semi-final of 1967 will be remembered for all the wrong reasons.

The Oulart/Alley combination lost to arch-rivals Rathnure by 4-4 to 2-6 in St Patrick's Park, but the game was marred by a *near riot* as simmering tensions spilled over. Most of it had nothing whatsoever to do with the Oulart-The Ballagh contingent.

JUST FIVE WEEKS earlier, and at the same venue, Rathnure had comfortably accounted for a Buffers Alley side contesting a first-ever senior county final by 4-13 to 1-4.

Some bad blood lingered from that contest, and it spiralled out of control.

It was a black day in the history of Wexford GAA, one report stated. *An unpleasant undercurrent was evident at an early stage. It became more pronounced between the contestants as the game wore on, and erupted into a raging fury in the second half.* For Mick Jacob, a sportsman to his fingertips, he had no interest in getting involved in anything other than playing the ball.

And amid all the ill-feeling, it was notable that both local newspapers singled him out for special praise.

Michael Jacob was the losers' Man of the Match, The People noted. *He was matched with and beat a succession of the stars of the opposing side and generally improved his chances of joining brother Christy on the inter-county senior panel before long.* While The Echo scribe observed: *A sweet striker and unceasing worker, his unyielding spirit saw his side out of many dangerous situations. He can remember this game with pride.*

◄◄◆▶▶

MICK WASN'T SORRY to bid a final farewell to his goalkeeping duties, but it did serve a useful purpose in his overall development.

'I wasn't going to be an outfield player anyway when I was still only a juvenile, I was too young for junior,' he says. 'Tommy Leacy was in the goal for Oulart before me, but they needed someone and turned to me at the time.

'I was only delighted to be asked to play, sure it didn't matter to me that it was in goal at first.

'I was still able to play a lot of under-age hurling out the field, and I knew that was where I was going to end up at some stage.

'And then when Johnny Parle came along, we had a real goalkeeper for the club. He was a natural. But I must say that being a goalkeeper gave me a lot of experience and responsibility.'

HIS FIRST MAJOR exposure to an outfield role on the county scene came with the Wexford intermediate team in 1966.

Three years after keeping goal with them in the Leinster final, he was back to carry on the family's strong involvement in the grade.

Wexford went all the way to another All-Ireland intermediate decider in 1965, with Robbie and Christy manning the left half-back and left corner-forward positions respectively.

After high-scoring wins over Kilkenny and Offaly, with Christy contributing 4-1 in total, they beat an Antrim team competing in Leinster at the time in the provincial final in Croke Park.

That secured a direct passage to the All-Ireland 'Home' final, but Cork came up to St Patrick's Park and edged a tight affair by 3-7 to 2-6 before 4,839 spectators.

Even though the under-21 selectors couldn't find a starting place for him, Christy's displays with the intermediates earned a call-up to the county senior team for the 1966 championship.

He was one of three men promoted from that All-Ireland final side, along with centre-back Mick Kinsella and goalkeeper Nick Power, who deputised for Pat Nolan in his absence owing to illness.

June 19, 1966, was a very big day for the Jacobs.

Nowlan Park was the scene of a double-header, starting with a 3-9 to 1-12 win for the county intermediate team over Kilkenny.

It was Mick's big break outfield, as he was paired with Oliver Cullen from Liam Mellows – also a stylish footballer with the county senior team – and they combined very well. Cullen was rated Man of the Match in one newspaper report which added that *Michael Jacob gave him solid support, doing a lot of good hurling.*

He scored a couple of points from frees and one from play, with a column written under the byline *Outsider View* saying he was particularly good *when the going was tough and the game in doubt near the end.*

After a quick change into his clothes, Mick hurried back out that day to watch Christy doing very well on his senior debut, scoring 1-2 from right corner-forward in a 3-18 to 4-5 Leinster semi-final win over Dublin.

His selection came as a surprise, because mentors Nickey Rackard, Mick O'Hanlon, Jim Byrne, Larry O'Brien, Nick Cardiff and John 'Dough' Murphy hadn't used him at all in the league campaign.

That day in Kilkenny represented the high point in the summer of 1966 for both Jacob brothers.

IN A TWO-WEEK period in late-July, they would lose Leinster finals with their respective teams.

First up were the seniors, with Christy getting a pulled goal to lead Kilkenny by 2-5 to 0-7 at half-time in the Leinster final.

An all-out collapse followed, with a pointed free from Horeswood's Dick Shannon the only Wexford score of the second period as they surrendered the title on a 1-15 to 2-6 scoreline.

The big news before the intermediate final in Carlow on the last day of July was the recall to the centre-back position of Billy Rackard, for his first county game since the 1964 Leinster senior semi-final.

He was living in St Helen's, near Rosslare Harbour, at the time and opted to play his club hurling with St Martin's, the nearest senior club. This was a big deal for Mick, to be performing alongside one of his boyhood heroes.

It was just over a decade since he waved him on as the cavalcade of cars passed the Jacob house at Coolnahinch en route to Croke Park.

And then there was the thrill of that experience in 1962, when they travelled together to the same venue. Now, Mick was going out on the field alongside Rackard for the first time.

Alas, there was just one opportunity to be teammates, as Dublin denied Wexford the title by 2-9 to 1-8.

Mick and Oliver Cullen struggled to get into their usual flowing style, with the heavy going not suiting a pair with an abundance of natural skill between them.

It was a missed opportunity for another Leinster medal, but those two games – the Kilkenny one in particular – clearly showed Mick's outfield talents were now being taken seriously.

'I was midfield on Harry Dalton against Dublin, and Billy was in behind me at centre-back. It was a big deal for me to be playing with Rackard. We were turning around and watching him catching balls, and it was mighty for us to see that.'

Robbie remembers the impact of that game on his youngest brother.

'You can clearly see the influence Rackard had on him. He doesn't remember the detail from a lot of matches, but he remembers that one. Billy had a great personality too.

'He was most encouraging, and never had any big ideas about himself.'

◄ ◄ ◆ ▷ ►

NO MATTER WHAT happened with county teams during the summer months, the club was always waiting with open arms to welcome the Jacobs back.

After the initial promise shown in 1962, the quest for promotion stalled in the following years. Getting out of the minefield otherwise known as the Enniscorthy District Junior Championship proved easier said than done.

A small thing could have changed the outcome in 1963, when eventual county runners-up Blackwater beat them in a replay. It might have been a different story if Christy had been available for the drawn game.

There could be no excuse for 1964, as the preparation was lacking and the favourites were deservedly caught out by Monageer-Boolavogue.

However, that Bunclody tournament revitalised Oulart-The Ballagh, culminating on March 7, 1965, when they beat Duffry Rovers by four points in the final at the Bridge Meadow.

The team appeared to be well primed for another strong bid for the District title, only for a bombshell to be dropped later that month.

When the great Pat Nolan captained Oylegate-Glenbrien to the county senior hurling title in 1963, the club had assistance from a strong Ballyhogue contingent comprising Phil Wilson, Joe Foley, Eddie Walsh, Willie Foley, Nick Fortune and Liam Swan.

Two years later, that amalgamation disbanded, with the pair deciding to go their separate ways.

There was an assumption among the junior clubs in Enniscorthy District that Oylegate-Glenbrien and Ballyhogue would both compete in the intermediate grade. And when it emerged that they were actually being accommodated in junior instead, all hell broke loose in the boardroom.

Cloughbawn objected to their placement, and they were supported by Oulart-The Ballagh, Blackwater, Monageer-Boolavogue, St Vincent's (Bunclody), Duffry Rovers and Davidstown-Courtnacuddy.

However, a motion to rescind that decision failed to get the required two-thirds majority at a county board meeting in Asple's restaurant, Enniscorthy.

With 31 votes required, only 21 were secured.

It prompted Duffry Rovers delegate Tom Dunne to voice the frustration felt by the seven affected clubs.

'We're wasting our time playing the championship this year as with two senior teams regraded, the best thing to do would be to hand out the medals,' he said.

Ballyhogue duly drove on to the county title as predicted, seeing off Na Fianna from Wexford in the final by 10 points.

Their six medal winners from 1963 were all still on board, and two of that number – Phil Wilson and Joe Foley – would win junior club medals three months after featuring with Wexford in the All-Ireland senior final loss to Tipperary.

And by 1965, the 'Hogues had been strengthened even further by the addition of Nick Power – the county senior netminder in the following year's Leinster Championship. Two young county footballers who also represented Wexford in hurling – Denis Asple and Pat Leacy – figured on that team too, making them exceptionally difficult to beat.

And it wasn't much consolation for Oulart-The Ballagh that they did at least give them a serious rattle in the District semi-final.

AFTER A ROUTINE win over Shamrocks, a shock was on the cards with 15 minutes left in that game held in St Patrick's Park on September 19. Having led by 3-3 to 1-3 at half-time, Oulart-The Ballagh were still ahead by six points entering the last quarter.

Mick and Robbie were pitted against Phil Wilson and Nick Fortune in the middle of the field, and they were giving their all.

It needed a two-goal haul from Wexford dual star Joe Foley to get the wind-aided Ballyhogue over the line, with their very strong finish yielding 3-2 without reply to earn a 4-8 to 3-6 success.

They were made fight every inch of the way for that win though, and it stood to them in the subsequent District final because Duffry Rovers brought them to a replay.

In fairness to Oulart-The Ballagh and the Duffry, the general view was that both played above themselves and really rose their respective games in the face of adversity.

It was hard to see Ballyhogue losing from the off, but they certainly didn't get it easy. Oulart-The Ballagh grew into that semi-final after a slow start, and it looked like they were going to spring a surprise after scoring a couple of goals before half-time. Robbie netted direct from a '70', before Phil Redmond and Jimmy Roche combined to set up Tom Kehoe for a tidy finish.

There was a chance of an upset at that stage, but Oulart-The Ballagh left Enniscorthy that evening resigned to another year stuck in junior ranks.

'When they allowed Ballyhogue to be regraded, we had a new hill to climb.

'And we nearly had them turned over that day. With a bit more belief, we would have beaten them.'

The clubs of the Enniscorthy District agreed on a short-lived new approach for the 1966 championship.

Oulart-The Ballagh and Duffry Rovers were granted places in the semi-finals, and kept on opposite sides of the draw. Marshalstown, Monageer-Boolavogue, St Vincent's (Bunclody), the second team of Ballyhogue, and the Rathnure 'thirds', were left to battle it out for the right to meet Mick and his colleagues.

In order to remain sharp while the preliminaries took place, Oulart-The Ballagh played in as many tournament games as they possibly could. It was still the era of the straight knockout in every grade, meaning that an entire year's preparation could be shattered in the space of 60 minutes.

And it explains why clubs were always so eager to be included in any tournaments organised in their locality.

After their success in Bunclody, the club took up an invitation from Liam Mellows (Coolgreany) to participate in a competition that started with a notable win over an established senior team.

Ferns St Aidan's provided the opposition in Gorey on March 20, 1966, and Oulart-The Ballagh's 3-8 to 2-5 success was largely down to the handiwork of Mick and his brothers – Christy scored 2-3, while Mick chipped in with a five-point haul.

Another victory followed over Craanford in the semi-final, and it set up a game that was eagerly awaited in the parish.

BUFFERS ALLEY WERE in their first year as a senior club, fresh from winning the intermediate title of 1965, and they made it to the Coolgreany tournament decider with wins over the Forestry College from Arklow, and the host Liam Mellows club. Sadly, that final didn't go ahead at the time due to county commitments, but Oulart-The Ballagh would cause another major stir in a tournament game just a few short weeks later.

Enniscorthy St Aidan's were the outstanding club team of the 50s, contesting every county final from 1952 to '59 and winning seven titles.

They embarked on a gradual slide after losing the 1961 decider to Rathnure, and were lagging behind Shamrocks as the top team in town by the middle of the decade.

Nonetheless, they were expected to be well able to handle the Oulart-The Ballagh juniors when they met in the Keegan-Parle tournament in St Patrick's Park on June 26. Not alone were they defeated, they were humiliated, losing on a 4-10 to 2-2 scoreline. Eyebrows were raised when a junior club – struggling for many years to win a county title – put such experienced opponents to the sword.

It was another sign that Oulart-The Ballagh were on the rise.

'When we played the Aidan's and beat them, that was a big thing for us,' Mick confirms. 'It brought on the team immensely, and we were getting stronger all the time.

'We had been building from 1962, but it was tough. There was nothing soft in Enniscorthy District, and any win over a strong team in a tournament would build more confidence.

'Christy getting picked on the county senior team was a kick-start for everyone too, myself included. Our young fellas now had a clear goal to aim for, trying to get picked for Wexford in minor and under-21. Now they could see that was possible.

'The selectors never missed a game either. They were seeing our lads in tournament games, and watching them perform well. That gave us an even bigger drive when we knew they were there.'

Before getting a tilt at junior honours in 1966, Mick actually got to play in the senior grade for the first time.

It was decided to allow the four Districts to enter teams in the top grade, comprising hurlers from their intermediate and junior clubs.

They played off among themselves first, with Enniscorthy emerging as the representatives for the championship proper thanks to wins over Gorey and Wexford respectively. Mick showed his versatility with that side, lining out at half-forward and contributing tallies of 1-1 and 0-4.

As well as Robbie and Christy, the key men on the team included three more club colleagues in Tony Byrne, Billy Dunne and the versatile Willie Cullen – All-Ireland junior light-middleweight boxing champion earlier that year. The 1960 All-Ireland winning brothers, Pat and John Nolan from Oylegate-Glenbrien, were influential on that side too, as well as Jim Earle from Duffry Rovers.

Enniscorthy District departed from the senior race with a 2-10 to 3-3 loss to Geraldine O'Hanrahans, but it was a very decent performance considering their New Ross rivals went on to win the 1966 championship.

Mick partnered Larry Whelan from Blackwater at midfield in that game and scored an early goal from a 21-yard free. They went on to lead by 2-0 to 0-3 at half-time, before a further contribution of 1-1 from Christy on the restart left the Geraldines in a spot of bother.

They needed a goal and a point in the last eight minutes to secure victory, but Mick had once again made the best possible use of his opportunity in the 'shop window'.

'I was playing on Martin Lyng in that game, and he had been on the county team at centrefield in the All-Ireland final of 1962,' Mick says.

'He was a good bit older than me and very experienced, but I got on quite well on him. That would be another thing working in your favour, to hold your own on an established player like that.

'It was great to be togging out on the same team as John and Pat Nolan. John was very supportive of the younger players, there wouldn't be a word out of him if a mistake was made.

'It was special to be putting on the same jersey as John, after what he did in 1960 when he came out of nowhere to mark Jimmy Doyle out of it in the All-Ireland final.'

Given the geographic closeness of the two places, there was always a big connection between Glenbrien and The Ballagh. Indeed, they had asked Jim Mythen to be part of the set-up for their senior hurling success in 1916, and he was happy to oblige.

After the preliminaries were sorted, St Vincent's (Bunclody) emerged from the chasing pack to take on Oulart-The Ballagh in the District semi-final of 1966.

Mick and midfield partner Jimmy Carr *gave their front lines a good service of the ball* in a convincing 7-5 to 2-2 success. There was a talented new kid on the block for the winners, with St Peter's College and Wexford minor star Tom Royce contributing 2-2 up front.

With Christy as sharp as ever and weighing in with 3-2, the path to the final was straightforward, but surprise opposition lay in wait. A Cloughbawn side powered by two 50s veterans Tim Flood and Billy Wickham had first taken out Oylegate-Glenbrien before defeating Duffry Rovers, the other seeded team, on an 8-5 to 4-9 scoreline.

This time around Mick had Billy Dunne for company in midfield. And after a gap of four years, that elusive District title was finally regained with another handy win by 6-12 to 4-2.

'Tim Flood looked dangerous in that semi-final, but we hit a very good day. Cloughbawn had come back from intermediate, and we wouldn't have been too sure against them.

'We had Willie Cullen on Tim and he did a very good job. He had won an All-Ireland boxing title and was very young, very fast. He was a stopper as much as a hurler, but he got the job done.'

IT WAS AN immense relief more than anything for Oulart-The Ballagh, and a familiar foe awaited in the shape of St Brendan's from Craanford in the county semi-final.

Mick and company knew what to expect after their tournament meeting earlier in the year, and the outcome was similar as the north county men were beaten by 6-8 to 4-5. It was 4-3 to 1-2 at half-time in a game that fell below expectations, with the teenage Tom Royce in devastating form.

Mick and Christy also stormed into proceedings when they were needed most, after Craanford fought back to leave just three points between the teams.

There was no panic in the face of pressure, as a late Oulart-The Ballagh goal made sure of success.

However, there was a twist to the tale, and it centred around that late clinching score. Craanford objected to their rivals, and their county board delegate was ideally placed to outline the reason why.

Not alone was Dan Kennedy the man who did the talking for his club, he was also their left corner-back.

And on the day in question, he recalled his direct opponent Eddie Carr going off with a head injury near the end of the game. Oulart-The Ballagh had already replaced three players at the time, including Jimmy Carr who was still standing behind the goal.

According to Kennedy, Jimmy rushed in again when his brother went off and duly scored the goal, without giving his name to referee Paddy Brosnan from Ferns St Aidan's.

Robbie confirms that version of events. 'Fr Staples ordered Jimmy to go back on, and he did what he was told!'

It was hot and heavy for a while at the county board meeting to discuss the objection, with two esteemed clergymen going head-to-head – Fr Staples in the Oulart-The Ballagh camp, and Fr Michael O'Regan with Craanford.

Seán Browne TD had been in the chair since 1950, and he was highly regarded. 'He never wanted to throw teams out, that would always be a last resort,' Robbie says. 'He was a real hurling man.'

Robbie Sinnott defended the club to the last, stating at one stage in the debate: 'We gave them a good beating twice this year and that was good enough for any team.'

The upshot of it all was that a re-fixture was ordered, but that wasn't the end of the matter.

'Let's just say that the debate continued out on the street afterwards,' Robbie says with a laugh. 'Fr Staples wasn't out there genuflecting, I'll put it that way! He never minded a bit of controversy.'

A 10-week delay ensued before the game could proceed in Bellefield again, on November 27.

In that timeframe, Mick played three All-Ireland under-21 finals against Cork, along with the county semi-final and final at that level, so he was razor-sharp.

Tom Royce was unavailable as he was boarding in St Peter's, but his colleagues made no mistakes in his absence.

This time around it was a dominant display from start to finish and, for the avoidance of any doubt, the mentors opted against using substitutes on this occasion! Craanford were crushed by 6-7 to 1-3. Mick contributed a goal and three points.

'That objection brought a right bit of tension for the replay, but we never played better than we did in that game,' Robbie says.

Oulart displayed nothing but confidence from the opening whistle. Powered by the three Jacob brothers, they made all the running – Michael and Robbie gave them a big pull in the midfield exchanges, The People *noted.*

Given the onset of December, the county final against Shelmaliers was delayed until the new year.

After the disappointment against Our Lady's Island in 1962, a more experienced team now had a chance to make amends.

◄◄◆►►

MICK AND HIS clubmates were men on a mission in 1967.

And while they reached their destination before the year was over, they certainly didn't do it the easy way. Indeed, it took them not one, but two, campaigns before they finally emerged from junior ranks on an emotional day for Oulart-The Ballagh.

And they had a new man in their corner whose influence was profound.

The good relationship between the local gardaí and the club stretched all the way back to George Jacob's playing days in the 30s, when he struck up that great friendship with Pat Hernan from Donegal.

In early 1967, Sergeant Frank Donnelly arrived in the barracks, situated close to Cooney's pub and shop in Oulart village, and word quickly spread that this man might have something to offer.

He was a member of the panel 14 years earlier when his native Armagh went all the way to the All-Ireland senior football final before losing to Kerry. He also played with Sligo when work brought him to the north-west, and now he had arrived into a parish with a county final against Shelmaliers foremost on the agenda.

'We discovered this man would fit in very well, and he started to do the physical training,' Robbie says. 'We had lost some momentum after the Craanford game, but we started to train properly again. Frank Donnelly got us into shape, and the lads really took to him.'

OULART-THE-BALLAGH sought an April 2 date for the final, but it was fixed for a fortnight later on an 18-15 county board vote. That decision denied them the services of Tom Royce, who wouldn't be released from boarding school in St Peter's College. It was a crushing blow to his team's hopes.

There was no such thing as players minding themselves before big matches during Mick's career.

On the two Sundays prior to the final, he was in action with Wexford teams. His last-ever game in goal came first, a 4-11 to 2-6 win over Kildare in the Leinster Under-21 Championship in Athy.

One week later, Mick was at right half-forward and scored four points from frees as Kilkenny dumped Wexford out of the race for Leinster intermediate honours by 2-6 to 1-6 in New Ross.

Robbie lined out at left half-back, but only goalkeeper Pat Nolan lived up to his reputation according to the match report. He was eligible for this game after missing Wexford's two senior championship matches in 1966 owing to illness.

With those games done and dusted, it was finally time for the showdown with Shelmaliers, near neighbours from down the road in Castlebridge, Curracloe and Screen. A close game was expected, but most observers felt the Enniscorthy District men would be a little sharper.

A fair turnover of players was evident in the time between the county finals of 1962 and early '67.

Of the 18 men used in that loss to the Island, seven didn't feature against the Shels – Nicky Sutton, Jimmy Roche, Johnny Murray, Pat Quigley, Tony Sutton, Hugh Bolger and Jim Doyle.

Oulart-The Ballagh deployed 17 hurlers for the 1966 final, and netminder Johnny Parle, Jimmy Prendergast, Matty Ryan, Tom Kehoe and the Carr brothers, Jimmy and Eddie, were all new faces.

SURPRISE DEFEAT FOR OULART IN THRILLER, read the headline afterwards in *The People*.

It was a teak-tough affair, with Mick in the wars more than once, but he soldiered on regardless.

The Shels dominated the first-half and led by 2-6 to 0-6 at the break, with Pat O'Leary their stand-out player. Paddy Prendergast was the third defender given the task of curbing him after his goal in the 19th minute, and he finally succeeded.

The Oulart-The Ballagh mentors started Christy Jacob at left corner-forward, but the service in to him was non-existent. Mick began the game at centre-forward, but a series of half-time switches involving the three brothers bore immediate fruit.

Mick went to midfield, Christy came out to the left wing, and Robbie moved to left half-back.

Christy pulled a goal back after three minutes, and they drew level in the 43rd minute when Robbie's '70' was pulled overhead to the net by Freddie Jeffs, an earlier replacement for Willie Cullen.

When Christy pointed at the start of the last quarter, Oulart-The Ballagh led for the one and only time. And after Josie O'Leary equalised for the Shels, eight barren minutes followed before the game's decisive moment.

Johnny Parle saved a shot from Owen Cash, but the ball broke into the path of Noel Ryan and he slammed the rebound home. Oulart-The Ballagh fought until the bitter end, but their only reward was a point from Billy Dunne. They lost 3-8 to 2-9.

There was one golden chance near the finish, but veteran substitute Phil Redmond couldn't get a decent connection on a ground stroke and the Shels held on.

It was another crushing blow for Mick and company, but he was heroic in defeat.

The three Jacobs were the stars... but it was Michael that followers really warmed to, The People reporter wrote. Seldom, if ever, has a player worked so hard under such a handicap as this youngest of the Oulart hurling trio. He received a very nasty eye injury before the interval – one that would mean a termination of interest in the game for most players.

But not this player, and he took his place at midfield at the change-over with his head swathed in bandages and his sight impaired by the dressing.

Half way through the game, he received a second and even more serious wound on his other eye.

With blood streaming down his face and in considerable pain, he once more resumed to do everything one player could do to sway the fortunes of his team, and in the last minute was once more the victim of misadventure and gained a third head wound.

It was clearly no place for the faint-hearted, but Mick's bravery didn't go unnoticed. Old-timers leaving Bellefield after the game concurred – George Jacob's youngest lad was going to be a really good one.

'That was a raw enough game alright,' Mick recalls with typical modesty and understatement. 'I got a few stitches, but sure I hurled away anyway. The adrenaline would get you through it. I think the Shels had a more mature team than we had. That bit of added experience helped them in that final.'

Robbie says Mick, 'hurled okay in the first-half at centre-forward, but we weren't getting the best out of him in that position. Then he went to midfield… the further back Mick was going, the better he was getting.

'With the bandaged head in the second-half, he really started to play. He hurled out of his skin in the middle of the field. It was a great personal display.'

That final defeat happened on April 16, but by October 1 it was erased from memory.

TWENTY-FOUR WEEKS after that second crushing county final disappointment, Oulart-The Ballagh finally captured the elusive Junior Hurling Championship title.

Mick and Robbie are adamant about one aspect of 1967 – without the influence of Frank Donnelly, that recovery would never have happened. 'Frank was only starting really with us at the time. He was still a fresh voice, and he was able to inspire us mentally. He picked us up and made sure we really went for it again. There was no feeling sorry for ourselves. Without him, it might have been the same as in 1962 when we lingered on that defeat.

'This time the boys stayed with him, and believed in him. He had a good personality for the job. He could be tough when it was needed, but he was very good with players.

'He got training really well organised, and everyone was at it,' Mick continues. 'Everyone drove on hard and that was important; he got the backing of all the players. We all loved him, and what he brought to our set-up. He got us very fit. He made all the difference. He provided the spark that Oulart needed. He was the ideal man to come in at that particular time.'

The seeding system in use for the District championship of 1966 was a short-lived experiment. It was ditched after one year for financial reasons, with officers alarmed by the drop in revenue when well-supported clubs like Oulart-The Ballagh and Duffry Rovers weren't involved in the earlier rounds.

By August 27, these two powerhouses had safely negotiated their paths to another District final showdown. And this time the treasurer was very happy, because Bellefield was packed to the rafters. It was a cracking contest, and the Jacob boys were all centrally involved in the key move that secured the title on a 3-12 to 3-9 scoreline.

In the dying minutes as Rovers strove to snatch a winning goal, Robbie Jacob saved his lines in brilliant fashion and charged through a ruck of players to send a lengthy delivery to his brother Michael at midfield.

The latter sent a perfect centre into the Duffry Rovers' goal area where it was firmly grasped by the third member of the family, Christy, who flashed it between the posts to make victory secure.

The Jacob brothers had combined to put the final nail in their opponents' coffin.

Tom Royce was back to partner Mick at midfield, and it was the first big game for 16-year-old wing-back Tom Byrne, who would captain Wexford to All-Ireland minor glory one year later.

Frank Donnelly had three weeks to fine-tune his charges before their next big test, and it was one they were fortunate to survive.

It was almost inevitable that they would meet Craanford again. They were their most frequent rivals of that era, and the latest showdown was another county semi-final, this time in Gorey. Given the history between the clubs, and the objection of the previous year, it was no surprise either when the animosity on both sides sparked off a violent after-match row.

Oulart-The Ballagh won by 3-10 to 3-6, but their goal lived a charmed existence late on.

A relieved Mick turned to shake the hand of his nearest opponent after Cork-born referee Paddy Brosnan blew the final whistle. 'The Craanford man pulled on me. And immediately one of my great friends and loyal Oulart supporter Johnny Hayden clocked him. Sure all hell broke loose after that,' he says. An out-and-out sportsman, Mick had no interest in what happened next, so he stepped back as tempers frayed.

The game was played in a downpour which increased in ferocity in the second-half. In this period the rain was so heavy that it was almost impossible to see the players, and certainly it must have been extremely difficult for the players to see the ball, The People reported.

Immediately the game was over, a mini-riot, involving players and spectators,

*erupted in the centre of the field, and fists and hurleys were freely used. With the big
crowd milling around the fighting and struggling participants, it was impossible to see
what was going on, but it is understood that a number of those involved received minor
cuts and bruises.*

MICK WAS ONE of those in need of treatment, but there was also a funny side
to it.

'They were doing development work around the field in Gorey, and they had
dug a big trench in one place. By the end of the game, it was full to the brim with
water. I looked around at one stage, and here was Tommy Kirwan down in a heap
in the trench, with half of Craanford in on top of him!'

Tommy, a great friend of the Jacobs, would serve the club as a key official for
many years. A very capable hurling referee, he took charge of three county senior
finals and also handled games at inter-county level for a while.

He was a selector with the Wexford senior camogie team at the time of his
sudden death in 2005.

And on that wet day in Gorey, Tommy needed some urgent assistance from
his colleagues to save his bacon!

'That was a tough match. One of the Craanford lads had pulled on me in the
second-half and got the line too,' Mick says. 'It was unbelievably wet, and there
was a fierce wind. The pitch wasn't great either. There was long enough grass down
one side and the rest of it was even worse.

'Fr O'Regan was a great man over Craanford that time… himself and Fr
Staples would have fierce battles. Craanford started to come back in the second-
half. There was a scramble one time, and a big gush of water fell out of our net
when they got a goal. Fr O'Regan jumped about five or six feet into the air when
they scored.

'They got about four 21-yard frees late on. Mylie Donohoe took them, he
would have played with us on the county intermediate team around the same
time. Myself and Christy went back in the goal beside Johnny Parle, and we saved
some of them. If Mylie had hit them all over the bar, we were probably beaten.

'I'd say we only got the ball into their half twice in the last few minutes. We
had Freddie Jeffs at full-forward, and he was a very good first-time hurler.

'He let go on a ball, and we got a goal out of nowhere. Only for that, we were gone. We got out of jail completely. We were hanging on, and really they should have won.'

AFTER SUCH AN almighty scare, Oulart-The Ballagh simply weren't going to slip up on their third county final appearance of the decade.

They finally bid farewell to the junior grade in Bellefield on October 1, 1967, and they did it with a considerable degree of comfort. In conditions similar to the semi-final – a high wind and a downpour of rain – St Abban's (Adamstown) were beaten by 2-14 to 0-4.

'We got a great start and never looked back. We really missed Freddie Jeffs when he couldn't play in the 1962 final, but he got an early goal that day and it settled us. He was playing full-forward on Jimmy Furlong, who was on the Wexford panel with me in 1968. That scare in the semi-final didn't do us a bit of harm. We didn't play well against Craanford, but we survived against the odds.

'Frank Donnelly instilled the fighting spirit in us, and we were fed up of those dark days when we lost the finals to the Island and the Shels.'

Mick *struck up an effective partnership with Billy Dunne* at midfield against Adamstown, scoring one point from a '70' as the pair got the better of Jimmy Galway and Joe O'Reilly. *Of course, the three Jacob brothers were to the fore as usual,* The People reported.

Michael was his industrious self at midfield, and his accurate centres usually ended in a score, while dashing Christy was the will-o'-the-wisp that none could fathom and, in their anxiety to curb him, Adamstown defenders often left Tom Royce all the time he required to extend his team's lead.

It was one of the most popular wins in the grade for many years, with neutrals recognising the strenuous effort behind it.

With such a tough hurdle finally cleared, promise abounded for 1968. The newspaper noted: *A team has never won a county junior championship more deservedly than Oulart. The frustration that comes with repeated defeats never infiltrated their ranks. Rather, those repeated disappointments seemed to foster a sense of loyalty and dedication to their club, and, in the steadfast belief that success would come eventually, they battled gamely on.*

Between the posts... Mick guarding the net for the Wexford under-21 team in their Leinster Championship first round win over Kilkenny in Nowlan Park on May 9, 1965.

Brothers in arms... Christy, Robbie and 16-year-old Mick side-by-side in the Oulart-The Ballagh team photograph prior to the county junior hurling final of 1962 against Our Lady's Island.

The breakthrough team... Mick (front, extreme right) and his colleagues show off the silverware in the company of legendary club official Robbie Sinnott after finally winning that elusive county junior hurling title in 1967.

« CHAPTER 4 »

THE OLD-TIMERS weren't the only ones impressed by Mick's heroics in that junior final loss to Shelmaliers in April 1967.

Five weeks later, he got the big call from the county senior selectors for the first time. Wexford were playing Cork in a tournament in Mallow on a Sunday evening, a game attended by an estimated 5,000 crowd according to *The Cork Examiner*.

Padge Kehoe was managing the team, with the backroom crew also comprising Nickey Rackard, Art Bennett, Peter Hayes, Nick Cardiff and Larry O'Brien. The game ended in a 3-7 each draw, with Mick coming on for the injured Willie Murphy. The presence of Christy made it that bit easier to assimilate, with his big brother scoring a point from the right half-forward slot.

One very heartening aspect of the game was the display of two of the newcomers, Jim Berry and Michael Jacob, The People reported.

Mick lined out at midfield after Murphy departed, with the latter's slot at wing-back occupied by Jim, who arrived at the same time. The St Anne's man was more noted as a footballer, along with his brother Jack, who would light up the hurling scene in 1968.

Mick was clearly on the selectors' radar.

WHEN WEXFORD CLAIMED the National League title with a 3-10 to 1-9 win over Kilkenny in Croke Park, Christy came on for Fergie Duff, making a key contribution by scoring a goal and a point, but that big game arrived a little too soon for Mick, who wouldn't feature with the seniors again for the remainder of 1967. While the Cats turned the tables in the Leinster final nearly two months later, the one consolation was that Christy had passed the test and started that game at right half-forward.

Mick would have to wait until 1968 to nail down a regular place on the squad, although that wasn't a bad year to start as it turned out! 'It was winning the junior against Adamstown later on in 1967 that really put me in line for the county senior team,' Mick says. 'I can remember Robbie Sinnott saying it to me, and also to Christy, that we were going to be in the reckoning. We were making strides all the time, and Christy had already taken his chances when they came along.

'I was gaining a lot of experience through under-21… that really stood to me. It was my last year at that level in 1967, and all those games were very helpful. With the county team going so well in the grade, too, it added another edge to it.'

MICK KNEW HE was ready for the highest level with the dawn of 1968.

He had confidence in his own ability, and was itching to be given a chance. The big opportunity arose in the first National League game after Christmas, a clash with the old enemy that attracted 6,000 onlookers to Nowlan Park on February 4.

The selection committee had altered significantly. While two former greats, Kehoe and Rackard, remained, along with Nick Cardiff, the trio of Bennett, Hayes and O'Brien were replaced by Syl Barron of Rathnure, Tom Donohoe from Buffers Alley, and another playing stalwart of the 50s, Horeswood's Mick O'Hanlon.

Wexford struggled at midfield in the first-half, with neither Jimmy Galway from Adamstown nor Jack Berry making any headway on Frank Cummins and Paddy Moran.

'I played on Paddy in the second-half, and I thought I did well enough,' Mick recalls. The game ended in a 1-10 to 1-7 loss, but the local reporters were suitably impressed. *Galway was replaced at the interval by Mick Jacob, whose accession had a wonderful effect, The Echo* enthused.

'Paddy Moran was a very experienced midfielder. That was a big step up in class for me, but I was happy with how I got on,' Mick says. 'It was simple enough really. I knew I just had to get out there and give one hundred percent. I always had that attitude, no matter who I was playing on. Whether he was the worst or the best, the aim was to make sure he didn't get the ball.

'That was the approach I took everywhere. If I was pucking around in the front yard at home with someone, I'd want to be on the ball the whole time. And then when I went in to train with Oulart, I'd be the very same. I think that really stood to me in every game I played, because I didn't know any other way.

'I was just obsessed with getting to that ball ahead of my opponent. I always had a fierce competitive streak.'

The year 1968 would unfold as one of the most special in Wexford's hurling history, and it was marked by a series of notable breakthroughs for Mick. After that competitive debut off the bench in Kilkenny, he only had to wait another fortnight for his first start. That was when Tipperary travelled to O'Kennedy Park in New Ross in the league, and it proved a fruitful day all round.

Initially selected to partner local lad Mickey Gardiner in the middle of the field, Mick lined out at right half-back instead when Tom Neville was ruled out through injury. He found himself up against no less an opponent than the honours-laden Donie Nealon, but this big test was passed with flying colours. Wexford won by 3-12 to 0-10.

Robbie remembers a conversation he had with Oulart-The Ballagh stalwart Phil Redmond after that game. Phil had a friend from Tipperary who told him Nealon wanted to know afterwards about the new lad that marked him. Clearly, Mick had made an instant impression.

'I remember him giving Nealon no space at all, he did a really good job,' Robbie says. As for Mick, his outlook – then and now – is modesty personified.

'Playing as a back, I'd always play tight and play close, and make sure I was well covered by the other lads around me. I was a greenhorn that time, and you'd have to be up for it from the word go against a player like Donie Nealon. You wouldn't have time to be nervous, that's for sure.'

Another landmark followed a fortnight later, this time in a 3-8 to 2-9 win over Waterford in Dungarvan. Christy hadn't featured against Kilkenny or Tipperary, so that game marked the first time the Jacob duo played together in a competitive senior outing.

That first extended run in the Wexford team hit a roadblock with a 1-19 to 5-5 loss to Tipperary in a league play-off in Croke Park on March 24. This time Mick had another new midfield partner in Phil Wilson of Ballyhogue, and he must have harboured high hopes of retaining his place for the championship.

As it happened, though, the selectors had other ideas.

He was confined to one outing in the Intermediate Championship instead, partnering Jimmy Galway at midfield in a 4-7 to 2-11 exit to Dublin in Gorey, with Robbie at right half-back while Billy Dunne came on.

The senior mentors had done a lot of tinkering with the two midfield slots since the start of the year. Indeed, in those four competitive games pre-championship, Mick was one of six players utilised in that department, along with Jimmy Galway, Jack Berry, Mickey Gardiner, Paul Lynch and Phil Wilson.

And funnily enough, none of that sextet featured in the number 8 or 9 jerseys for the Leinster semi-final against Dublin in Nowlan Park on June 16!

A FORTNIGHT EARLIER, Mick's first-ever overseas trip brought him to Wembley for the annual Whit weekend exhibition game, a fixture on the GAA calendar from 1958 until '76.

He didn't feature in a 3-16 to 1-8 win over Cork on the Saturday, although he was one of five alterations 24 hours later when the same opponents were beaten again, this time by 3-17 to 4-12, in Coventry. *The newcomers played as if they were regulars, and Michael Jacob did well,* the report in *The People* said, after he slotted in efficiently for Willie Murphy at left half-back.

Of more relevance in the context of the championship team was the strong showing from the youthful pair of Dave Bernie and Ned Buggy at midfield. After doing well there in a drawn under-21 championship clash with Dublin in May, their displays on foreign soil convinced the senior selectors of their worth.

Bernie's inclusion, in particular, was a bolt from the blue, but he made the most of his chance.

In time, the Ferns St Aidan's clubman would form a strong midfield pairing with Mick, most notably in the 1970 All-Ireland final loss to Cork. But in early 1968 he wasn't on the radar for senior selection, and actually started at corner-forward for the under-21 team in their first championship game against Laois on the last day of March.

In late April, he was right half-back with the county footballers in an early Leinster exit to the same opponents.

Many felt that would be the extent of his senior involvement in 1968, but just a few short months later Bernie would join Jack Berry from that side on the long list of Wexford dual performers.

Dave's hurling debut wasn't the easiest, with another truly gifted performer in both codes, Des Foley, the stand-out Dublin player at midfield in spite of his team's 3-15 to 1-11 loss.

The experienced Phil Wilson, unavailable for that game, was an automatic selection for the Leinster final versus Kilkenny. And when Ned Buggy, the original choice to partner him, was unavailable, Bernie was retained and never looked back.

Mick remained on the fringes and didn't get a chance on the field, but he wasn't too far removed from the action either. Indeed, any objective analysis of Wexford hurling in 1968 would mark him out as the most unlucky player on the squad.

From a tally of 14 matches in official competitions, he started nine and came off the bench in another two; the only three he didn't feature in were those championship successes against Dublin, Kilkenny and Tipperary that brought the Liam MacCarthy Cup home after a gap of eight years.

And as well as playing in Coventry on that weekend trip, he was involved in tournament outings against Waterford and Cork, in Walsh Park and the familiar stomping ground of Mallow respectively.

Mick paired up with Dave Bernie for the first time in between the Leinster and All-Ireland finals.

That was in Croke Park on July 28 when, in the delayed Walsh Cup final of 1967, Kilkenny were obliterated by 8-16 to 3-7.

Three weeks later, they featured at midfield once more when the semi-final of that competition for 1968 resulted in another runaway win, this time by 2-22 to 1-6 against Offaly. However, Wilson was back to partner Bernie for the All-Ireland final, with Mick resigned to biding his time.

'IT WAS A great few months. Going to Wembley was a brilliant experience for starters, my first time outside the country.' That was more than a mere social weekend too, as Robbie points out.

'There's a picture at home of Christy and Nickey Rackard taken on that weekend. After that trip, Rackard said they were going to win the All-Ireland, he was convinced.

'A declaration was made, and he was proven right. They got a lot out of that, in particular the younger lads coming on to the team. It had a big significance for later in the year.

'Rackard was a great fan of Christy's... he liked the way he played and recognised that he was a goal-scoring opportunist.'

The events of 1968 prompted Robbie to marvel at Mick's stoic demeanour once again. 'Mick should have been disappointed with his lot from that year, but he never showed it.

'He always had such a great attitude. Not making that championship team would only make him more determined to go harder again for the next year. Bitterness or annoyance would never come into it.'

The winter of 1967 and '68 was Mick's first experience of working under renowned Wexford trainer Ned Power, the Kilkenny native and teacher in St Peter's College, who had masterminded the school's All-Ireland breakthrough success of 1962.

'We started training very early for '68, in the previous November I'd say. That would have been unusual enough at the time,' Mick says. 'It was nearly all done in St Patrick's Park, apart from maybe a few sessions in Wexford Park. We probably should have got out of St Patrick's Park a bit more, because it was very tight in comparison to the wide open spaces of Croke Park.

'I hadn't much personal experience of trainers before Ned got involved with us.

'I was always fit myself really, no matter who was training me. I'd get ready myself nearly, certainly from the physical point of view. On the farm I'd be working with horses and doing an awful lot to stay naturally fit.

'I might be making cocks of hay all day for example... or thinning turnips. I could be pitching bales, and then after a hard day's work like that I'd go in to Patrick's Park. We had a lot of farmers on those teams, significantly more than nowadays, and they would have built up their own strength.

'In later years, after I got married and moved to Oulartwick, I'd often run from the farm to the house. That would be about four miles across the fields, and sometimes I'd do it in wellington boots.

'Going back to the earlier days, I always cycled to Mountdaniel for training, so fitness was something that came naturally to me.'

Robbie's admiration for his youngest brother knows no bounds, and he is keen to highlight his close attachment to the land and how it stood to him as a hurler. 'A good bit of the farm was on the side of Oulart Hill, with some very long fields. Often times, Mick would have to go out after the sheep, and he'd always be very active that way.

'Even when he was working, it would still be a form of training in his mind. He loved the challenge of going into the fields, and he'd never sit at home doing nothing.

'In the evenings, he'd head off with the dogs again, after the farming work was done. He was a hunting man too, and he nearly got as much enjoyment out of that as hurling.

'On the field, Mick was determined to give none of the opposition even a sniff of the ball. He was very mean in that sense, but in a good way. He wanted every ball.

'He had a great attitude, great judgement, and unbelievable stamina. That fitness he had came from working on the land, from hunting, from running home as part of his daily routine.

'He had a great desire to get the very best out of himself, always. He didn't look a big man, but he had a body like granite. I remember one particular day when we were playing against Rathnure.

'Mick was stooped over this ball, and he tightened up his body when he spotted an opponent driving at him out of the corner of his eye. The Rathnure man ended up with a few broken ribs. Mick was like concrete,' Robbie recalls.

'It was a solitary enough existence for him on the farm, too. The day after a big game in Croke Park, it would be the same as if he had never set foot in the place. He might have a brief discussion with his uncles about the game, and then he would head off to get the work done.

'It was an isolated enough spot, with a rough road going into it, and hardly any cars appearing.

'Mick would love to see some lad arriving in the farmyard that wanted to talk about hurling. There were never any airs or graces about him, he'd happily mix in with anyone. He could spend all day talking with some of the local people about the matches at that time.'

AND THERE WAS certainly plenty to analyse and discuss in 1968.

'The build-up to the All-Ireland final was great,' Mick recalls. 'It was a novelty for myself and Christy, our first venture together with the senior team… sure we loved every second of it. I can remember one night inside in Patrick's Park, Con Dowdall and 'Shanks' Whelan got into a row and tore into each other.

'You'd have to be on your toes to win the ball in there. It was a great experience to be getting ready for an All-Ireland final and to be a direct part of it. In the first half hour it was looking grim for Wexford. They hurled poorly and Tipp were completely on top.

'But the selectors made two or three changes and the whole game was transformed. Tony (Doran) went to full-forward, (Paul) Lynch went to centre-forward, and John Quigley came on at wing-forward.

'The backs got completely on top. Willie Murphy, Dan Quigley and Vinny Staples were unreal, they all had powerful games. The full-back line was steady, and (Phil) Wilson came out of his shell in the second-half.

'Wexford finished very well in that All-Ireland final, and all the hard training helped in a big way. It might have been strange to have started so early, in the previous November, but it paid off. It was a great day for every single Wexford person there. It was something special for Christy and myself.

'It meant a lot for the Oulart-The Ballagh club to have two people on the squad. And then you had Tom Byrne captaining the winning minor team on the same day, with Paddy O'Connor on that panel and Robbie Sinnott a selector.

'Tom lived across the fields from us when we were in Ballincash. He went on to the CBS in Enniscorthy after that and he was a classy hurler.'

Rather than linger on the disappointment of not making the team, Mick was intent on putting the experience gleaned from being around such quality players to optimum use.

'Training was very competitive that year, and everyone was gunning hard for places. They used to line out the team in the way they were intending to pick it. So for any fella not on that 15, you were always going to try that bit harder. It made the substitutes and everyone else on the fringes so much better too. Anyone who got a chance was ready.

'Of course I was mad to get a run, especially on All-Ireland final day, but it just didn't happen and there was nothing more I could do about that,' Mick says.

IN A MORE innocent time, far removed from the slick approach to every aspect of sport nowadays, Breda Jacob recalls her future husband sitting among the substitutes on September 1, 1968, wearing a sports jacket over his jersey. Tracksuit tops weren't an option in those days!

'I can remember travelling up to the final in a fleet of hackney cars, and we were based in the International Hotel in Bray,' Mick says. 'Christy was a big support to me that year, and when he made the team sure I was mad to get on it with him. You'd learn your trade fast playing against Wilson and those fellas in training.

'We came home on the Monday and visited Gorey and Enniscorthy with the senior and minor trophies. We ended up in Wexford and had something to eat in the Talbot Hotel. I would have been back on the farm on the Tuesday, although that would have been a lazy day by my standards.'

FOUR WEEKS AFTER winning his sole All-Ireland senior medal, and two years after England won the real thing in Wembley, Mick got to play in a World Cup final!

That was the rather grandiose title given to what was, in effect, a challenge game against New York, held in Wexford Park on September 29, when he partnered Phil Wilson at midfield in a 1-17 to 3-5 win.

By the end of the year, Mick and Dave Bernie were firmly established as the first-choice midfield pairing. They were together for the last four county matches, adding a couple more medals too in the space of a week with final wins over Clare in the Grounds tournament, and Kilkenny in the Walsh Cup.

Prior to that, he made a big impression when replacing Teddy O'Connor in an Oireachtas semi-final loss to Cork in the Athletic Grounds. *Substitute Michael Jacob in the brief period he was in action showed that he was too good to be left on the sideline for so long.*

That earned him a start for the league opener against Offaly in Gorey, won by 6-14 to 5-8.

Wexford's only sector in which they had no worries was midfield, The People enthused. *Here Michael Jacob had a faultless hour and, with wonderful support from David Bernie, Wexford ruled the roost absolutely in this zone.*

The Grounds tournament was annexed with wins over Tipperary and Clare respectively, the latter on a 4-6 to 2-8 scoreline in Croke Park. A second Walsh

Cup medal in just four months followed with a 3-15 to 0-5 demolition of Kilkenny in St Patrick's Park. His two points were the first scores in either half, with Christy contributing 2-2 – and he was still gunning for action just ten days before Christmas.

In that era the Leinster champions played the rest of the province in a challenge to select the Railway Cup team. Wexford won by 6-9 to 2-12 and… *Michael Jacob and Dave Bernie left their stamp on the game with infectious enthusiasm* after facing up to a formidable pair in Paddy Moran and Pat Henderson.

THERE WAS MORE to 1968 than Wexford sweeping the boards in senior and minor hurling, senior camogie, senior colleges hurling with St Peter's, and senior handball.

By the end of that magical year, Oulart-The Ballagh were a top flight club. And after all the trials and tribulations involved in the escape from junior ranks, there was an almost embarrassing ease attached to conquering the intermediate grade.

Club officials were so keen to get a crack at senior that they tabled a novel motion for the county convention of 1968. They wanted the Intermediate Championship to be held early, with the winners then being entitled to take part in the senior campaign of the same year.

However, the motion was withdrawn, in favour of one from Shelmaliers looking for the intermediate grade to be played on a league basis. With the apparent guarantee of additional games, Oulart-The Ballagh decided it would be better to go down that route instead.

As it transpired, just three matches were required to win the title, all of them against the second strings of senior clubs. A mere six teams entered, divided into two groups of three to abide by the stipulations of convention.

Oulart-The Ballagh were in with the reserves from Rathnure and Enniscorthy St Aidan's, but they only played one match before the semi-final.

The town team withdrew after losing to Rathnure, ensuring Mick and his colleagues were actually through before their opening game in Bellefield on July 21. One week after Wexford's Leinster final win over Kilkenny, Mick *had a great hour at midfield* in a 6-13 to 4-7 success. Shelmaliers, the only other first team in the intermediate grade, beat Faythe Harriers and Geraldine O'Hanrahans to top the other group, with the Ross men winning the all-town battle to also advance.

The county semi-final in Bellefield on August 4 was most notable for its final scoreline, with Oulart-The Ballagh beating the Barrowsiders by 10-9 to 7-4. Mick, Robbie and Tony Byrne were described as the *outstanding workers* on a day when he was partnered by Matty Ryan at midfield.

The final was played two months later, but Christy was out after sustaining a hand injury in that 'World Cup' win for Wexford over New York.

Rathnure had done Oulart-The Ballagh a massive favour by seeing off Shelmaliers in the other semi-final, killing off the prospects of a repeat of the 1966 junior decider. And they couldn't live with their Mick Jacob-inspired rivals on the day, as a one-sided encounter ended on a 5-10 to 1-3 scoreline.

This time he was at centre-back, scoring one of the goals, and *the outstanding player on view. The Echo scribe concurred with his colleague from The People. For the winners, Mick Jacob played one of his best games: between his clever passing moves and his score (a goal) he was a major force in Rathnure's undoing.*

Returning to *The People*, there was generous praise for what Oulart-The Ballagh had accomplished, and for the role of Mick and his brothers in making it happen. *Some years ago hurling followers would have scoffed at the suggestion that Oulart would shortly become a senior hurling force. But, just as Buffers Alley did three years before them (although the latter did not win the lesser competition), their neighbours and under-age allies are now following.*

But, Oulart has always been a hurling stronghold. The arrival on the scene in recent times of the Jacob brothers gave the struggling club that much desired boost and, though defeats in the last four years were often heartbreaking, they struggled on gamely.

THERE WAS A lot to look forward to at the start of 1969.

Mick had already pocketed Leinster and All-Ireland senior medals by the age of 22, and his beloved Oulart-The Ballagh were about to play in the top flight for the first time after so many years of trying. There was a significant change, too, on the home front.

Christy had shown an aptitude for carpentry and working with his hands from an early age – those skills were honed in Enniscorthy Vocational School for a few years.

After completing the Group Certificate, he returned to work full-time on the farm, with his mother delighted to have another family member alongside Mick and his two uncles.

While Mikie concentrated on buying and selling cattle, Owen and the two youngsters focused on the hard physical work, sowing the corn and tending to the sheep and cattle.

The land situation had improved, of course, with an increased workload resulting directly from some shrewd acquisitions made by Mikie.

Christy was still working on the farm for the All-Ireland win of 1968, but shortly after that he branched out into the building trade. By the end of that year, he was constructing his first houses, leaving Mick, Owen and Mikie as a formidable three-man team on the farming front.

THE OULART-THE-BALLAGH AGM, held on January 5, 1969, agreed they were strong enough to proceed in the senior championship without calling on assistance from any neighbouring parish.

And a singular honour was bestowed on Mick, as he was appointed captain for the maiden campaign.

On the county scene, the Jacob/Bernie pairing had firmly established itself in the final months of 1968. And they took up where they had left off when the National League resumed with a 2-6 to 2-4 win over Kilkenny in Wexford Park on February 9.

The midfield partnership is maturing into one of the most consistent that the Slaneysiders have had for some years, The People remarked. The high praise continued one month later, after Tipperary were pipped by 3-12 to 2-14 in Thurles. Michael Jacob worked like a Trojan from first whistle to last and kept a very tight rope on John Flanagan, one of the more prominent of the Tipperary players. Jacob worried and harried him all the time and curbed a serious threat to the Wexfordmen.

After an easy 7-13 to 1-11 hammering of Waterford in New Ross, neither Mick nor Dave had to over-extend themselves in their next match, with the strong run of results continuing as Laois were demolished by 11-8 to 2-3 in Portlaoise. It was considerably tougher in Nowlan Park on April 20, but there was a strong sense of personal achievement after Mick contributed a great deal to a hard-earned 2-5 to 1-6 semi-final win over Limerick.

Two weeks later, Mick had another Croke Park date against Cork. Two and a half years after his first big outfield assignment in the second replay of the 1966 All-Ireland under-21 final, he had a lot more experience under his belt as he sought a first National League medal.

And although defeat was his lot once more, this time by 3-12 to 1-14, he clearly left a lasting impression among the 31,963 crowd. *Midfielder Michael Jacob was the man-of-the-match to followers of the Munster county as well as those of Wexford, The People* exclaimed. *Slightly built and red-haired, Michael has never had an hour like this. He treated his much-vaunted opponents, Gerry (sic) McCarthy and Roger Tuohy, with contempt and his first-time striking on the ground or in the air, allied to his boundless energy, gave Wexford a decided advantage in these important exchanges.*

Losing star centre-back Dan Quigley after just two minutes with a broken hand was a big blow to the team's prospects, not just for that final but for the short-lived championship campaign to follow.

Full-back Eddie 'Dow Dow' Kelly and attacker Jimmy O'Brien had retired since the All-Ireland win, with Jimmy Furlong and John Quigley taking their places.

And as Mick and Dave Bernie were playing too well together to be broken up, it meant Phil Wilson was now at left half-forward. Christy was the unfortunate one to miss out in the shake-up that followed, although he scored a point after replacing 'Shanks' Whelan in the second-half.

WHILE THE OUTCOME was a disappointment, it still left the team in an apparently good place ahead of the Leinster Championship semi-final against Offaly. Mick remained eligible to play in the intermediate grade, as a result of not featuring on the field with the seniors in 1968.

And he was a rock at centre-back in a first round win over Carlow (6-10 to 4-5), flanked by clubmate Jimmy Prendergast and Davy Doyle from Craanford. There was a very strong Oulart-The Ballagh representation overall, with Tom Byrne at midfield, Tom Royce scoring 2-2 from centre-forward, and Robbie replacing Jack Hanrahan of Duffry Rovers in the course of the game.

With Robbie retained at centre-forward for the next round versus Wicklow in Aughrim, exactly one-third of the starting team hailed from the club. However, they couldn't prevent a 3-7 to 2-8 defeat.

Interestingly, the fathers of two famous modern faces also wore the purple and gold that day. Liam Walsh's son Billy brought boxing fame and glory to Ireland before embarking on his current coaching journey in the USA.

The Na Fianna clubman, who died in 2014, was Wexford's goalkeeper, while the sole substitute used was Seán O'Leary – father of Dermot, the popular TV presenter in England.

'I think I played on Billy Hilliard that day in Aughrim and did well. Billy was a top-class forward from Carnew,' Mick says. Along with those intermediate games, he managed to get another cross-channel trip under his belt before facing Offaly.

However, his second journey to Wembley – and first time to actually line out there – wasn't a memorable one as Wexford lost heavily to Tipperary by 2-10 to 1-2. One day later, with Mick at centre-back this time, the visitors drew with London on an unusual 7-3 to 4-12 scoreline in a challenge game watched by 2,000 eager exiles in New Eltham.

There was still nothing to suggest the first defence of the Leinster and All-Ireland titles would also be the last. In the absence of Bernie, the selectors took a gamble by selecting Pat Sinnott to partner Mick at midfield.

In similar fashion to Christy's introduction three years earlier, he was brought in for his first-ever senior outing in the championship, with no league games under his belt beforehand. However, club form with Shamrocks was strong from a man known to one and all in his native Enniscorthy as 'The Bull'.

It was a somewhat misleading nickname, given he was of similar build to Mick, small and sleek rather than the battering ram that moniker might suggest.

Sinnott was one of three other championship debutants, along with Ned Buggy at centre-back and Mick Butler at corner-forward, while there was a recall at right half-forward for Ballyhogue's Joe Foley, playing his first game at this level since the All-Ireland final of 1965. The Quigley brothers Dan and John were notable absentees along with Dave Bernie.

Despite the much-changed Wexford side, few foresaw the strength of the Offaly challenge. And by the time they realised the extent of it, the midlanders were too far down the road to be overtaken.

The People noted that the holders were *diabolically bad* in the first-half, and trailed by a staggering 5-4 to 0-5 at half-time. Joe Foley moved to centre-back for the second period and was a *revelation*, while Christy made a *very favourable impression* after his introduction at right half-forward.

He scored a couple of points, but Wexford were always playing catch-up and, although Tony Doran (two) and Mick Butler pulled back goals, they were dumped by 5-10 to 3-11.

After the highs of 1968, the result was a severe shock to the system. 'A bit of complacency definitely set in before that game,' Mick accepts. 'Offaly were starting to come good at that time. Paddy Molloy was an unreal forward, he scored 3-4 that day.

'Damien Martin was in goal, and Johnny Flaherty was corner-forward. I was marking Declan Hanniffy at midfield, and he was a good one too. They were only beaten by two points by Kilkenny in the final afterwards. Once Offaly got going, they were always good hurlers.'

THERE WASN'T MUCH time – none at all, in fact – for Mick to come to terms with that unexpected defeat.

Just one week later, Oulart-The Ballagh were up against the might of reigning champions Buffers Alley in only their second senior championship game. They had fared pretty well in preparatory matches, but this would be the ultimate test – they lost 5-15 to 4-5.

In the first round in Bellefield on May 11, Oulart-The Ballagh had been in fine fettle against Geraldine O'Hanrahans – champions as recently as 1966. And although a losers' group was in operation for only the second year in Wexford, they had no desire to go down that route.

Robbie vividly recalls that maiden senior campaign of 1969. 'When the draw was made we reckoned it would be a tough match against the Geraldines. We had played against them for the District three years earlier, when they went on to win the championship. But we had fierce enthusiasm and had prepared very well. We certainly hadn't worked so hard to get to senior, just to be regraded again. Buffers Alley had won it the year before for the first time, and that had proven to us what was possible.

'We turned up against Ross to have a serious go. We hurled well on the day and we were delighted to win our first-ever senior championship match. Soon afterwards, we played the Shamrocks, a well-established senior team, in three tournament matches and I would say, that year, we made the Shamrocks,' Robbie says. 'We beat them first in *The Echo* Shield. I think that might have been in a replay, but we hurled really well.

'Then they invited us in for the Strawberry Fair tournament, and we hit our county final form from the previous year. The trouble was, we were starting to get over-excited about ourselves. We started to think we could beat anyone.

'Buffers Alley had won the championship, and they were picking up on a little bit of boasting coming from us. It wasn't from our players, I must stress that, but others close to the team were talking us up too much.

'The pride of the Alley was at stake, and they ended up getting five goals, with another one disallowed. Tony Doran did a good bit of damage that day.

'We got a rude awakening. It was a tough experience, with no prisoners taken by the Alley.

'But it was a lesson we had to learn. Some of our supporters could get a bit over-excited, and that result stopped them in their tracks. The most important thing was, that defeat wasn't going to knock us or set us back. It was all part of a new experience for us… we knew we'd learn from it.'

Shamrocks went on to beat Buffers Alley in the semi-final by 3-12 to 4-6.

'After that they had a big win over Ferns – who had surprised Rathnure – in a fairly one-sided final.'

Oulart-The Ballagh's own campaign had come to an end in early July. And for the next 12 months, the future of Mick Jacob as a Wexford senior hurler was in considerable doubt.

A VERY SERIOUS situation was about to emerge. The decisions of the new Wexford selection committee for 1970 would meet with stern resistance from the Jacob brothers.

A squad of 23 to meet Laois in round one of the National League in Gorey on October 26 was printed in the *Irish Independent* on the previous Wednesday. Mick's name appeared among the substitutes, but there was no place for Christy.

Their twin omission wasn't appreciated.

Mick didn't tog out for that game against Laois; in fact, he wasn't seen in a Wexford jersey again until the following year's All-Ireland semi-final against Galway. But Mick's career didn't stall after that dispute in the winter of 1969-70. If anything, he came back even stronger after forcibly making his point. In doing so, he was showing that his mild-mannered nature off the field did not make him a soft touch. And, just as importantly in his eyes, he was making a stance on behalf of his club.

WHAT EXACTLY PROMPTED Mick and Christy to voice their disapproval in late 1969?

'There was a bit of a falling out with the selectors,' Mick explains. 'We felt we weren't getting a fair crack of the whip from them.

'We were very disappointed with the way the new selection committee carried on around that time. We felt they just wouldn't pick two from Oulart-The Ballagh on the same team.

'It took an awful long time for the club to gain the respect it deserved. Even though we were senior by that stage, I would say some people still looked down on us. If you were to ask when that finally changed, I would say that realistically it didn't happen until we drew with Rathnure in the county semi-final of 1972.

'That's how long it took for us to be treated as equals and for everyone to realise we were a serious hurling club that demanded full respect. We really had to earn our stripes.'

Wexford's two pre-Christmas National League games in 1969 were staged without Mick, and it became a major topic of public interest in the spring months of 1970.

In fact, *The People* devoted a lengthy piece on the subject under the headline… *WHY OULART BROTHERS ARE NOT ON HURLING SELECTION* in its edition of April 25, with county secretary Paddy Roche sent out to bat on behalf of officialdom.

While the newspaper article lacked balance without an input from the Jacob side, a man of Mick's reserved disposition had no interest in a public debate. Neither had he any desire to sit around a table to try to iron out any perceived differences. What he did firmly believe was that the only place to show one's true worth was inside the white lines.

'I missed out on a Leinster medal in 1970 over that, but I was happy myself in the decision I had made,' he says. 'I kept myself in good nick training-wise, and I was going to prove myself worthy of a place again by playing as well as I possibly could with the club.

'I stayed going to some of the Wexford matches and had a look at what was going on. I know Syl Barron approached us as well at one time, along with Paddy Roche, about coming back, but we didn't travel.'

In the Jacobs' absence, Wexford didn't advance to the knockout stages of the league. Promising wins over Tipperary and Waterford in early 1970 were followed by a deflating last-day defeat away to Offaly, when a miserly 2-3 was scored in an eight-point loss.

Mick's entire focus at that point was on the club campaign, with Oulart-The Ballagh's fortunes plotted by Fr Staples, Phil Redmond, Bobby Walsh, Robbie Sinnott and Lar Dempsey. The championship started on a high in Wexford Park on May 24, when he was joined at midfield by Matty Ryan in a 4-9 to 1-11 win over the Berry-powered St Anne's/St Patrick's.

On the county front, a routine Leinster semi-final win over Dublin was followed by a second provincial title in three years. With Dave Bernie and Phil Wilson at midfield, and four Quigley brothers on board, Kilkenny were beaten by 4-16 to 3-14, with Mick looking on from the stand.

However, the local newspapers in early August brought bad news. *The People* lamented in a headline… *SENIOR HURLERS' ALL-IRELAND HOPES SUFFER SEVERE SETBACK*, before explaining Willie Murphy, Ned Buggy and Wilson were all ruled out through injury.

The unfortunate dispute between the Jacob brothers and the county selectors could again prevent Michael Jacob getting the position (neither side has relented in this confrontation) but another young Oulart star could be the answer to the problem. Selectors could do worse than call Tom Byrne into training.

On that same weekend, Oulart-The Ballagh recorded another convincing championship win. They travelled to Gorey and crushed Ferns St Aidan's, the runners-up of 1969, by 1-15 to 1-6.

Robbie joined Mick at midfield in a dominant performance. *The Jacob brothers were in tremendous form and completely eclipsed Dave Bernie and Donal Behan – though the latter gave a very wholehearted display.*

AS THEY LEFT the field that day, Nickey Rackard made a direct approach to Mick. He asked him to come back into the Wexford fold. And it was hard to say no to a man of that calibre.

Whatever else had happened with team selections, Mick didn't bear any ill-will towards this hurling giant whom he had revered since his own childhood.

That Ferns match took place just one week before the All-Ireland semi-final against Galway.

Mick agreed to Nickey's request, bringing his self-imposed exile to an end, and he would remain a faithful servant of the Wexford senior hurling squad until serious injury robbed him of that privilege all of 14 years later.

'Missing that Leinster final had no real effect on me, if I'm honest. Others might be sorry about losing out on a medal, but I didn't look on it that way.

'I just kept hurling and hurling, and worked my way back. Nickey asked me to return on the strength of my performances on the field with Oulart, and that's what I wanted all along.

'I had to show my mettle then against Galway when I got the chance.'

That was the first year of the short-lived experiment of playing championship matches from provincial finals onwards over 80 minutes, and Athlone was selected as a somewhat bizarre neutral venue. Galway had played, and struggled, in Munster over the previous decade, so perhaps it was an act of benevolence to stage the game so close to their county boundaries.

It was the one and only time in the history of Wexford hurling that the county played competitively at the midlands venue.

The day started on a low note, with the minors losing to a Galway side featuring future Ireland rugby captain Ciarán Fitzgerald, of 'Where's your f*****g pride?' fame.

And the senior game was no walk in the park either, with fancied Wexford eventually pulling through by 3-17 to 5-9. As predicted, young Tom Byrne got the nod for a midfield start and ran himself into the ground.

Not alone that, he appeared to be conscious of the need to offer game-time to his returning club colleague. *Newcomer to mid-field, Tom Byrne, played himself to a standstill, The People* said. *In his time on the field, he lived up to the very high reputation he earned in age limit ranks in recent years and, in fact, it was partly his own decision to move to the sideline to make way for Michael Jacob.*

Mick remembers being 'very lucky' to come out of Athlone with a win that day.

'Tom Ryan from Tipperary was playing with Galway, and he caused us a lot of problems. It wasn't a great display on the whole, but we got over the line.' If the performance left room for improvement, the return of Wexford hurling's prodigal son was universally acclaimed.

A further chance to acclimatise to life as an inter-county hurler once again arose seven days later.

Mick won a third Walsh Cup medal on the trot when Dublin were beaten in the delayed final of 1969 by 6-13 to 3-18 in St Patrick's Park. With Dave Bernie unavailable, he partnered clubmate Tom Byrne at midfield and scored four points from play.

And while the youngster made an immense contribution to that campaign, deep down he must have known that Mick would get the nod ahead of him for a starting berth on All-Ireland final day.

Cork lay in wait, and the preview in *The People* highlighted the potential in this talented pair.

Such was the majesty of Bernie at Athlone that it is difficult to see any midfielder lasting eighty gruelling minutes beside him. Jacob, the man who came out of 'inter-county retirement' at the request of the selectors and sat on the sideline for sixty minutes in the All-Ireland semi-final, is worthy of his place.

MICK AND DAVE certainly kept up their side of the bargain in Croke Park on September 5, 1970.

So, too, did netminder Pat Nolan, but otherwise it was a dismal day for Wexford hurling.

Although 5-10 was a decent tally to rack up on All-Ireland final day, they conceded 6-21 and never really stood a chance against a county that Mick would never beat in his championship career.

Nonetheless, the local press were loud in their praise of the midfielders' contribution, with *The Echo* headlining one piece... *JACOB AND BERNIE WERE STARS.*

Pitting the relatively new midfield partnership of David Bernie and Mick Jacob against Cork's Gerald McCarthy and Seamus Looney was one of Wexford's biggest successes of the few that resulted in the 1970 final.

Undoubtedly the youthful duo – Bernie is aged 23, and Jacob 24 – gave Wexford a vital, very much wanted 'edge' in this sector.

The People chimed in: *Wexford's stars were few and far between. One might say that there were only three who came up to expectations and, indeed, two of them did much better than many people considered possible. They were midfielders Dave Bernie and Michael Jacob.*

'A soldier is not a soldier until he goes to war, and then you know whether he is a real soldier or not.' Dave Bernie uses this analogy to sum up the sterling contribution of a man he went into the hurling trenches with for a full decade from 1968 to '78.

'Mick Jacob was a soldier on the field of play… a warrior, a motivator, and the heartbeat of all teams he played for,' he says. 'It was my great honour to have partnered him in so many memorable battles. We complemented each other with our contrasting styles of hurling.

'Mick always performed to the maximum of his ability. More importantly, he knew how to win, and when to drive on… when victory was in sight.

'Our partnership commenced versus Kilkenny in Croker in 1968 before the All-Ireland. It was a Walsh Cup final that resulted in a big win for us. We were to have many more memorable battles including the All-Ireland final of 1970, although beaten by Cork. We carried the day in that midfield battle, and many more also, too numerous to mention,' Bernie recalls.

The pair lined up together for a throw-in with Wexford on 25 occasions in all, with all bar two of those games taking place between 1968 and '71, before Mick made his successful switch to centre-back.

After Nickey Rackard persuaded him to return for the All-Ireland semi-final of 1970 against Galway, the midfield display of Mick (front row, third left) was one of the few bright aspects of Wexford's subsequent heavy loss to Cork.

Mick was a virtual fixture with Wexford for another 14 years after 1970. Bogey team Offaly inflicted narrow defeats in 1982 (left) and again in 1984 (above) as Mick clears his lines under pressure from Paddy Corrigan, 17 days before a serious eye injury forced him into retirement.

« CHAPTER 5 »

MICK JACOB WILL never forget the solemn promise made to him by Mylie Ryan.

In 1962, on the eve of his first-ever adult match, the full-back approached his goalkeeper and vowed to protect him, no matter what the cost.

On that day, a bond initially formed when they cycled together, night after night, to training in Mountdaniel was solidified. Not alone that, it was never broken. Mylie remained true to his word; all Mick had to do was worry about the ball, and Mylie would look after the rest. These lifelong friends were always there for one another.

And after the tragic events of October 18, 1970, it was Mick's turn to step up and put a protective arm around his stricken colleague. The memory of that deeply upsetting day still sends a shiver down his spine.

IT WAS SIX weeks after the All-Ireland defeat to Cork, and the focus was back on the club scene. Oulart-The Ballagh met St Martin's, with a place in the county semi-final the attractive prize on offer. The game didn't go well for the relative newcomers, even though Mick scored 2-2 from his midfield partnership with Robbie.

OULART STILL HAVE A LONG WAY TO GO, ran one newspaper headline, and that was quite evident in the 5-11 to 3-7 result in favour of St Martin's.

Mick was *the best man, the finest player on view, who lacked even the minimal support. Jacob was flying all over the field, and his play got Oulart 'off the hook' on many occasions.*

It was another typically defiant display from a man hitting his hurling peak, but on this occasion it paled into insignificance.

Mylie, a sterling servant of the club as it rose steadily through the ranks, had passed the 30 mark by this stage and watched the early part of that match from the sidelines. However, with Oulart-The Ballagh under pressure, he was called upon to enter the fray in his familiar stomping ground of the full-back line.

His goal was the same as ever, to look after the colleague behind him; the only difference was that now it was Johnny Parle, rather than his great friend Mick who was further upfield.

As the match entered its closing stages, there was no way back for Oulart-The Ballagh, but Mylie wasn't ready or willing to stop trying; that simply wasn't part of his nature.

With his team defending the Bellefield Road end, a high, dropping ball was delivered towards the square from the side of the ground where the pavilion currently stands at the Enniscorthy venue.

Mylie engaged in a physical tussle for supremacy with his direct opponent that was part and parcel of the game in those days. He had done this literally thousands of times, grappling with a forward as the sliotar arrived around the danger zone.

This particular contest had a chilling conclusion, though; it ended with Mylie writhing in agony on the ground, clutching his face and in immense pain. All interest in the game dissipated as he was treated with care for a lengthy period, but nothing could be done.

His injuries were severe, resulting in the loss of his right eye.

It was an incredibly traumatic day for Mylie first and foremost, but also for the Oulart-The Ballagh club as a whole.

And nobody felt the after-effects of those few seconds that altered a man's life forever with greater force than Mick, his firm friend. 'That was a very upsetting time for me, and for everyone that knew Mylie. It had an awful impact on the club, and on the rest of the players. Mylie was such a great warrior with us for years and years. For him to lose his eye was something unreal.

'I remember for weeks and weeks after it, I just couldn't stop thinking about him. He was on my mind the whole time. No matter what I did or where I was, I was wondering about him.

'He lived a life of hardship afterwards, and my heart went out to him. The eye was always troubling him, and he was prone to picking up all sorts of infections.

'That man had given so much to the club through all the lean years. In those bad times, playing junior and intermediate and struggling on many occasions, Mylie was constantly there in the full-back line, giving his all,' Mick says.

'When he got the chance to play senior hurling himself, he thought it was out of this world. He couldn't believe how lucky and privileged he was, it meant so much to him. He would have closely followed the great teams of the past like Enniscorthy St Aidan's in the 50s, but he knew that he was never going to be inter-county standard himself.

'So, for him, to be playing senior against the likes of Buffers Alley was the exact same as playing in an All-Ireland final.'

Mylie hailed from Kilcormack and was one of a family of six, with four sisters and one brother Willie. He never married but had a close network of siblings, nephews and nieces that helped him through the tough times that followed.

And then there was Mick, and his regular visits.

'Mylie was a great friend of mine. I used to call in to see him every Friday night without fail.'

Those trips to his house meant everything to a man who passed away in January 2017, at the age of 78. It was only in the last few weeks of his life that he had to move to a nursing home in Enniscorthy.

Prior to that, he remained in the homeplace and relished Mick calling in to share the latest news. It gave him a lifeline, something to look forward to. And in those few hours, Mylie's troubles would fade into the background as his heart warmed with hurling talk and local chit-chat.

Even if Mick had a big match coming up on the Sunday, he never missed calling to his friend every Friday. It might be late, particularly if training was in full swing on a bright summer's evening, but Mylie knew Mick would never let him down.

'Sometimes we would stay in the house, and other times I'd bring him over to the pub in Raheenduff so he could have a few drinks. He'd always say, "No matter what you do… come over Friday". And if I was going to be late, he might go over to the village without me and then come back.

'He'd say, "I'll leave the key out for you. You make the tea for yourself when you arrive. Hang on for me until I get back." We used to have great chats about all the games, the memories of going to Croke Park… the top players and teams.

'Mylie was a big man for Tipperary, but only in certain circumstances. Any time Tipp were playing Kilkenny, he'd be certain that Tipp were going to win… nothing would convince him otherwise.

'But if it was Wexford playing Tipp, then there was never any doubt in his mind, he'd be backing Wexford all the way.

'Peter Keane is another good friend of ours, and I'd say to him, just for the craic, "Go over and tell Mylie that Kilkenny will walk Tipp into the ground on All-Ireland final day".

'Mylie wouldn't be having that at all. "I've never seen a Kilkenny man walking a Tipp man into the ground yet, and I've been around a long time," he'd say. We'd have a right term with him.

'He was like a father figure to me. I loved those chats, and that ritual of calling to him every Friday night.'

It was as much a part of Mick's regular routine as getting out of bed every morning, and the bond between the pair was special. 'Mylie was a fine singer, with a great twang in his voice. In later years, I used to bring him up to the pub in Raheenduff on the Monday after a big win, to join in the celebrations. The lads on the team would always look for a song from Mylie.

'And he would belt out his favourite… *The Rose of Mooncoin*.

'Or *Slaney Valley* to rapturous applause.

'He really loved those occasions and they maintained his connection with the club. I would always ring Mylie after matches, to keep him informed on how the various club teams were progressing – he took a great interest in how our under-age teams were doing in their championships. I would give him a run-down on the matches, and I think he would visualise what had happened on the field.'

Even now, four years after Mylie's death, he misses his dear friend.

MYLIE SUSTAINED HIS injury three years after the same fate befell Kilkenny forward Tom Walsh – the man denied a goal by Mick's late save in the 1964 Leinster Under-21 Championship – during the All-Ireland senior final of 1967.

'Tom made contact with Mylie a good while later and spent a fair bit of time with him. It was a kind gesture he always appreciated,' Mick says. 'The three of us got together for a meal in Ferns one night… I'd say about 10 years before Mylie died, and he really enjoyed himself.'

WHILE MICK JACOB would make the centre-back position his own as his career blossomed, for a long time it appeared his calling lay at midfield.

His partnership with Dave Bernie continued into 1971, starting on a high note when they shone in the annual challenge game against the Rest of Leinster to pick the Railway Cup team. He had a brilliant hour, scoring two points in a 3-11 to 2-13 win in Bellefield on January 24. That game was also notable for Christy's return to the county fold, but there was disappointment and surprise when Mick only made the substitutes.

The National League group campaign that followed was a mixed bag of three wins and two losses for Wexford, with the Jacob/Bernie partnership featuring on three occasions.

The attack failed to capitalise on their good service in New Ross on St Valentine's Day, with a 4-7 to 2-7 success for Tipperary helped by their decision to move Mick Roche to midfield.

The absence of Michael Jacob was a major blow one week later, with the 'flu ruling him out of a 1-16 to 3-6 defeat to Cork in the Athletic Grounds.

He was back for the visit of Limerick to Bellefield, but the poor form continued as the visitors prevailed by 1-17 to 2-7. Indeed, according to *The People, for the first time in nine months, Dave Bernie and Michael Jacob did not form a consistent midfield partnership.*

Thankfully, the sight of the Kilkenny jersey prompted a positive response in Wexford Park on March 21. Mick's insatiable appetite for work was praised in a 2-12 to 2-9 win, as *Wexford's midfielders exerted clear superiority over Kilkenny pair Mossie Murphy and Michael Brennan.*

A doctor's cert declared him unfit for a one-point success over Galway in Ballinasloe, before a play-off was secured thanks to a handy home victory against Dublin. Mick returned for that one, and success earned them another crack at

Kilkenny, this time in Waterford's Walsh Park, with Christy coming off the bench and shooting two vital goals in the course of a 5-8 to 3-13 victory.

That bid for league honours came to an abrupt halt in Thurles just one week later, with Clare in command from the off on the way to a 4-10 to 1-7 quarter-final success.

Mick created the Wexford goal, with his delivery in the 27th minute clipped overhead to the net by Con Dowdall. However, in the context of his overall career, there was a far more significant occurrence... a first opportunity to shine at centre-back.

Reporter Billy Quirke of *The People* was in no doubt that this move was long overdue. Always a great fan of the Oulart-The Ballagh operator, he was the only local journalist who always referred to him as Michael, never Mick. And he wrote glowingly on this occasion.

Few Wexfordmen emerged from the test with reputations untarnished. But if there was a bright note it was the display of Michael Jacob. What a big-hearted player this is! With players all around him in the early stages just refusing to give him their best support, and later, as those same players, frustrated, could not do as they wished, the Oulart man worked tirelessly and unselfishly.

He played a lone hand at midfield, assisting a harried defence and prompting a subdued attack. Then he was moved to centre half-back, and this is the reason why Clare scored only two points in the last twenty-two minutes of the game.

At last, selectors decided to give Michael Jacob a run in the position in which he can assist his county best. But it was only in desperation that they did so.

How badly Wexford need a capable centre-back, and how long it took to give Jacob his chance! He will be missed at centrefield, but the assistance he can give to his defence and his lengthy striking (he was the only Wexfordman capable of hitting a ball more than forty yards) will benefit half-forwards.

The selectors had tried three men in the No.6 slot during that campaign: Jack Russell, John Quigley, and Mick Kinsella. However, they had seen enough in that cameo against Clare to convince them that Jacob was the man for the job.

ON HIS 30th outing for the county senior team, Mick started at centre-back for the first time in the Leinster semi-final against Offaly in Croke Park on June 27, with Dave Bernie and Phil Wilson at midfield.

Flanked by Colm Doran and Willie Murphy, he had another excellent game in a straightforward 2-14 to 2-6 victory. Kilkenny, as ever, were waiting in the long grass.

Their team of the early-70s was one of the most formidable to ever emerge from the county, and they started five years of provincial dominance with a 6-16 to 3-16 final victory in Croke Park on July 11.

Reporter Larry Larkin noted: *Mick Jacob did an excellent job on Pat Delaney, but was not so successful on Mossy Murphy.*

It marked the first use of a Kilkenny tactic that would be deployed more than once in the years to come. Delaney, a player of immense physical strength, preferred to go through an opponent rather than around him.

And after giving his all in that one-to-one battle, Mick had a lot to contend with then once the fresher Murphy was moved out to the '40' in a direct swap with Delaney after starting at full-forward.

Little did he know it at the time, but four more frustrating summers lay in store before Mick would win his first Leinster senior medal on the field of play.

OF MORE IMMEDIATE concern in 1971 was the club championship, with Oulart-The Ballagh facing a must-win game in the losers' section after an earlier reversal to Rathnure.

It took a long time for the club to warm to the task of another senior campaign, even though Frank Donnelly was back on board as trainer after a brief absence. Bobby Walsh, Phil Redmond, Lar Dempsey, Johnny Martin and John Storey were appointed selectors at an AGM in January that saw the club vote 44-3 in favour of removing the infamous 'Ban'.

However, they struggled to build the required interest in the early part of the year.

For starters, Mylie Ryan's teammates were pre-occupied with working on the fundraising appeal that sought to compensate him for his loss of earnings. A sum of £900 had been raised by the end of January 1971, and the efforts were ongoing.

Another direct consequence of Mylie's injury was the retirement of his brother-in-law Tony Byrne.

The club's regular centre-back throughout the 60s, he also represented Wexford at intermediate level and was a very important figure in the rise to senior hurling.

Tony was married to Joan, Mylie's sister, and saw at first hand the devastating impact of his injury.

It prompted him to hang up his boots, and that, in turn, led to Mick's redeployment to centre-back with Oulart-The Ballagh.

However, for the championship opener against Rathnure on May 23, he was posted on the right flank of the defence, with a specific purpose in mind. That was to keep tabs on county colleague Martin Quigley, and he certainly succeeded, holding this outstanding young forward scoreless.

It was all in vain, though, as Oulart-The Ballagh lost by 3-12 to 3-8.

However, it was a replay against the same opponents in 1971 that raised Oulart-The Ballagh's game to another level, and also helped immensely in lifting the gloom that surrounded hurling in the parish after Mylie Ryan's injury.

'Buffers Alley had bought land for a new pitch down in Ballinastraw, and they held a big festival as a fundraiser,' Robbie explains. 'A hurling tournament was the main attraction, and they got massive crowds to the games played on summer evenings. We were drawn against Rathnure, and there was a great atmosphere at it.

'People were swarmed along the sidelines. Spectators would have to step back out of the way whenever a player came racing down the wing.

'Mick was put centre-back for that tournament, and we had a great game against Rathnure.

'There was nothing in it, our lads were going flat out for every ball. Rathnure got a goal to go three points up, and it was close to the last puck of the game.

'Tom Byrne caught our puck-out, playing at centre-forward. He turned and headed for goal, got to the '21' and tore the roof of the net out of it with a rocket.

'We got the draw, and there was a major buzz afterwards, the fact that we had been able to do that. After losing to Rathnure a short while before in the championship, it was another sign of progress.

'Tom Byrne had to go to Paris for a week to work, and we weren't willing to play them again without him.

'We waited until he came back, and beat them in the replay. It was a very significant win for our club, although – like with the Shamrocks in 1969 – we possibly won the championship for Rathnure on the strength of it. They learned a lot from those games too.'

While those tournament ties nailed down Mick's new club spot at centre-back, they had to do without him for the championship clash with Duffry Rovers in Bellefield on August 8.

This was do-or-die, and the extent of his loss with an injury was evident in the end result.

Oulart-The Ballagh scraped home by 2-7 to 1-9, in a game regarded as the best in the championship for some years. Robbie stepped up in his baby brother's absence, driving the team on from right half-back despite the nuisance of having two fingers strapped together.

One week later, Mick was back for the clash with Enniscorthy District, but it was a bridge too far as an opposition powered by Ballyhogue, Oylegate-Glenbrien, Cloughbawn and Half Way House-Bunclody players prevailed by 2-11 to 2-8.

The District team had been good to the Jacobs before their own club reached the top flight, affording them a first opportunity to play senior hurling. However, they saw the other side of the story on this occasion.

'It was one small parish playing against five or six, so it was disappointing to lose in that way.'

MICK IS THE last man who would seek controversy in any shape or form.

A renowned sportsman, all he ever wanted to do was play hurling to the very best of his ability.

And yet, he was unwittingly part of a further confrontation with the county board in late 1971.

The start of another inter-county season had provided a notable family feat.

Wexford beat Galway in an Oireachtas quarter-final in Ballinasloe on September 19, and it was the only time that Mick and Robbie played together on the county senior team. Mick was alongside Dave Bernie at midfield, while Robbie came on at wing-back and marked Pádraig Fahy.

What a pity Christy didn't feature too, because the three brothers never lined out alongside each other on any Wexford team, despite a lifetime of collaboration with the club.

The National League campaign was set to start against Cork in New Ross on October 10 but, shortly before, Mick got an offer he simply couldn't refuse.

'Mylie Doran from Kilmuckridge was over the Wexford hurling team in New York. He got in contact with myself, Dan Quigley, Dave Bernie and Teddy

O'Connor to see if we'd come over to play in a game. Naturally enough, we said we would. It was my first time in America, and sure I was delighted to be asked.

'Anyway, the day of the game, didn't the heavens open. It absolutely spilled down, and Gaelic Park was unplayable. The match was postponed, and we had to stay over for a week until it could go ahead.

'Mick Morrissey from the Wexford team of the 50s was living over there… he was working in a bakery at the time. So I went with Mick to work there. He'd collect me in the morning, and off we'd go.'

Dave Bernie also has fond memories of that particular week. 'Mick Morrissey managed a bakery in White Plains, outside New York, and he provided jobs for a few of us while we were there.

'Dan Quigley and Mick were masquerading as two mechanics, and Teddy O'Connor and I were two bakers. Productivity was at an all-time high in our time there!'

The most important thing was that Wexford won the match when it did go ahead at the iconic Bronx venue, particularly when the opposition was provided by the Kilkenny team in New York.

That was all that mattered to Mick Morrissey, manager of the victorious side.

However, little did the Wexford quartet know that a storm was brewing at home in their absence.

A FEW DAYS before the Cork game, journalist Billy Quirke explained that all four were named on the team. *A spokesman for the Co Board informed me during the week that if any or all of the players fail to answer the call to turn out for their county, they will receive lengthy suspensions,* he added.

Wexford duly lost to Cork in their absence by 6-7 to 3-8, and the matter of the 'missing players' was passed on to the disciplinary committee when a county board meeting took place one night later.

'We got home to be told they were going to suspend us,' Mick remembers.

'A meeting was called, and they wanted the four of us to be there. I didn't go, I stayed at home, but I think the other lads might have gone alright.

'I decided that if they were going to suspend me over something like that, sure let them off. I didn't see any value in wasting a night by going in to a meeting.

'We weren't suspended anyway… there was no more about it.'

Thankfully for everyone, there was a quick realisation that banning four of the county's top players would be of benefit to nobody, apart of course from Wexford's main rivals.

'I had a great time in New York. To get out there, especially as a young lad, was really special.

'There was right fun going with Mick Morrissey out to his bakery. And the hurling was very good too, there would always be a few county lads on all the teams.

'Joe Foley was out there at the time, he played with me in 1969 when Offaly beat us. If Joe was in the mood, he'd hurl Christy Ring, he was some stickman.

'I played with Seamus Hearne at midfield in New York, and he was still some man to go. That was an honour for me, because he was on that great team of the 50s. He wasn't a big fella, but he was like a terrier, even then when he was getting on in years. He had some engine.

'We were looked after very well when we were over there. Mylie Doran was a great sort, and sure he knew all about the Jacobs because of his Kilmuckridge roots.

'He looked out for us, and showed us the places to go, and the places to avoid. That was important, because some parts around Gaelic Park were rough enough at the time.

'I think I ended up visiting New York about nine times altogether. It's a great city, and I'll always cherish that first trip.'

ALL WAS FORGIVEN a fortnight after that missed game against Cork, with Mick and Dave Bernie back in harness for the second round of the National League against Tipperary in Thurles. They drew 3-12 to 4-9. Jimmy Galway of Adamstown was his partner next time out versus Offaly in Gorey, and Mick *was his usual industrious self at midfield, covering acres of ground* in a 3-8 to 2-3 success.

Bernie returned for the clash against Limerick in the Gaelic Grounds on November 21, but the home side prevailed quite comfortably by 3-6 to 0-8. The year ended with another loss, and another new midfield partner.

Jim Higgins of Rathnure was handed a debut after a strong club campaign, but Kilkenny beat Wexford by 1-14 to 1-9 in Nowlan Park on the first Sunday in December.

And in their desire to give this newcomer the full hour in his favoured position, there was an unusual posting for Mick. He ended up at corner-forward after a series of positional switches, the start of an ill-advised brief dalliance with an attacking role.

It only continued for the first three games of 1972, but it did yield his one and only goal in a Wexford senior jersey.

First up was a 2-13 to 2-8 Walsh Cup win over Offaly in St Patrick's Park, with Mick selected at centre-forward and scoring two points.

It was one of three notable experiments, with Phil Wilson at centre-back and Colm Doran at midfield. And on a first viewing, one local reporter actually felt it might be worth pursuing.

All three were at their very best, and many followers were overheard complimenting the selectors on the changes and expressing the hope that they would be permanent.

A lot can change in the space of a week all the same.

That sole goal for Wexford arrived in a heavy 4-6 to 1-4 National League loss to Clare in New Ross, and it won't be remembered as a classic.

It came from a ball struck in from 60 yards, with the normally reliable Seamus Durack getting his stick to it but only succeeding in helping it to the net.

Larry Larkin covered that match for *The People*, and he knew a thing or two about the GAA. After all, he had played on the Wexford minor football team in the All-Ireland final of 1950, and then with the seniors in the Leinster final of 1953.

A journalist who always called it as he saw it, he didn't spare Mick. He wrote that *he looked a complete misfit... apart from his well-taken goal, he made very little contribution.*

Mick laughs when he hears this description of his performance in attack, nearly 50 years later. 'I wonder what I ever did to upset poor Larry,' he jokes.

Thankfully for everyone, this short-lived experiment was dispensed with a fortnight later.

He again started at centre-forward in the delayed Walsh Cup final of 1970, flanked by Con Dowdall and Martin Quigley against Kilkenny in Nowlan Park. The hosts won by 3-9 to 1-10, but not before Mick was moved to partner Phil Wilson at midfield.

They took control against Frank Cummins and Paddy Moran, and the pair combined effectively once more in the last National League game of the campaign, a 4-13 to 5-6 win over Dublin in Croke Park.

The year 1972 was set for another incredible twist.

Mick would return to centre-back – his championship role for the first time 12 months earlier – and be selected as the best No.6 in the land on the strength of two outstanding performances versus Kilkenny.

◄ ◄ ◆ ► ►

'For his sparkling hurling style, his intelligent understanding of the game, and his refusal to give up in the most difficult situations.'

Mick Jacob's citation for winning Wexford's first-ever Carroll's All Star award in October 1972 summed up his abundant qualities in a succinct 22 words.

His club and county rejoiced as the good news spread. It couldn't have happened to a more popular individual, and the man himself was thrilled with the recognition. 'I remember getting a letter to tell me I was picked, but I had to keep it a secret until the team was publicly announced. That wasn't an easy task,' he laughs. 'Players were nominated for specific positions in those days, but it never came into my head that I would make it until I got that letter.'

There was no limit to the numbers that could be shortlisted in the early years of the All Stars.

Indeed, in 1972, just the second year of the scheme, the grand total of 82 hurlers stood a chance, including 10 Wexford players.

As well as being in the hunt for centre-back, Mick was also among the 16 nominations for right half-back along with Colm Doran, with that position going to Kilkenny's Pat Lawlor. His other teammates in the running were Pat Nolan, Tom Neville, Teddy O'Connor, John Quigley, Martin Quigley, Phil Wilson, Christy Keogh and Tony Doran.

He was pitted against Kilkenny giant Pat Henderson, Mick Roche of Tipperary, Limerick's Pat Hartigan (selected at full-back), Kildare dual star Pat Dunny, Ted Murphy of Galway, and John Kirwan from Waterford, for that coveted No.6 jersey.

Mick's secret emerged on Monday, October 23, when the second All Stars hurling team was announced at a press reception at the PJ Carroll & Co Ltd headquarters in Grand Parade, Dublin.

His beaming smile appeared in the following day's newspapers, flanked by Pat Lawlor and Con Roche of Cork in a formidable half-back line.

And as the well wishes flooded in from near and far, this modest man savoured an extraordinary sense of achievement. At 26 years of age, his elation was infectious.

'Being picked at centre half-back on that team meant the world to me. It felt like I was in the big time, up there with the best hurlers in the country.

'I was absolutely thrilled to get that position. I always had it in my mind that I wanted to be a star.

'I wanted to be the very best I could possibly be in every game I played, whether it was only a practice match, or a big championship final in Croke Park.

'It was also a great shot in the arm for Oulart-The Ballagh to have the first All Star in Wexford. That's something that can never be taken away from the club, they will always have that.

'I felt like I'd come a very long way from my time as a child in Gorey, cheering on the Wexford team of the 50s.

'I remembered being picked on the Oulart-The Ballagh team for the first time and working my way up. I thought about all the people who had been involved with me since my under-age days, helping to build me up.

'There was Fr Staples at the start, and then Frank Donnelly played a big part. And Robbie of course, as the eldest… he got us gelled into the whole thing when we were very young.

'My mother and uncles were thrilled too, and it also sowed the seeds for the rest of the club to go on and achieve great things. It got everyone in the parish interested in hurling, that's for sure.

'And people in the rest of the county finally sat up and took notice. They thought to themselves, *By God, Oulart have produced an All Star here.* It was another sign that we were finally recognised as a club.'

NOBODY, LEAST OF all the man himself, could have seen this coming ahead of the 1972 championship campaign. Indeed, he wasn't even on the field for the first game on June 18, a routine 4-13 to 2-5 Leinster semi-final win over Dublin in Nowlan Park.

Mick has 'no recollection whatsoever' of a disciplinary measure that was apparently taken by the selectors against six players. He was among that number, along with clubmate Jimmy Prendergast, Dave Bernie, Matt Browne, Con Dowdall, and substitute goalkeeper Pat Nolan from New Ross.

Reporter Billy Quirke stated in his match preview that, *The selectors have decided to ignore those who do not turn up at training.* After the match, *The Echo* commented that, *If Mick Jacob changes his attitude, then Wexford will be a side to be feared by the best.*

It ended as a storm in a teacup, one of several affecting the county hurling camp in the early-70s.

Under the headline… ABSENTEE HURLERS ARE INVITED BACK, it was reported, *Wexford selectors have invited the players who were disciplined for the Leinster senior hurling semi-final to rejoin the panel.*

Oulart-The Ballagh had comfortably beaten St Anne's/St Patrick's in a championship clash on the Sunday prior to the Dublin game. Perhaps Mick missed a county training session in order to focus on that match, but his attitude to playing for Wexford, or commitment to the cause, didn't deserve to be questioned.

As ever, he preferred to let his hurling do the talking on the pitch. Give him a chance, and he'd never let the side down.

Before the Leinster final against Kilkenny on July 9, John Quigley was named at centre-back with Mick on the left flank. However, when referee Mick Spain from Offaly threw in the ball, the duo had swapped positions, and Pat Delaney was his direct opponent for a high-scoring thriller.

'Coming into that Kilkenny game, all the talk was about Pat and what he could do to Wexford,' Mick recalls. 'I always loved a challenge, so I was all out to prove myself against this lad. From the word go I got stuck in.

'I caught a few balls starting out, and I had him on the back foot for most of the game. It was a real ding-dong of a match… typical Wexford against Kilkenny.'

It ended in a 6-13 each draw, with the holders relieved to survive after the dismissal of corner-forward Mick Brennan in the 19th minute of the second-half for a foul on John Quigley. For a mild-mannered man off the field, Mick took on a different persona once he went inside those white lines.

'The better your opponent is, the more you have to stand up to him and match him stride for stride,' he stresses. 'Playing on the front foot like that won't work all the time, but when you're up against the best you have to be at your own very best, it's as simple as that.

'You have to go out with the attitude that, *I'm going to hurl this fella*. I always felt in those days that if we could get the real Wexford spirit going in the course of a game, then we were good enough to beat any team.

'I was well prepared for Pat Delaney, and I felt I had the indian sign over him, I never let him get by me. Kieran Purcell was a different type of player, he was tall and had a great hand. He'd come out on me maybe after half an hour, fresh from being inside at full-forward.

'I'd always be thinking about the match, Sunday night… and all through Monday, I'd go through everything in my head and work out for myself what I needed to do better.'

While it would be unheard of nowadays, Mick played two games in between the draw and replay of that Leinster final in 1972.

First up seven days later was a five-point Oireachtas semi-final win over Limerick in New Ross, and that match helped to cement his role at centre-back. And then, just one week before the replay, Oulart-The Ballagh advanced to the semi-final of the county senior championship for the first time with a hard-earned 1-7 to 1-5 dismissal of Geraldine O'Hanrahans.

Buoyed up by that victory, Mick was primed for another battle with Pat Delaney, and he lorded it over him for more than half the game before the Kilkenny mentors took decisive action.

There was no doubt regarding the move of the match in the eyes of Mitchel Cogley in the *Irish Independent*. He stressed that Kilkenny's 3-16 to 1-14 win *will be remembered most for the dramatic effect of the big switch, when Pat Delaney moved from centre forward to full forward after ten minutes of the second half, with Wexford six points up and apparently in control.*

The Johnstown star went on to score the goal that sparked his side's recovery, and created most of the havoc in the opposition defence that was reflected in that eventual eight-point winning margin.

Cogley noted, *Delaney had made no impact when on the '40' opposed by Mick Jacob, who was far and away the best of the Wexford backs.*

Should the Wexford mentors have instructed Mick to follow his man to the edge of the square? It would have been an alien position for him, but Cogley certainly felt it was the required action.

Yet, when Delaney moved in to full forward, Jacob was not moved with him – and Delaney went to town.

It was a major talking point among the 22,745 onlookers on an afternoon when Mick gave the performance above all others that secured that precious award.

Although Wexford's championship campaign was over, there was another opportunity for him to grace a high-profile occasion before the All Stars team was selected.

The Oireachtas final against Tipperary was the curtain-raiser to the All-Ireland football final replay between Offaly and Kerry in Croke Park on October 15, and he stood out once more in a 2-13 each draw.

The teams met again one week later in the National League opener in New Ross, with the home side comfortable winners on this occasion by 4-15 to 2-9. *The ever-consistent Mick Jacob deserved a five star rating, The People* enthused. *He was slow to get into his stride and had difficulty with the hard ground and fast ball in the early stages, but once he found his feet he was a 'tour de force'. His anticipation, handling and enthusiasm left nothing to be desired.*

And when the All Star team was announced in late October, it made a front-page headline in *The Echo. BRAVO, MICHAEL JACOB!*

The People effused, *This is just reward for one of Wexford's most consistent players. The citation sums up this giant-hearted man who has done more solid, hard work for Wexford teams as a defender and midfielder than any single player could be expected to contribute.*

THE EAGERNESS OF his own people to salute Mick was reflected in the bumper crowd of over 300 that flocked to Murphy-Flood's Hotel in Enniscorthy for Oulart-The Ballagh's sixth annual dinner dance on the first Sunday in December.

Mick had missed a National League defeat to Kilkenny earlier in the day as he was suffering from 'flu, but his name was on everyone's lips at the function. Trainer Frank Donnelly led the tributes, calling him, 'A great Gael and sportsman on and off the field'.

An equally overjoyed Fr Staples described Mick as 'a trainer's dream', and urged that all players, particularly the younger men, train with the same wholeheartedness and dedication of their All Star member. He then made a presentation of a wall clock to the club's favourite son.

Mick Jacob and Breda McClean were 'an item' by that stage, and Breda remembers his award having the desired knock-on effect. 'It was great for youngsters in the parish, to know that somebody who grew up in Oulart could achieve that.'

The award 'brought on the rest of our senior players, and gave them a big incentive,' Mick adds. 'I never lost my head over it; when fellas get a big ego they're going nowhere.

1972 WAS UNDOUBTEDLY the break-out year, both for Mick in his inter-county career, and for the Oulart-The Ballagh club in their quest to attain respect from the hurling hierarchy in Wexford.

However, it was also marked by a tragic loss of life that rocked the parish to its very core.

When Billy Dunne died in a car accident on November 8, he left behind a grieving wife Catherine and an infant son Robert, who would go on to play with distinction on the club's first-ever senior-winning team 22 years later.

Mick had known Billy since their days in the schoolyard in Oulart in the late-50s. They had formed midfield partnerships for the club on numerous occasions, and also played together with Wexford in the Leinster Intermediate Championship of 1968.

With Robbie Sinnott for a father-in-law, Billy always gave his all for the club. A county minor with Robbie and Christy in 1960, he was a mechanic by trade and had a huge interest in cars.

His last two outings in the red and black colours were as a substitute in the drawn and replayed county semi-finals of 1972, when Oulart-The Ballagh came up against the mighty Rathnure.

The sides had clashed earlier in the year in an *Echo* Shield game, with the reigning county champions winning by 2-17 to 3-8.

Oulart-The Ballagh subsequently won their championship opener against St Anne's/St Patrick's pulling up by 3-24 to 2-12, but they weren't as impressive when squeezing past Geraldine O'Hanrahans by two points. Nobody apart from their own crew felt they had a chance in the semi-final in Bellefield on August 27, but they were agonisingly close to pulling off a shock victory.

Mick was paired with a promising youngster in PJ Harris at midfield, and

Oulart-The Ballagh led Rathnure by nine points at half-time. And although the holders recovered and the game ended in a draw, there was still glowing praise for the underdogs.

Those who thought that Rathnure's qualification for the final against Rapparees was but a matter of form, got a grave shock, The People reported.

It was Oulart's greatest hour. They were razor keen and what they lacked in championship experience, they made up for in courage and determination. Mick Jacob had a brilliant hour, and it's difficult how anyone could have expected more from this superbly fit and courageous hurler.

It was felt that the excellence and craft of the old hands rescued Rathnure, with their second-half comeback so strong that Tom Byrne had to knock over a late free to ensure a 3-9 each draw for the underdogs.

And now that they were forewarned, the Quigley-powered champions weren't going to be caught napping by these upstarts a second time. The crowds flocked back to Bellefield for the replay a fortnight later, and Oulart-The Ballagh were always playing second fiddle.

With two minutes left, and Rathnure leading by 2-14 to 2-8, the pitch was invaded after a heavy tackle on diminutive netminder Johnny Parle.

Amid the commotion, an announcement was made on the PA that the game would be awarded to Rathnure if the field was not cleared. Although stated with the best of intentions by a young, green official, his words backfired as it prompted large numbers to stay put.

Eight days later, Rathnure were awarded the match by 20 votes to 8 at a county board meeting, with Oulart-The Ballagh's call for a replay rejected.

Robbie Sinnott, combative to the last in the boardroom, memorably told fellow delegates that, 'The first man to start the row was a Rathnure man, and the little man he hit was only about six stone weight'.

Bobby O'Dowd, a Wexford town garage owner from the St Fintan's club, refereed the game but hung up his whistle for good afterwards.

All of the fault for the unsavoury incidents lay with spectators rather than players or officials, and this was confirmed in a statement released by the county board's disciplinary committee.

Mick's class shone like a beacon amid all the chaos. *I do not feel like repeating myself in singing the praises of Michael Jacob, but it is a pity that he was not allowed to remain as an attacking midfielder.*

That was the verdict in *The People*, while *The Echo* reporter couldn't resist an obvious temptation to play on his surname. *Michael Jacob once more 'took the biscuit' as far as class and skill were concerned, and greater still his refusal to quit.*

Mick remembers the quality of the hurling rather than the unruly scenes at this far remove.

'They were magnificent games against Rathnure in 1972, the hurling was unreal. The supporters were everywhere; I remember looking up and seeing lads hanging out of trees behind the country end goal.

'We were always up for Rathnure in a big way. There was very little in those games, maybe the puck of a ball. The excitement was something else, and the quality of hurling was top class.'

Robbie Jacob's recall of past matches is precise, and the events of the drawn game in 1972 remain etched in his memory. 'With one minute to go, we were still a goal up. Teddy O'Connor took off on a solo run from their half-back line, and he was tripped just beyond midfield.

'The free was landed into our goalmouth, and John Quigley doubled on it to the net with a one-handed flick. There was no way we should have let them back into it.

'I'll always remember Robbie Sinnott at that game. He had been with us through thick and thin, back to the time when we were only a down and out junior outfit.

'Now we were nine points up against this seemingly unbeatable Rathnure team, and he was actually crying as we went back on to the field for the second-half.

'This was beyond his wildest dreams, and he was bristling with pride and emotion.'

The battles with the men from under the Blackstairs mountain were only beginning. And for Mick Jacob, three generally frustrating years would follow. Apart from winning a National League medal, the period from 1973 to '75 would produce more lows than highs.

Mick's selection as Wexford's first-ever All Star is marked with the presentation of a wall clock by his early mentor Fr Frank Staples at the Oulart-The Ballagh dinner dance on December 3, 1972. The pair are joined by proud club officials Bobby Walsh, Fintan Cooney and Tommy Kirwan.

The life-changing injury sustained in 1970 by his great friend Mylie Ryan (left) had a lasting impact on Mick, seen here on the right in the official photograph that accompanied his selection at centre half-back on the All Stars hurling team of 1972.

« CHAPTER 6 »

MICK JACOB OFTEN wonders how the Wexford hurlers would have fared if the back-door option was open to them in the early-70s.

From 1971 all the way through to '75, their summers ended in the same abrupt manner... defeat at the hands of a powerful Kilkenny team in the Leinster final.

And with no second chance to avail of, all they could do was lick their wounds and focus their energies on the ultra-competitive club scene instead.

The highlight of that period for Wexford arrived in Croke Park on May 13, 1973, when Mick won his sole National League medal with a 4-13 to 3-7 success over Limerick.

However, the Shannonsiders learned more lessons from that game than their conquerors; while Kilkenny would go on to ambush Wexford yet again on provincial final day, Limerick would upset them in turn in the All-Ireland final.

Mick played in 16 of the county's 18 competitive games in 1973, with all bar one of those appearances in the centre-back position he had made his own by that stage. More often than not, he was flanked by Colm Doran on the right, and Willie Murphy on the left, although the half-back line also featured two of his clubmates Jimmy Prendergast and Paddy Kehoe at different stages as well as Ned Buggy and Jack Russell.

There was also one brief reprise of his midfield partnership with Dave Bernie, for a National League loss to Waterford at the start of the 1973-74 campaign.

The Doran-Jacob-Murphy axis was used first in the 1971 championship, but really flourished two years later. There was a good start in the old Cork Athletic Grounds on February 4, with Wexford's 1-9 to 1-7 win ending the home side's title hopes. *Colm Doran, Mick Jacob and Willie Murphy were unbeatable over the hour – the rock on which Cork's National League aspirations perished.*

A low-scoring 1-9 to 2-2 win away to Clare followed, before reporter Seán Dwyer rated Mick *Wexford's outstanding player* in a 4-14 to 2-1 demolition of Galway in Gorey – a fitting way to mark his 50th competitive appearance in the county senior jersey.

There was a setback in Bellefield on March 11 in the form of a 4-11 to 2-12 loss to Limerick, although that outcome would be suitably rectified just over two months later.

In between, Mick added a couple more strings to his bow.

ST PATRICK'S DAY saw his first Railway Cup medal collected on the field of play, following on from 1971 and '72 when he was an unused substitute. His versatility saw him partner Kilkenny's Frank Cummins at midfield, as the No.6 shirt went to the formidable Pat Henderson.

And with Wexford colleagues Teddy O'Connor, Martin Quigley and Tony Doran also on the field – Colm Doran and Paddy Kavanagh were held in reserve – Mick and the rest saw off Munster by 1-13 to 2-8.

By the following weekend, he was on the far side of the world, enjoying his first All Stars trip to San Francisco along with his good friend Pat Nolan, who travelled as the replacement goalkeeper.

Indeed, the Oylegate-Glenbrien veteran's brilliance between the posts was the main reason for Kilkenny losing the main exhibition game by 5-10 to 3-14, while Mick was also credited with turning in a fine display.

It was on that tour that he first formed a lasting friendship with Craanford native Jackie Kavanagh and his family. 'San Francisco was the nicest of all the places I visited, and I've been back a good few times. The city was more spread out than New York, and the weather was really lovely too.

'At that time the players would stay in the houses of Irish-American families, and I was sent to Jackie Kavanagh and his wife Theresa. They showed me all the sights and looked after me so well, and sure they were only delighted to have someone from home staying with them.

'I remember playing one game under floodlights against Kilkenny, and the ball was flying around. It was all a new experience to me, and I got to know hurlers like Con Roche, Pat Lawlor, Frank Cummins, Denis Coughlan, Francis Loughnane, Pat Delaney, Eddie Keher, Ray Cummins and Eamonn Cregan on those trips.

'There was always strong competition in the games, because Kilkenny would never want to be beaten. All those lads were genuine and I had great craic with them. Everyone was mixing and some lasting friendships were made.'

Refreshed from the holiday and raring to go, he came home in time for a National League quarter-final against Waterford in Nowlan Park that ended in a 1-9 each draw. And although the extra game wasn't planned, it did sharpen the rough edges as Mick formed one-third of an effective half-back line along with Colm Doran and Willie Murphy in a 2-16 to 4-7 replay win.

MICK AND COLM had to tend to family matters before meeting Kilkenny in the semi-final in Waterford on April 29.

Bridie Jacob married Bill Doran on the previous day in Oulart parish church, uniting two of Wexford's best-known sporting dynasties.

Mick's only sister was a household name in her own right by that stage, having played in the All-Ireland senior camogie final of 1971, when Cork beat Wexford. And that memorable weekend was crowned the next day when the hurlers pipped Kilkenny by a point (2-10 to 2-9).

'Willie and Colm were two really good wing-backs to play beside,' Mick says. 'You knew they were going to give one hundred percent all the time, and you could depend on them with your life.

'Colm was a hardy lad and I think he was under-appreciated. I don't recall ever seeing him play a bad game with Wexford. He didn't get the credit he deserved. He was on the top wing-forwards in the game all the time and they didn't get much off him.

'Willie had a great flair about his hurling, and I always thought it was a terrible pity he had to move to full-back for the 1976 and '77 All-Irelands. It's a different game altogether in there, and I felt he was always a better asset to Wexford out on the wing.'

Limerick lay in wait in the National League final set for Croke Park a fortnight later, on May 13, and Wexford were on high alert after losing to the Munstermen in Enniscorthy earlier in the campaign.

In hindsight, it was the best thing that ever happened, as Mick and his colleagues struck 1-2 in the last two minutes to copper-fasten an impressive 4-13 to 3-7 success. He performed a sound marking job on Eamonn Cregan, 'a very stylish player and hard to manage' as he recalls.

And making this win – his only national title secured on the field of play – all the more special was the presence of four club colleagues to share in the success. Jimmy Prendergast featured at right corner-back, and was replaced by Paddy Kehoe when he picked up an injury, while Tom Byrne lined out at left half-forward and Johnny Parle was reserve netminder to Pat Nolan.

All those years vying to win respect within the county had been worth it, and the point wasn't lost on local reporter Billy Quirke.

The feat of Wexford's smallest senior hurling club Oulart-The Ballagh in having no fewer than five players on the National League-winning selection is no mean one, he wrote. *The great St Aidan's teams of the 50s and 60s and subsequent Rathnure side have bettered Oulart's performance, but it is worth noting that the latter have had a selector to 'put forward' their players.*

Mick returned to Croke Park just six days later to pursue another new angle to his career, assisting Ireland to a 2-16 to 2-7 win over Scotland in a hurling/shinty international along with Tony Doran, Christy Keogh, and Marshalstown native Johnny Walsh, who had established himself in the all-white jersey of Kildare.

The National League win heightened hopes of overturning Kilkenny's championship dominance, but Wexford would not reach the same level of performance from mid-May again.

The Leinster semi-final win over Offaly in Nowlan Park by 2-14 to 2-9 was a forgettable affair.

The less than convincing performance did prompt the selectors into one notable decision, as Christy Jacob was recalled to the attack for the final.

It was his first appearance since coming off the bench in a league game in March of the previous year, and naturally enough Mick was delighted to see him back in the fold.

The game was one to forget, though, a rare occasion when Mick and his regular half-back colleagues Colm Doran and Willie Murphy were completely over-run.

Kilkenny cruised to victory by 4-22 to 3-15, with *The Echo* stating that, *The great half-back line was torn apart by a quicksilver Kilkenny half-forward line* that comprised Mick Brennan, Kieran Purcell and the bespectacled Pat Broderick.

There was the admittedly small consolation of another All Star nomination for centre-back three months later, although Mick never realistically stood a chance of collecting a second award after the county's less than stellar campaign.

He was one of eight from Wexford shortlisted, but only Colm Doran and Martin Quigley made the team. Pat Henderson collected the award for centre-back.

IF REDEMPTION WAS once again sought on the club front, it certainly wasn't forthcoming in 1973.

Three shrewd men were in place as selectors, namely Fr Staples, Frank Donnelly and Phil Redmond, but they took a calculated gamble for the straight knockout championship clash with Rathnure and it spectacularly backfired.

It was Oulart-The Ballagh's misfortune to be drawn against the holders yet again, this time at the first hurdle and without the chance to build momentum against weaker opposition beforehand.

OULART CRUSHED BY RATHNURE MACHINE, ran the headline after a 1-19 to 2-10 defeat in Bellefield on July 22, but the losers didn't help their own cause. *By placing Jimmy Prendergast at centre-forward, it played into Rathnure's hands, as he was the best defender on view in the Leinster final, The People* explained.

And although Mick was listed among his side's best players in both local newspapers, the prospect of building on the progress made in 1972 was crushed in one hour's hurling.

'Playing them in the first round was a big handicap. It was always better to get a game under your belt and gather up steam before taking on Rathnure, but it wasn't to be that year.'

With a large chunk of the summer still in front of them, Oulart-The Ballagh took a keener interest in football than would normally be the case. The club's last title in the code had arrived in 1936, when George Jacob and his colleagues claimed the Gorey District championship for the second year running.

And now, 37 years later, but competing in Enniscorthy District this time around, that gap was bridged. Mick wasn't playing when Marshalstown were beaten by six points in the semi-final, but he made a big contribution to the 2-2 to 0-3 title-winning victory over Cloughbawn a fortnight later.

Starting at midfield alongside Jimmy Prendergast, his best work was done after moving to centre-back – certainly not the first time for this switch to occur in his sporting career. After waiting almost 40 years for a football victory, there wasn't even a cup to be filled afterwards.

The intermediate grade was re-introduced after a long gap in 1973, and the District committee decided that the junior football trophy, the Bunclody Co-Operative Society Cup, should now be presented to the intermediate winners instead. They simply hadn't got around to sourcing a replacement by the time of Oulart-The Ballagh's win!

As the final scoreline would suggest, it was no classic.

It was a long way removed from the glamour of playing for Wexford on a big day in Croke Park, but Mick was equally committed to the cause whenever the club colours were on his back.

Unusually, he got to play in two county football finals in the space of six weeks in late 1973.

A new junior B grade had been introduced in 1972 and Oulart-The Ballagh – opting for Gorey District rather than Enniscorthy – beat Ballygarrett in the final by 13 points. The county semi-final didn't take place until December 10, when Mick was one of several players to the fore in a 1-4 to 0-1 win over St Martin's in sub-zero weather.

With hurling the obvious priority, it wasn't until October 14, 1973, that the decider was staged. Oulart-The Ballagh, with Mick at right half-back, were pipped by Clongeen (2-3 to 0-8), but the game was perfect preparation for that year's higher-grade junior semi-final, held just a fortnight later!

And after seeing off Adamstown by 2-3 to 1-4, there was another showdown with Shelmaliers in a repeat of the 1966 hurling final. It was an odd contest, with the Shels scoring the first two points before their rivals responded with 1-4 without reply.

However, Oulart-The Ballagh didn't register at all in the second-half. Shelmaliers edged home by 1-5 to 1-4. 'I was good at getting the ball because I was so fit, but I wasn't into solo runs. I used to just catch it and lay it off. Christy was a handy footballer alright.'

While naturally disappointed to lose in any game, a football reversal would never hurt or linger in the same way as a similar outcome in hurling.

The small ball was king in the parish, and there was no point pretending otherwise. Ironically enough, there was a football background to the use of the red and black colour combination.

'I was fascinated by that great Down team of the early-60s, with Paddy Doherty, Seán O'Neill, Joe Lennon and all the rest,' Robbie says.

'I was at the 1961 final, part of the biggest All-Ireland crowd ever, and there was a real style and swagger about them... their combination, movement and speed. Their colours stuck in my mind.

'We were actually wearing black and amber then, and we used to have green jerseys one time too. In January of 1962, I had a chat with Phil Redmond about the colours, that maybe we'd get a bit of luck if we changed and tried something new.

'There was no club meeting to discuss it or anything. We just ordered a Down set from Gorvan's of Wexford Street in Dublin, and Phil went up to collect them. We wore them for the first time in a tournament game against Buffers Alley.'

WEXFORD'S DEFENCE OF the National League title started on a firm footing in the first two rounds of the 1973-74 campaign, with Mick on board at centre-back for narrow wins at home to Cork and away to Tipperary.

After 21 successive outings at No.6, since the Leinster final of 1972, he returned to midfield to partner Dave Bernie against Waterford in round three in New Ross on November 4.

And even the very best need time to find their feet in different surroundings, as this game proved.

The usually reliable Jacob seemed to need to get acclimatised to the position, one report noted, and Waterford would fashion a 3-10 to 2-8 win. Restored to centre-back for the trip to Kilkenny in early December, he was *outstanding in defence* along with Teddy O'Connor and Colm Doran.

However, that wasn't enough to prevent a seven-point loss, and Mick's absence due to 'flu was felt in a 1-11 to 1-9 defeat away to Limerick one week later.

He also missed the first outing of 1974, with a hand injury ruling him out of a big win over Clare.

That came a few weeks after his *startling omission* from the Leinster team for the Railway Cup, although he was later added to the substitutes for year four of their five-in-a-row.

He returned for the last round league loss to Galway in Ballinasloe, joining Christy Keogh at the outset at midfield but making a bigger contribution elsewhere.

A lot of Wexford's problems in the 70s would have been solved if cloning was an option.

Put one Mick Jacob at centre-back, and the other at midfield, and there wouldn't have been a team in the country to stop them.

If only.

THE WEEKEND BEFORE the first Leinster Championship game of 1974 saw Mick visiting pastures new.

Selected on the Ireland hurling/shinty squad for the second year on the trot, he started on the bench along with Martin Quigley as Christy Keogh, Johnny Walsh and the rest of the men in green beat Scotland in the return game in Inverness by 3-8 to 1-6.

'It was a totally different game to hurling. You'd want to be fairly close to their lads when they were pulling on the ball, because the longer sticks they had gave them a fierce reach,' Mick says.

'There was a big function over there that weekend, and I came home from it with a shinty stick. I still have it to this very day.

'It was a fast game, and I was impressed with the very high skill levels of the Scotland players. They could take a cut very well.

'In shinty it was all about moving the ball on as swiftly as possible. And I guess the two sports were well matched, because if you look at our game from 1968 all through the 70s, there was a fierce amount of ground hurling too.

'That's more or less completely gone from the modern game. You'd only see it on an odd occasion, like in the All-Ireland semi-final of 2019 when Seamus Callanan got that first-time goal against Wexford.

'In my time there was a lot more ground hurling, even around the goalmouth. And it was a great thing in a way, because it meant the backs always had to be on their toes for a quick pull.

'Players didn't have much time in those days to set themselves up, the ball was travelling so fast.'

The big talking point before the provincial semi-final of 1974 was the return of All-Ireland winner Vinny Staples for his first outing since coming off the bench in the Leinster decider three years earlier.

And with the St Martin's man to his right, and championship debutant Fr Martin Casey of Buffers Alley to his left, just one week after the Kerry native's ordination, Mick calmly anchored the half-back line in a handy 1-18 to 1-5 win over Laois in Nowlan Park.

An attempt was made to stir controversy prior to the Leinster final, with one reporter claiming it was *contrary to the wishes of the county selectors* when Mick and Tom Byrne played in a tournament game in Rathnure against The Rower-Inistioge on the Sunday beforehand.

Club secretary Fintan Cooney was quick to defend his men, stressing there was no such instruction given for the duo to step aside.

That 1974 final will be remembered as one of the greatest games of the 80-minute championship era, but also as another fitting snugly into the 'What If?' category from a Wexford viewpoint.

All seemed lost when wing-forward Phil Wilson, who was having a splendid game, was ordered off in controversial circumstances by referee Mick Spain approaching the interval.

Wexford trailed by 3-8 to 0-10 at the time, and it was 5-10 to 1-15 twenty minutes into the second-half before an incredible comeback yielded 1-7 without reply and established a three-point lead.

Kilkenny needed a second goal from Eddie Keher to steady their ship, and ultimately they edged through by the bare minimum (6-13 to 2-24).

John Quigley was an inspiration, and challenging him closely was Mick Jacob who outclassed Kieran Purcell and Pat Delaney in turn, The Echo *reported.* The only scope this pair got was when they inter-changed positions.

For Mick, it was another all-too-familiar outcome as a pretty constant pattern developed in that era.

'That was a tough one to lose for sure. Around that time, Wexford were capable of playing a really good game, but it always seemed like we lost the big ones by just a point or two. You'd be down and out for a day or two after it, but then you'd say to yourself, *We'll go again next year.*

'That was all you could do really. Get up and go again, go even harder if you could. You'd be sickened for a few days… then the club championship would come on stream again and everything would be forgotten about.'

Mick had great sympathy for Phil Wilson's plight, agreeing that 'it was unusual to be put off' for reacting to an opponent while receiving first aid treatment for a facial injury.

However, that dismissal actually played into Oulart-The Ballagh's hands.

Wilson, a Ballyhogue stalwart, had business interests in Enniscorthy town and duly joined the Rapparees for that 1974 campaign.

The club year started in rather tame fashion with a series of inconsequential league games, but it cranked up on the intensity front when the Caim tournament final was played on the Friday night after Wexford's championship win over Laois in June.

Even though Oulart-The Ballagh were set to face the Rapps in the knockout championship, that didn't stop them from locking horns in this appetiser just a fortnight earlier.

Mick partnered Tom Byrne at midfield and helped the men in red and black to a four-point win in a most exciting game, but it had nothing on the drama that would follow.

Phil Wilson was a huge addition to the Enniscorthy team, especially when he was paired with a player of the calibre of Christy Keogh at midfield.

This time Mick had another Byrne, Larry, for company, and they broke even with the Rapps duo in a fiercely contested clash in Wexford Park on July 7.

Mick's tussle with Wilson *was one of the highlights of the game* and, after a scoreless last tension-filled seven minutes, there was stalemate.

Oulart-The Ballagh's 2-11 tally was matched by the 3-8 recorded by the beaten finalists of 1972, for whom Davy Fortune contributed an impressive 2-2.

'I was well used to Wilson and the way he played from our time together with Wexford,' Mick says. 'I was familiar with his style, and I also knew I would really have to be up for it against him because he was always a fierce competitor.'

The replay took place a fortnight later after Wexford's Leinster final defeat and, in an era when suspensions were time- rather than competition-based, Wilson was a huge loss to his new club. Another hotly-debated refereeing call was central to the outcome, a second draw (1-13 to 2-10).

The Oulart-The Ballagh goal was *a typical Mick Jacob effort, which he finished to the net when he looked like losing possession.*

It came near the end and seemed good enough to steer his team through, only for a harsh free to be awarded against defender Willie Cullen – the former multiple All-Ireland winning boxing champion – as he broke out in possession. Henry Goff tapped it over, and the teams had three weeks to ponder their next moves before going at it again.

Paddy O'Connor had joined Mick at midfield for the replay. However, for that third clash he reverted to centre-back to keep tabs on Christy Keogh, while O'Connor and Larry Byrne went up against Ger Collins and Aidan Wildes in midfield, with Phil Wilson still out of bounds. And it worked a treat, as Oulart-The Ballagh were well on top this time and won comfortably by 3-11 to 2-5.

Robbie Jacob feels the Rapps did them a big favour in 1974. 'Our club was maturing overall, and the Rapps made a proper team out of us in those three games.

'We were coming fairly good that year. We started going outside the county to play practice matches in places like Camross, Castlecomer and Freshford, and we were serious about the thing.'

Those three games offered perfect preparation for the immense task that served as a reward. The county semi-final pitted Oulart-The Ballagh against Buffers Alley, and it was time to finally deliver.

THE INEXPERIENCE OF two years earlier was no longer a factor for several of the team's key men, and the outcome in Bellefield on September 8 engulfed the parish in joy.

Aided by the wind in the first-half, Oulart-The Ballagh powered into a 3-4 to 1-3 interval lead.

And they never relented, with their advantage extended to 11 points with five minutes left. True to form, Buffers Alley didn't fall easily, but there was a defiance from the underdogs that drove them to a stand-out success on a 5-5 to 3-6 scoreline.

Of course, nobody typified that better than their leader in spirit and deed, one Mick Jacob.

Mick Butler of Buffers Alley attempted goals from four 21-yard frees in the last quarter, but Mick *defied his best efforts.*

After struggling to make any headway on full-back Jimmy Prendergast, Alley powerhouse Tony Doran did pose a few problems for Mick when he moved to centre-forward.

Great contestant that he is, however, Michael Jacob quickly re-assessed the situation and proceeded to follow the example set for him by his full-back, Prendergast.

'The team showed really good form that day,' Mick says. 'We took the game to the Alley and that's how we had to go about it, there was no other way to beat them.

'We had learned a good bit from playing them so often before, and thankfully it all worked out.

'I remember the bad weather that day alright, especially the heavy rain near the end of the match. We were all soaked, but sure nobody cared.'

After finally downing one of the 'big two', it was no surprise that the other now lay in wait.

A Rathnure side going for four titles in a row would provide the opposition in Oulart-The Ballagh's first-ever senior county final. The team had three weeks to prepare in Mountdaniel, and it helped that September of 1974 was a very sunny month.

'With the Alley out of the way, we had a really big day to look forward to,' Mick says.

And Robbie hoped the sun splitting the trees would be a bright omen. 'It was a joy to be heading over to the field at 6pm on a sunny September evening to train for a county final.

'The weather made it even better. Everything we had worked so hard for was bearing fruit.'

THE WEXFORD SENIOR hurling final of 1974 will be remembered for two key reasons. The achievement of Rathnure in completing a four-in-a-row of titles was rightly lauded, the first club to do so since the immense Enniscorthy St Aidan's outfit of 1956 to '59.

But for every man, woman and child from Oulart-The Ballagh, not to mention the hordes of neutrals packed into Bellefield on September 29, it will always be regarded as 'The Mick Jacob Final'.

This was the afternoon, above all others, when he stamped his greatness on proceedings.

Old-timers still talk in revered tones about Mick's performance that day. While the team didn't hit the necessary heights on this maiden county final voyage, their star man was operating in an entirely different realm.

His defiance was as inspiring as it was extraordinary, a performance of such unrelenting quality that it was all the hurling folk of Wexford could talk about for months afterwards. Reporter Billy Quirke was so moved by his display that he wrote an accompanying piece to his match report in *The People* with an appropriate headline… *MICK JACOB… A HERO IN DEFEAT.*

This county final is one that will always be remembered – not because of the excitement generated but because it was the game in which Rathnure achieved a unique distinction and because of the brilliance of Oulart centre half-back, Michael Jacob, he wrote.

I have never seen anything to equal this performance in Wexford championship hurling. I can recall the magnificence of men like Jim Morrissey and Ned Wheeler, of Harry O'Connor, Padge Kehoe, Ted Bolger and Nick O'Donnell, of Bobbie and Billy Rackard, not forgetting Tim Flood, but I must give the red-haired Jacob pride of place in this elite company.

All of the above, and others, played with championship-winning teams. Michael Jacob was fighting a losing battle from the word go. But he refused to accept defeat and he refused to be overawed or intimidated by the reputations or tactics of a succession of opponents.

There is no point in asking Mick for a proper evaluation of his heroics in that 1974 final. A man for whom modesty is a by-word would never blow his own trumpet. Instead, we'll turn to big brother Robbie, who remembers a distinctive sound from that day.

'I was playing left half-back alongside Mick, and I was marking Martin Quigley so I had more than enough to be dealing with.

'But as soon as the ball went past me, from the very start of the game, all I kept hearing was a thud.

'It was constant… THUD… THUD… THUD.

'It was the sound of Mick connecting with the sliotar and clearing it back down the field. He kept the ball travelling in the other direction, and I'd follow its flight again beside Martin and wait for it to return. And as soon as it did, the very same thing would happen.

'Mick would be on it again and... THUD. He cleared balls from all over the place in that final. It was an unbelievable performance. It took a super-human effort on his part, but that wouldn't have registered with him. He didn't know he was doing it, and doing it so amazingly well.

'That was simply down to the natural ability he had. No matter where that ball was, he had it.'

Sadly, the Oulart-The Ballagh forwards could make no headway whatsoever against a defence comprising two Quigley brothers in Jim and Pat, the O'Connor brothers Teddy and Johnny, Aidan Somers and a youthful Seánie Murphy.

The final score says it all... Rathnure 2-8, Oulart-The Ballagh 1-5.

The challengers only registered 1-3 from play; Tom Byrne was the sole forward to contribute, adding a goal and a point to a couple of converted frees, while midfielders Larry Byrne and PJ Harris chipped in with a point apiece.

Rathnure, with Dan Quigley at left corner-forward, were restricted to 2-5 from play thanks in the main to Mick's heroics, but it was still sufficient to get the job done. His direct opponent was held scoreless, while the wing forwards were confined to a point apiece.

That came as a direct consequence of Mick's covering and sweeping across the entire half-back line, along with the diligence of Robbie and Paddy Kehoe in their man-to-man duties.

After that final, a feeling intensified among hurling supporters throughout Wexford, and it grew even stronger with every passing year.

It was a sentiment expressed with such regularity that it was printed as a headline in 'Just A Memory', a book of Wexford GAA tales and recollections penned for the centenary year of 1984: *I'd love to see Mick Jacob win a senior championship medal.* Sadly, that never came to pass, and it remains a source of immense sadness to anyone who watched this gifted stickman in his prime.

Mick's influence after that final was every bit as important as his contribution on the field, as Robbie explains: 'Clearly we were lacking a bit of experience at the other end of the field, and it didn't help that our forward line in general wasn't physically that big. We must have had at least sixty-five percent of the ball, because of Mick in particular, but we didn't make the most of it.

'Everyone was on a high going into that final; between players, mentors and supporters, the atmosphere in the parish was something else. And then, all of a sudden, the game itself goes by in a flash, and before you know it the whole thing is over. You have all these expectations built up in your mind, only to be knocked down on your back again.

'And that's where Mick came in. His influence was always powerful in that type of situation. Of course, he would be as disappointed as the rest of us, but he wouldn't say much about it.

'Instead, he'd be the one reminding us of next year and the next chance. He was always great for focusing on the positives, and looking at what we could take from a defeat like that.'

One of the immediate moves made afterwards was to organise a four-team parish league for the young boys who had packed into Bellefield to cheer on the local heroes.

'Myself and Tom Dunne ran that league and got a lot of players out of it. I'd say eight or nine of them were involved in the club's first senior win in 1994, the likes of Martin Storey, Seán Dunne and John Rossiter.

'Mick inspired them all. I've never seen anything like it, before or since.'

As for the man himself, one sporting gesture immediately after the match struck a chord.

'I suppose it's nice to play well even when you don't win, but really it's all about winning on the day.

'Right after the final whistle, Bobbie Rackard came across the field to me, shook my hand, and congratulated me on the wonderful game I had,' Mick says. 'I felt I must have done something right when a man of that stature went out of his way to have a quiet word with me. I had never spoken to Bobbie in my life before that, so it meant a lot to me. It's something I'll always cherish.'

Looking back on 1974, Mick feels, 'Rathnure were only a small bit better than we were, although 1-5 was a very poor return for an hour's hurling.

'I'd never seen Bellefield as full in my life. It was absolutely packed to the rafters. Rathnure had the five Quigleys and a lot more county men, and they were used to winning senior finals.

'If we had won that day, we'd have come on in leaps and bounds. We were a lot like that Wexford team of the early-70s, so near and yet unable to make the breakthrough.

'The club was building gradually all the time, getting to quarter-finals first, semi-finals, and then finals. We were improving, but it was incredibly hard to win one in those days.'

TAKING A BREAK never entered Mick's head, especially after a big disappointment.

If there was a game to be played, and he was fit, then he would always make himself available.

Take 1974 as a prime example: for six straight Sundays after that galling county final loss, he was back in the thick of it.

The new National League campaign started in Walsh Park with a 3-5 to 2-7 win over Waterford, and he didn't take long to give it his complete focus. *Mick Jacob, after his epic performance in the county final on the previous Sunday was subdued over the first half hour, The People* reported.

He opened his shoulders in the second half and was one of the men chiefly responsible for the rallies that first brought the team level, then eventual victory.

One week later, Oulart-The Ballagh surrendered their Enniscorthy District junior football title to Monageer-Boolavogue, winners of their first-ever championship by 2-5 to 1-6. Mick partnered Nicky O'Toole at midfield and was listed among his side's best players.

The next four Sundays brought a mixed bag of results, with defeats to Cork and Clare in the Oireachtas and National League respectively followed by a draw with Tipperary and a handy victory over Limerick in the latter competition.

He had a new partner in the half-back line for most of those games, as Eddie 'Heffo' Walsh of Faythe Harriers managed to nail down a regular spot to his right.

Colm Doran and Willie Murphy were still on the scene that winter too, and others to fill roles on the flanks alongside Mick were Larry Byrne of St Anne's/St Patrick's, Dave Lawlor from Adamstown, John Stamp of Buffers Alley, and the versatile and experienced Ned Buggy from Faythe Harriers.

Mick also earned a third successive All Star nomination, along with a club colleague for the first time as Tom Byrne – then the Town Clerk of Cashel in Co Tipperary – also did enough to merit consideration.

They were two of six from Wexford on the shortlist along with Martin and John Quigley, and Tony and Colm Doran. Pat Henderson nailed down the centre-back slot for the second year running, but there was good news for the

Quigleys as Martin also retained a position – this time at centre-forward – while John earned his first award in the right corner.

The year ended with some more super news for Mick on the individual accolades front.

The Powers Gold Label Sports Star awards had come into being in 1964, recognising excellence in every sporting discipline in Co Wexford. The previous list of hurling winners read like a who's who of the game's greats in the county.

Netminding supremo Pat Nolan was honoured in the inaugural year and again in 1969, while Phil Wilson, John Quigley, Tony Doran, Dan Quigley, Dave Bernie, Matt Browne, Willie Murphy and Martin Quigley also adorned this glittering list.

In 1974, they were joined by Mick Jacob, with the award citation singing his praises.

Mick Jacob of Oulart-The Ballagh has been acclaimed the greatest half-back Wexford has had since the great men of the 50s. During the year his displays at club and county level at all times left nothing to be desired.

However, his performance in this year's county hurling final surpassed the imagination of all hurling followers and could be only classified as superb, which proved that he is the most elegant and energetic player in the game today.

High praise indeed, but so thoroughly deserved.

'Nicky Kirwan, the boxer from The Ballagh, got a Powers award that year too, so it was a good double achievement for the parish,' he says. 'It made up a small bit for not winning, and I suppose it was nice to be recognised for my commitment to the game.'

As Mick looked forward to another year and celebrated his 29th birthday in early 1975, he was clearly a hurler at the peak of his powers.

And he received another nice little boost with his selection as one of two All Stars replacements from Wexford, along with Teddy O'Connor, to accompany the Quigley brothers on the annual tour to San Francisco and New York.

'I was still going to Jackie Kavanagh's, it was like home at that stage, and we also stayed with another Irish American named Jack Scannell.'

That trip took place in April, some three weeks after playing on the left flank in a Leinster half-back line that also featured Kilkenny pair Pat Lawlor and Pat Henderson.

The Railway Cup five-in-a-row was completed at Munster's expense in a tight affair on St Patrick's Day, with Tony Doran and influential substitute John Quigley getting the goals in a 2-9 to 1-11 victory.

Some players were intent on simply seeing the sights and having a good time on those All Stars tours, and there was nothing wrong with that.

However, Mick's character and temperament was such that he always threw himself wholeheartedly into the exhibition games organised to give the exiles a true taste of home.

Indeed, he excelled to such an extent in the three matches against Kilkenny on that 1975 trip that he returned home with the MVP (most valuable player) award, a staple of the US sporting scene.

'We played Kilkenny and I knew we would be coming up against them again in the summer.

'I wasn't going to bow to them. I was intent on putting down a marker, and I saw this as an ideal chance. I always believed that no matter what type of game I was playing in, there was no point going out half-hearted. I just couldn't do it anyway, it would be against my nature.

'I also felt we had a duty to give our best for the people watching. They really appreciated the All Stars coming out to them every year. It was only right that we'd give them a few good games to say thanks for their hospitality.'

ANOTHER LEINSTER CHAMPIONSHIP campaign was drawing near on Mick's return to base.

Offaly were kept comfortably at arm's length in the provincial semi-final, with the 1-29 to 1-18 success largely attributed to Colm Doran and Mick in that ever-reliable sector, along with goalkeeper John Nolan, Seánie Kinsella, and the All Star Quigleys, John and Martin.

Oulart-The Ballagh had a Wexford selector for the first time in 1975, with Phil Redmond part of the backroom crew along with manager Syl Barron from Rathnure, Pat Murphy of Faythe Harriers, Fr John Doyle from Buffers Alley, and Adamstown's Matt O'Neill, also a prominent referee.

Christy Jacob made a brief return, coming on in a National League loss to Cork in the Mardyke in early March, but he was no longer part of the plans by Leinster final day.

In fact, he never played again with the county, and Mick still feels he was cut loose too soon.

Would a forward of his cunning and experience have made a difference in yet another defeat to Kilkenny, the fifth final disappointment on the trot? One will never know, but it was difficult to sift through the wreckage and pick out anything of a positive nature after that particular setback.

The reigning All-Ireland champions prevailed by 2-20 to 2-14, and it was one of those rare days when even Mick struggled to impose himself on proceedings.

He started at centre-back and later spent time at wing-back and at midfield, but to no avail.

When pressed to name his three toughest opponents nine years later, he selected Kieran Purcell on top of the pile with Cork duo Justin McCarthy and Tim Crowley filling the second and third positions.

And Purcell was clearly the master on this occasion, although Mick did deal more efficiently with Pat Delaney in an earlier head-to-head. *One has come to expect Jacob's dominance from the centre-back berth, but on this occasion he was never happy, and could never come to grips with Purcell, The Echo* reported.

Robbie Jacob was a frustrated onlooker in the Hogan Stand, and he sensed that something was clearly missing.

'I would rate the second-half against Kilkenny in 1974 as one of the top four or five Wexford performances of the past 50 years. In comparison, they looked very flat in '75. The team never got going on the day and it was a very disappointing outcome.'

Oulart-The Ballagh already had one knockout hurdle cleared by that stage in their bid to build on the previous year's county final debut.

The same five selectors were on board, with Mick's uncle Mikie joined by Fintan Cooney, Freddie Jeffs, Bobby Walsh and John Doran.

Paddy Kehoe replaced Christy as captain, and this time it only took one game – rather than the three of 1974 – to dispose of Rapparees by 1-11 to 1-7. The big talking point was the presence of newcomer Johnny Murphy in the winning line-out, with Mick's county colleague scoring two points from centre-forward.

It led to one delegate – Tom Rowe of St Fintan's, the Wexford District chairman – describing the county board as 'a circus' at a stormy meeting on the following Monday night.

Crossabeg-Ballymurn, Murphy's home club, sought clarification on a controversial ruling in place at the time, allowing senior clubs to call on players from a second parish.

It meant they could be transferred in without changing address, and that's how Murphy played in just the one championship campaign before moving back to base in 1976. Johnny's house was right on the border with The Ballagh, and he often travelled with Mick to county training and games.

He joined the Wexford squad in 1974, after playing in the All-Ireland under-21 final loss of the previous year to Cork when Robbie was a selector.

And he was a regular on the side over the next 10 years, proving a particularly tough opponent for Kilkenny's Frank Cummins.

'I met Frank one night at a function, and he told me that himself,' Mick says. 'Frank liked a lad who would stand beside him and go hip-to-hip for the ball with him, but Johnny never did that.

'He was a great man to attack the ball for a small fella. He was really good on his feet, and he had this knack of arriving at the last minute to flick it away from Frank.

'It took some clever timing to be able to do that. Johnny was always a nightmare for Cummins, and Wexford made a mistake by not playing him a little more in midfield. A lot of his matches were at wing-forward, but I think he was more suited to the middle. He had a great brain for hurling.'

Another new face with the team in 1975 was Ferns native Tony Dwyer, who moved on after 1976 and would actually end up playing with Buffers Alley against Oulart-The Ballagh in the county final of 1982.

A third semi-final in four years was the prize for beating the Rapps, and it was time for the second behemoth to fall.

MICK AND HIS clubmates never seemed to get a favourable draw, and it was no different on this occasion as holders Rathnure provided the opposition in Bellefield on August 10.

Crucially, though, the players didn't fear a team seeking five titles on the trot by that juncture. They might have been over-awed on their first big coming together at the same stage in 1972, but now it was different.

Oulart-The Ballagh knew they were a better team than they had shown in the

1974 final, particularly in attack, and they were hell-bent on proving it. It went to two games again, just like in '72, but this time around they were able to hold their nerve between draw and replay.

Ten minutes from the end of that first meeting, Oulart-The Ballagh led by six points.

However, they conceded two late goals as Rathnure reeled them in (1-12 to 3-6), and in the end they were steeped to survive after Dan Quigley missed a golden chance for the winning point from a 35-yard free.

Robbie recalls learning one of the best lessons he ever picked up on a hurling field in that game.

'It was a lot like the draw in 1972 in many respects. Because we hadn't won a title, we lacked that bit of composure to close it out. We let them back into it… a couple of simple mistakes left a bit of a gap at the back for their two late goals.

'We got a sideline ball with about seven or eight minutes to go, and Mick left the centre to take it.

'It wasn't one of his best strikes ever, and by the time he got back to the middle, the ball had ended up in our net. I swore after that incident that I would always get the wing-back to take the lineball. Like all of those tough lessons you learn along the way, it never left me.'

Oulart-The Ballagh looked outside the parish for assistance in 1975, and it certainly paid off in the replay against Rathnure. Mick Quigley came from a boxing background and his work as physical trainer had the entire squad in the shape of their lives.

And after the forwards didn't function in 1974, they turned to a stylish star of the 50s in a bid to impart some of his knowledge.

Harry O'Connor from Enniscorthy had done the business both with Wexford and the formidable St Aidan's, and the main reason for bringing him on board was an attempt to add some punch to that attack.

'Harry had a lot of experience from his own career, and we all looked up to him,' Mick says. 'He was really enthusiastic about training us, and was very good at driving us on.

'He had the knack of making you feel really motivated, and we hurled very well in that replay.

'Although he wasn't a county player, Johnny O'Connor was the man for

Rathnure around that time. If he played well, then Rathnure played well too. But we did a great job of nullifying Johnny that day, and it showed in the result.

'Harry wasn't involved when we beat the Rapps. He came in before the first Rathnure match, and he very quickly convinced us that we would beat them. That was a big achievement in itself.'

Clashes between the two clubs had been box office since 1972, and another massive crowd witnessed one more piece of Oulart-The Ballagh hurling history... beating Rathnure in the championship for the first time.

In a tense affair, Mick's role in keeping tabs on Dan Quigley in general play went a long way towards securing the 1-9 to 1-5 win. With Wexford's 1968 captain very quiet by his own high standards, it took a lot of penetration out of the losers' attack and also allowed others to flourish.

One of the main men in that regard was midfielder PJ Harris, whose powerful performance that day was instrumental in his first call-up to the Wexford squad for the next National League campaign.

Christy was his partner in the centre, a new role for this out-and-out forward but one which he warmly embraced with a fine display in curbing the experienced Martin Byrne.

'It was unusual for me to be on Dan that day. He would normally be the opposite centre-back, but they had him playing centre-forward,' Mick recalls. 'He was a mighty man, and a mighty hurler. I had played behind him so many times, when I was the county under-21 goalie and he was the full-back.'

It was another wonderful afternoon for the club, but the job was only half done.

They had finally managed to beat the county's big two in championship hurling, but a burning question remained... could they do it now in the same calendar year?

THAT WAS THE only means by which Mick and company would get their coveted county medals, and the answer would be supplied when they met Buffers Alley in Wexford Park on September 14, 1975.

Not surprisingly, Bridie was in big demand to give her verdict in the days leading up to the final.

Bill Doran, her husband of two years, was a veteran member of the Alley team so, as the newspaper headline outlined, she was, *SITTING ON BOTH SIDES OF THE FENCE.*

However, her colours were nailed firmly to the red and black mast, and that would have warmed the hearts of all those lapping up the preview in her native place.

Bridie is more Jacob than Doran (at this stage). She makes no secret of the fact that she will wear the red and black of famed Oulart and her dearest wish is to see the first county senior hurling title go to her native parish.

Breda also had divided loyalties, torn between supporting her boyfriend while watching two of her brothers Jim and Tony togging out for their keenest rivals.

Neutrals felt this might be the big breakthrough moment. That five-point win when the sides met in the previous year's semi-final was considered a factor, and the Alley were also going into battle without a key defender in All-Ireland medal winner Mick Kinsella.

Everything appeared to be set up for an Oulart-The Ballagh win, and that only made the crushing outcome even tougher to deal with.

The near neighbours battled their way to a third title in eight years, winning by 3-10 to 2-7.

Indeed, it would be another seven seasons before Oulart-The Ballagh made it back to the county final, and by that stage a number of the 1975 contingent had moved on.

Mick takes up the story: 'The final was in Wexford Park that year, and a lot of people said they were going down to see the row rather than the hurling.

'It was the first final between Oulart-The Ballagh and the Alley, and neutrals were expecting sparks. I suppose they got them too, because Jimmy Prendergast and Bill Doran were sent to the line.

'Bill was clever and cute, very experienced, and with a good head for hurling. But with all due respect to him, I think his loss didn't make the same difference to them as losing Pender did to us.

'It left a decent opening near our goal in terms of space. They made the most of it, although the game was tight enough for long enough.' This defeat was even tougher than in 1974, and on this particular occasion Mick didn't have a glut of games to distract him.

HE DIDN'T PLAY again after September 14, and it was the first time he had an extended break both from club and county in his career, due to a troublesome hand injury.

Another All Star nomination eluded him, although a notable family double was completed in mid-November when Bridie was selected as the Powers Gold Label Sports Star winner for camogie.

It was the first time for a sister to join her brother on the prestigious roll of honour for a Gaelic games award.

Bridie was undoubtedly the star performer among the Jacobs in 1975, helping Wexford bridge a six-year gap with their impressive victory over Cork in the All-Ireland senior final on the Sunday directly after that county final. Bridie scored her team's opening goal in the 23rd minute, and the subsequent 4-3 to 1-2 victory was the high point of a career that also featured a loss to Kilkenny in the 1977 decider. She would go on to win an impressive five All-Ireland club medals from her six final appearances with Buffers Alley between 1978 and '84.

Have tractor, will travel... Mick hard at work around the farm in Monavullen in the early-70s and striking a pose for the front cover of 'Pioneer' magazine in 1973 (right).

Mick (back row, third left) and his colleagues in Bellefield on September 29, 1974 – his individual display on the occasion of Oulart-The Ballagh's first county senior final appearance is still regarded as one of the greatest ever seen on the playing fields of Wexford.

« CHAPTER 7 »

WEXFORD 2-20, KILKENNY 1-6.

In the long and storied history between these age-old rivals, the above scoreline from the Leinster final of 1976 is one that will always bring a smile of satisfaction to Mick Jacob.

A particularly special aspect of the runaway win was that nobody really saw it coming.

How could they, in fairness? Every year from 1971 to '75, Kilkenny had prematurely ended the summer for Mick and his colleagues at the same stage of the championship.

And when he left Monavullen for Croke Park on the morning of July 18, 1976, for once in his career there was a nagging doubt regarding his own fitness in the back of his mind.

A broken finger robbed him of an entire winter campaign.

And then, there was an added complication.

WEXFORD TRAVELLED TO the Mardyke on May 23, 1976, for a challenge game against Cork, which ended in a draw. Partnering Martin Furlong of Cloughbawn at midfield, *The People* delighted in reporting Mick *had a capital game* in his first outing in the purple and gold jersey for nine months.

'It went alright for me, but unfortunately I got another belt and broke a different finger,' he recalls.

The immediate upshot was that Oulart-The Ballagh succeeded in having their knockout championship game against Cloughbawn – fixed for the following Sunday – postponed.

In those days, if a player was injured while on county duty, it was more or less taken as a given that his club wouldn't be obliged to field without him.

The decision upset a Cloughbawn crew primed for battle, though, and it was the first of two high-profile incidents in 1976 that resulted in the rule being shelved completely.

Later in the year, the county senior football final between Castletown and Rathnure didn't go ahead because of injuries sustained by the teams' respective star players Mick Carty and Martin Quigley while representing Wexford.

An element of farce surrounded that fixture and – coming so soon after the Oulart/Cloughbawn saga – it was enough for delegates at county convention to remove such an unwieldy bye-law.

With that club opener put on the back-burner, Mick took on the role of a frustrated onlooker in Athy on June 13 when Wexford survived a major scare in his absence.

Johnny Walsh, the Marshalstown man long since exiled in Kildare, was in peak form at the time and his six points from play, plus another half-dozen from frees, almost masterminded a shock win that would have rocked the hurling world.

Eventually, Wexford made it through to a seventh successive Leinster final by 2-19 to 2-15, but it was far too close for comfort. 'That was a very tight game and we were lucky to win it,' Mick says. 'Johnny Walsh gave an exhibition, and his brother Ned was playing too in the full-forward line. Kildare had some great players at the time. Pat Dunny and Tommy Carew did well for them too; it was a fierce battle altogether.'

Mick's comeback to competitive fare with Wexford arrived almost 11 months to the day since his last involvement which had been in the Leinster final loss to Kilkenny on August 3, 1975.

On July 4, 1976, a fortnight before the great rivals' latest showdown, he returned at centre-back in a 2-12 to 2-9 Oireachtas semi-final defeat to Galway in Croke Park.

Reporter Seán Nolan wrote that the *only ray of hope to come from this otherwise dour display was the performance of Liam Bennett, Mick Jacob and Colm Doran in the half-back line.*

Jacob, in his first inter-county game since his injury against Cork some months ago, showed that he is the man for the troublesome centre-back position.

It took selectors Syl Barron, Pat Nolan, Tom Neville, Pat Murphy and Mick O'Hanlon somewhat longer to arrive at the same conclusion.

Martin Quigley, centre-back against Kildare, was moved to his more natural centre-forward role, while Colm Doran started in the No.6 slot, with Liam Bennett and Ned Buggy completing the half-back line.

For the first time in two and a half years, Mick was selected at midfield, but he had a new partner.

His last club game between the posts for Oulart-The Ballagh in 1964 was spoiled by the goal-getting instincts of Michael Rowsome, who put four past him that day.

Twelve years later, Michael's younger twin brothers Billy and Declan had burst on to the county scene.

And after doing well to hold his place following a first start in the National League in late 1975, Billy lined up alongside Mick for the throw-in on that memorable day.

'A Wexford team in the right frame of mind makes all the difference, and we had that for the Leinster final of 1976,' Mick says. 'A lot of things worked in our favour. We didn't play particularly well against Kildare, in fact we stumbled over the line.

'Kilkenny were the All-Ireland champions, and they had also beaten Clare in the replayed league final of 1976. That game didn't take place until June, and they had scored six goals, so we were written off in most quarters.

'But when a group of Wexford hurlers see the black and amber jersey in Croke Park, anything can happen. That was always the way, and it was one of the best days of all.

'I was named midfield on "Chunky" O'Brien, who was a very lively character if he was given the space to roam. He used to do a lot of damage against Wexford, picking off points from long range and running hard at our half-back line before popping a pass to his forwards.

'I decided there was no way I was going to let this lad pick up loose balls, because he was very good at that. I stayed between him and the ball, and it worked out well for me.

'Billy got on fine on Frank Cummins also, and really we were on top all over. We were so far ahead that we were able to savour it and enjoy it a little bit before the game finished. That was a rarity against Kilkenny.'

Galway lay in wait in mid-August, and they came with a strong pedigree. After winning the National League title of 1975, they would shock Cork in the All-Ireland semi-final before coming up short against Kilkenny.

They commanded the utmost respect from Wexford. 'Galway had a great team, with Joe McDonagh, Seán Silke and Iggy Clarke in a brilliant half-back line,' Mick recalls.

'Frank Burke, PJ Molloy, PJ Qualter and three of the Connolly brothers... they were all serious operators and we knew we were in for a tough time of it.'

TWO MONTHS AFTER the official opening of the new Páirc Uí Chaoimh in Cork, GAA officials were eager to show it off and to pay some of the bills.

And while eyebrows were raised in Wexford at the choice of venue, by the same token it wasn't nearly as surprising as the selection of Athlone for the previous semi-final clash between the counties six years earlier.

The summer of 1976 was one of the warmest on record, and it was absolutely roasting by the banks of the Lee on August 15.

'I'll always remember the heat that day, it was incredibly warm. And then the pace of the game made it even tougher; it was really fast, because the ball was flying around the new pitch.'

Both teams had their periods of supremacy, and when referee Frank Murphy blew for full-time they couldn't be separated. Goals from Tony Doran (two), Mick Butler (two) and a Ned Buggy free left Wexford on 5-14, while Galway replied with 2-23.

They would have to do it all over again, and that had a considerable knock-on effect. After a strangely subdued spell at midfield, Mick thrived after being moved to his best position.

'I went centre-back in the second-half on John Connolly, and I got on well there,' he says, while *The People* noted *he was absolutely flying in the closing stages.*

'Joe Connolly got a ball and managed to get by Jimmy Prendergast just before half-time,' Mick says. 'I don't know how he hit it wide because it was from very close range. We had luck on our side in that incident.'

The prospect of having to travel to Cork again in the stifling heat just seven days later didn't appeal to anyone. All of the major urban areas en route are bypassed nowadays, but the opposite was the case in 1976.

'I think it was unfair to bring Wexford down to Cork for the two games. Surely they could have played the replay in Croke Park. We went down in cars the first day, and it was an awful journey between the heat and all the hold-ups.

'For the second day, the County Board decided we would travel by train. We had our own carriage, but supporters were coming and going too, so it wasn't ideal preparation either.'

It was another close contest, but this time Wexford overcame the tough Galway challenge by 3-14 to 2-14. And when John Connolly began to cause Colm Doran problems on the '40', Mick once again made the move to centre-back and left his mark.

'We had to peak for those two games against Galway, whereas Cork were waiting in the wings. They were able to keep fresh and, because those games were in Páirc Uí Chaoimh, they could have a very good look at the whole situation.'

The science applied to all aspects of team preparation nowadays fascinates Mick. 'I wish we had that in our time. Just take those two Galway games for example, and the conditions they were played in.

'Some of us must have been dehydrated afterwards, but we trained away as per normal a couple of days later. Sure we didn't know any different.

'Nowadays all that is looked after... players are tested and everyone knows exactly where they stand. It's a pity we didn't have the same in our day.'

With just another fortnight to go before the All-Ireland final, the selectors finally decided to bite the bullet. What would be the point in starting Mick at midfield again, when it was almost inevitable he would be needed to firefight at centre-back at some stage?

This time he was named as the defensive pivot from the off, flanked by Liam Bennett and Colm Doran, with Ned Buggy partnering Billy Rowsome at midfield.

The match preview in *The People* featured a photograph of Mick's mother Ellen with a confident prediction in the caption underneath. *Of course they'll win. One always has to be wary of Cork, but if all our lads give of their best they should have the edge on them this time.*

Mrs Jacob needed convincing that the hurling field was a good place for her sons to be when they moved back to Oulart in 1956, but she was an avid fan 20 years later!

'WE HAD A great start that day, with two goals in the opening few minutes,' Mick recalls. 'Rather than being tired after the Galway matches, at first it looked like they had made us sharper.

'Cork had waited a long time since the Munster final, and they weren't up to the pace of the game for a while. They got back into it with a Ray Cummins goal coming up to half-time... he took a lot of steps and kicked it to the net.

'Paddy Johnston of Kilkenny was refereeing that day and I didn't think he gave us a whole lot. Tony Doran was fouled with about 10 minutes to go and we didn't get a free; they went down the field and scored a point in the same movement.

'Overall, we were very close but we fouled too much, and Pat Moylan ended up getting 10 points from frees.'

Although beaten by 2-21 to 4-11, Tony Doran and Mick were lauded for their heroics, with journalist Billy Quirke warming to his task in *The People*.

This was the eighth All-Ireland final in which Wexford was involved which I reported for this paper, he wrote. *Since that great first victory of 1955, and in many defeats, I have not known an encounter which was so completely dominated by two members of a losing team.*

My heart bleeds for Michael Jacob and Tony Doran. Such effort and brave endeavour, such courage and character cries out to be rewarded.

Billy's colleague Phil Murphy made comparisons with Bobbie Rackard in 1954, as well as Mick's own display in the county final of 1974. *Time after time he leaped and caught cleanly and set Wexford on the move with long clearances. He ran himself into the ground and gave his all.*

Mick adds: 'I felt in peak condition for this game and the moment I got onto the pitch I had great energy and appetite for the battle ahead. We had a dream start with the early goals and we were hurling really well, and not giving an inch to Cork.

'They put a lot of different forwards out on me. I played on four opponents during the course of the match – Brendan Cummins, Mick Malone, Ray

Cummins and Jimmy Barry-Murphy. My focus was on winning the ball and reading the game, and it didn't matter to me who I was playing on. I was going to win that ball, and nobody was going to stop me.

'Towards the end, we lost momentum, while some questionable decisions were given against us and we just didn't have enough in the end to get over the line.'

The sides would meet again just six weeks later in the last of the series of Wembley games that ran from 1958 to '76, normally on Whit weekend.

In a repeat of the All-Ireland outcome, Mick contributed seven points – from midfield this time – in a 3-14 to 0-17 loss. The announcement of the All Stars team in the same week went some way towards easing the pain of Mick and the three colleagues that joined him – Willie Murphy at full-back, Martin Quigley for the fourth year running (centre-forward), and Tony Doran at full-forward.

It was, indeed, a marvellous return after such a lengthy lay-off, lasting almost an entire calendar year.

'That was a high note alright. Four All Stars and the four of us all down the centre, it was great for Wexford to be so well represented after losing the final.'

UNFORTUNATELY, THE CLUB campaign was one to forget. After going so close in the previous two championships, the disappointment of those defeats meant that some players eased off in terms of commitment.

Harry O'Connor hadn't continued on as trainer, while Johnny Murphy returned to his native Crossabeg-Ballymurn. And when the postponed match with Cloughbawn eventually took place in Bellefield on August 1, Oulart-The Ballagh were lucky to scrape through by 0-11 to 0-9.

By the time of the county semi-final in Wexford Park on October 10, 'The organisation had gone stale', according to Robbie.

Wouldn't you know it, the opposition once again came from Buffers Alley, and they had it a lot easier than in the county final of 1975.

The sides had clashed in a stormy league match in Monamolin six months earlier that didn't go the distance. It was halted by Gorey referee Michael 'Duckman' Kennedy close to the end when a brawl broke out.

After the game, several players of both teams continued to fight for over 10 minutes – onlookers were shocked by the brutality, one local newspaper claimed.

Any ill-feeling that lingered from the championship clashes of the previous two years was put to bed that afternoon, because the 1976 semi-final passed off without incident.

'There wasn't much said about the row afterwards,' Mick notes.

'And there was no such thing as being ill about it. There was a lot of respect at the back of it all, and we backed each other one hundred percent when we were with the county. It was all about Wexford then… myself and Colm Doran used to go flat out together for every ball.'

'You quickly learn within families to manage these things,' Breda adds. 'We never got too hot and bothered about it. Sometimes the trouble would be generated by people with no direct involvement at all. Of course there was rivalry, but there was never any real animosity.'

Robbie concurs: 'We had played under-21 with them, so we were comrades in some ways when younger. And later there was a bit of pride to be either won or lost when we played each other.

'Within an hour of a match like that you could meet an Alley player and there would be no more said about it.'

WEXFORD SUPPORTERS WERE afforded a rare opportunity to witness some Railway Cup hurling right on their doorstep when Connacht travelled to Enniscorthy to face Leinster in the semi-final on February 13, 1977.

Mick knew every blade of grass around Bellefield like the back of his hand by that stage, and he was determined to put on a good show.

A crowd of 2,000 saw him paired off at first with Frank Cummins at midfield, before a move to centre-back in place of Dublin's Vinny Holden. In a tight game Tom O'Riordan of the *Irish Independent* said the difference between the 1-12 to 2-5 victory and defeat was the *display of three Wexford stalwarts… Mick Jacob, Colm Doran and Martin Quigley.*

After surrendering their crown to Munster in 1976 by a one-point margin, Mick and company would return to winning ways in Croke Park on St Patrick's Day with a comfortable 2-17 to 1-13 success over the same opposition.

Although he had turned 31 a couple of months earlier, that All-Ireland final form from the previous September was carried into the new year.

Indeed, when the National League resumed post-Christmas with a low-scoring draw against Limerick in the Gaelic Grounds, Mick's display on Eamonn

Cregan had one of his biggest fans in the media piling on more praise.

I will forever remember the magnificence of Michael Jacob, Billy Quirke purred. *He was even better than he was in the All-Ireland final – if that is possible.*

Eddie 'Heffo' Walsh was the main man on his right in a one-point win over Cork in Wexford Park, but a setback followed when Offaly's 1-12 to 1-8 National League quarter-final triumph in Nowlan Park was attributed in large part to their success in curbing the influence of Mick, Martin Quigley and Tony Doran in the first-half.

Prior to focusing on another Leinster Championship campaign, there was some unfinished club business from 1976 to deal with.

However, it wasn't high on the list of priorities for Oulart-The Ballagh, principally because it was in football rather than hurling!

That point was emphasised by the events of March 20. Immediately after pipping Oylegate-Glenbrien in an early throw-in for the delayed Enniscorthy District junior football final of 1976, most of the players rushed to cars ferrying them to Kilkenny for a hurling tournament first round versus Brian Cody's James Stephens in the afternoon!

Mick didn't feature in that football tie, but he was back alongside Wexford hurling colleague Jimmy Prendergast at midfield for the county semi-final win over Adamstown three weeks later.

And before the final could take place, there was the very appealing sideshow of an early-May holiday in Los Angeles with the All Stars to face Cork.

Wexford's own Jim Berry managed the hurlers, with Willie Murphy, Tony Doran, Martin Quigley and replacement Johnny Walsh assisting Mick on the field.

Castletown's Mick Carty was also called up with the footballers for that trip of a lifetime and, who knows, maybe he even passed on some tips to Mick in preparation for his forthcoming final with Oulart-The Ballagh. Their fathers had been teammates on the junior county-winning Tara Rocks football squad of 1948, after all.

Whether or not that happened remains lost in the mists of time; what's fresher in the memory is that an unfancied team pushed Wexford town side Dan O'Connells all the way before going down by 2-4 to 1-5 in Gorey on the last Sunday in May.

Their rivals were a 'football-only' club, albeit with prominent Faythe Harriers hurlers such as Willie Murphy, 'Heffo' Walsh and Con Dowdall on board.

And even though, as Robbie stresses, 'there's no way we should have been able to give them a game', in actual fact Oulart-The Ballagh had more than enough chances and even missed a penalty.

Mick, starting at left half-back, showed up well there but was even better when pushed forward after the interval, combining with Nicky O'Toole to create a goal for Peter Storey in the 37th minute.

After a hectic spell since late January, a three-week respite from games followed, giving the Wexford hurlers ample time to prepare for the Kildare challenge.

They were on high alert after that scare in Athy one year earlier, and this time the Wexford Park venue was more favourable.

'Athy was a tighter pitch and they played like they had nothing to lose, but down here was a different ball game altogether,' Mick says.

'Kildare were an ageing side and they weren't able for us in 1977, but we had a lot of respect for them. Pat Dunny was on the Leinster teams with me and he was a wonderful hurler. And as for Johnny Walsh – I always thought more should have been done to stop him going to Kildare, I think Wexford could have held on to him in the 60s if they really wanted.'

This was one of Johnny's rare quiet afternoons, though, as Wexford romped home by 2-25 to 0-10, but not before Mick was laid low with another injury.

The lack of basic first-aid equipment at the main county ground came in for criticism because, after receiving a blow to his right knee in the 22nd minute *he had to be man-handled off the pitch.*

A stretcher couldn't be found, but happily the knock wasn't as serious as first feared. And although Mick missed a challenge game against Galway in Rathnure two weeks later as a result, there was still ample time to get himself right for the county's eighth Leinster final on the trot versus Kilkenny.

THAT WAS THE great Eddie Keher's last hurrah, and Wexford were thankful for a late save by John Nolan from one of his shots as they retained their crown on a 3-17 to 3-14 scoreline.

Given that he continued playing inter-county hurling until 1984, it seems scarcely believable now to be reminded Mick's last major honour arrived on that late July afternoon in 1977.

With 'Heffo' Walsh, Colm Doran and Billy Rowsome forming the half-back line, it also proved to be his final time starting a championship game at midfield.

He lined up alongside Ned Buggy, and also had the distinction of contributing a point from a lineball as Wexford retained their provincial senior title for the first time since 1956.

Now the team faced a different dilemma than 12 months earlier, when two energy-sapping clashes with Galway in the sweltering Cork heat depleted their reserves.

It was the turn of the Leinster champions to have the bye directly into the All-Ireland final, and in Mick's considered opinion they nearly had too much time on their hands.

Only one game was played – the first-ever Kehoe Cup final, named in memory of the late Mícheál Kehoe, one of two former GAA presidents from Wexford, who had died earlier that year.

While it would develop into a competition for the non-senior counties in Leinster, that initial venture saw Wexford pipping Kilkenny by 2-13 to 1-15 in Bellefield. Mick's accuracy from '70s' was a notable feature, as he pointed five times to show he could offer cover for the regular free-taker Ned Buggy if needed.

'I thought we over-did it right through that month of August with the amount of hard running at training. There's a time and a place for that, but we were doing it at the wrong stage of the year.

'We did a fierce lot of stamina work but it completely backfired. It got to the stage where all the players were talking about it among themselves.

'I used to come home after training, and have to go straight to bed, but then I wouldn't be able to go asleep. All the lads were complaining in the same way.

'And then we were dead as ducks in the morning when we tried to get up for another day's work.

'The training we did to prepare for that All-Ireland was the type that all teams should be doing in January, not in August. We left a lot of energy a team should be bringing to Croke Park on All-Ireland final day at home.

'The selectors were convinced it was fitness that beat us in 1976, but it wasn't.'

Their efforts to over-compensate meant Mick and his colleagues only started to get into their full flow when time was rapidly running out. 'If that game had gone on for another five minutes I firmly believe we would have won.

'Close to the end, I caught a ball at midfield that John Horgan had mishit. I came in with it a good bit and gave it to Christy Keogh, but Martin Coleman brought off a great save from his shot.

'After that John Quigley had another effort, and Coleman saved it on his same right-hand side. Wexford could have stolen that game, but it wasn't to be.'

The final score was 1-17 to 3-8.

That late surge goalwards to set up a chance for Christy Keogh arrived after Mick's move to midfield. Many felt it should have been tried earlier. Of all the defeats endured in such a long and distinguished career, that All-Ireland final of 1977 was the one that hurt most.

Even an eternal optimist such as Mick, a man brimming with positivity, found it very hard to take.

'There was fierce disappointment within the group. The atmosphere on the last day we were together that year was unreal. We really were on such a downer.

'That was three times in the 70s Cork had beaten us in an All-Ireland final. It wasn't easy to get going again after that.

'That team had put so much into it against Kilkenny, so it was an awful disappointment for that group of players not to get an All-Ireland. That would have been something special.'

Breda also detected a noticeable difference in the atmosphere after the finals of 1976 and '77.

'It was fairly upbeat in 1976, and there was a positivity and a belief that the next year would be better,' she says. 'But it was the total opposite in '77. Everyone was completely worn-out and downhearted.'

Mick would never again experience the thrill of racing out of the Croke Park dressing-rooms on All-Ireland final day, no matter how hard he tried.

And he feels Wexford didn't help themselves over those two years with the calibre of experienced players that weren't involved. 'I know Phil Wilson was very disappointed that he wasn't asked to stay on for 1976. Our Christy was playing exceptionally well with the club around that time but wasn't considered, while I believe that Seánie Kinsella, Vinny Staples and Dave Bernie could have contributed a lot that year as well.'

AND THEN THERE was the case of 'Big Dan' Quigley, the All-Ireland winning captain who played his last game for Wexford in 1972 after disagreements with the county board.

'A few of us went to see Dan before the 1977 All-Ireland final...Willie Murphy, Tony (Doran) and myself. We were hoping to get him back, but we couldn't persuade him.'

Mick is an avid Davy Fitzgerald fan and would like to have had the opportunity to experience the modern scientific approach that is now deployed in order to achieve peak performance. 'I'd love to be starting out again with a man like Davy in charge. He gets that extra five or ten percent from players which can get teams over the line.

'Personally, I don't think Cork played all that well themselves in 1977, and that's what made it even harder to take. The game was fairly close all the way along.

'I knew it was going to be very hard to get back there again after losing two on the trot. Kilkenny were going to be coming stronger and stronger after being beaten by us twice.

'Our best chance for winning an All-Ireland with that team was gone.'

THERE WAS ONE silver lining to the cloud that enveloped Mick Jacob and Wexford hurling in the autumn of 1977.

Twelve of the players received nominations for the All Stars from an overall list of 82 – with only Mick and Christy Keogh making the grade. On the shortlist for centre-back and midfield, he got the nod at No.6 for the second year running, and third time in all *for his continued excellent play and undiminished skills in a most demanding position*.

With another trip to the USA as the reward, Mick and Breda devised a plan.

They were engaged to be married, and duly set a date for the wedding that would allow the All Stars tour to double up as their honeymoon! Only a couple with a deep-rooted love for the game could have come up with the idea, but it made perfect sense.

'It was a little bit of a consolation to get another All Star, but it was surprising that only two Wexfordmen made it after reaching the All-Ireland final.

'It just showed how well a Wexford hurler would need to play in order to be recognised by the selectors. Kilkenny always seemed to get more recognition in the years when they lost finals.'

There was something else to look forward to also in 1978 – the appointment of older brother Christy as a Wexford senior hurling selector, three years after his last appearance with the county.

As for the local hurling campaign, even the presence of another Wexford legend as trainer wasn't enough to get the club over the line in 1977.

NED WHEELER HAD an endearing personality along with an outstanding pedigree, and when he agreed to give one year to the Oulart-The Ballagh cause it revived special memories for Mick and Christy of travelling with him to Croke Park along with Billy Rackard 15 years earlier.

'Ned commanded a lot of respect. The players had great time for a man like that, although I was with Wexford so much that I missed out on a lot of club training before the All-Ireland final.'

Round one was a mere formality in mid-April, with Adamstown overcome by 4-15 to 1-4. More than three months elapsed before a quarter-final clash with Naomh Eanna, and Mick needed to have his wits about him to marshal his defensive colleagues against a lively forward line.

In the end, it required three opportunist goals from a newcomer – county minor Richard 'Butch' O'Connor – to secure a fourth successive semi-final spot by 3-12 to 3-10.

However, the latest showdown with Rathnure in early October didn't go according to plan, with Christy's absence through injury sorely felt in a 1-15 to 1-9 loss.

Mick, partnering Willie Sunderland in midfield, had a tough battle with John Conran, but – not for the first time against these opponents – the forward line didn't click.

Robbie remembers Ned Wheeler's wonderful personality. 'He was always in great form, a big, happy man. He was a complete nut on first-time hurling, and he tried to mould Oulart-The Ballagh into that type of team… he wanted us to let go on everything on the ground.

'He was fully respected, and we were like schoolboys listening to him. We were willing to go with what Wheeler wanted us to do, but the bottom line was that it wasn't our natural style.

'It was great for the good strikers of the ball, but some were doing well if they hit it 10 or 15 yards along the ground, when they were well able to drive it 50 or 60 yards out of their hand. It led to frustration.'

Mick could understand Wheeler's reasoning. 'Ground hurling doesn't suit backs. If the ball is travelling slower, then they will be happy.

'Cork used to be great for it back in Willie Walsh's time at centre-forward in the early-70s. He was a natural first-time hurler, but over the years they changed their way of playing altogether.

'Offaly used it to their advantage, and I always found it harder to settle into a game when there was a lot of play on the ground.'

Mick was an ever-present for all 10 of Wexford's matches in the 1977-78 National League campaign, culminating in a one-point loss to Kilkenny after extra-time in a replayed semi-final in Carlow.

On day one – a narrow loss to Offaly in Birr – he partnered teenage debutant Ger Flood from Cloughbawn at midfield, but for seven of the next eight games he was in his familiar centre-back slot, flanked by 'Heffo' Walsh and Colm Doran.

The sole exception was for a notable milestone, not that he knew it at the time. On February 26, 1978, there was one last hurrah for the old midfield duo of Mick and Dave Bernie – the latter retiring later that year.

Cork were handy 1-15 to 0-9 victors in Páirc Uí Chaoimh, but what Mick didn't realise was that it was his 100th senior appearance with Wexford; nobody kept track of such matters in those days.

The highlight of that campaign arrived in the last pre-Christmas match. Clare had made their home venue of Tulla a fortress, but Wexford ended their 15-game unbeaten run there which stretched back several years by 2-12 to 1-13 and Mick *never put a foot wrong.*

He had another problem to contend with by the time the semi-final with Kilkenny came around. A boil on the back of his left hand made for two uncomfortable afternoons, particularly in the replay when he was forced off at the interval.

He did return for extra-time, but Kilkenny edged home by 5-15 to 5-14. The date was April 16, 1978 – it would be April 8 of the following year before Mick wore the Wexford jersey again.

MICK AND BREDA were married in St Cormac's Church, Boolavogue, on Thursday, May 11, 1978 – four days after his appearance at centre-back for Leinster in a Railway Cup final loss to Munster in Páirc Uí Chaoimh.

They were photographed in *The People* the following week after passing through the traditional archway of hurls, formed by Robbie, Christy Keogh, Teddy O'Connor, and three of the Doran brothers Bill, Tony and Colm.

The newly-weds had to wait a few weeks before viewing that image, because they were thousands of miles away by the time it was published.

'We flew out the next day from Dublin on our honeymoon,' Mick recalls. 'We spent the first weekend in Boston, and then we travelled on to San Francisco and finished the tour in Los Angeles.

'We were staying in family homes again, so I was re-united with Jackie Kavanagh from Craanford, who had been so good to me on my previous trips, and again in Los Angeles with Arthur Close. We visited all the great attractions while in California.'

This time Wexford's Fr Harry Sinnott was the All Stars manager, as the custom saw that role filled by the central council representative of the previous year's beaten All-Ireland finalists.

Mick captained, and starred with, the team in an eight-point win over Cork, accompanied by Christy Keogh as well as Tony and Colm Doran, both of whom travelled as replacements.

However, that inconsequential victory was achieved at an immense cost.

An accidental blow from the teak-tough Cork centre-forward Tim Crowley left Mick with a broken finger that would have serious repercussions for club and county alike.

'It was more an awkward pull than anything else. I put my hand down to gather the ball near ground level and he let fly. I had it looked at by the team doctor at half-time, and he said he didn't think anything was broken. I hurled on, but the pain on the knuckle was unreal afterwards.

'We were coming home the next day, and I asked Dr Pat O'Neill, the Dublin footballer, to have a look at it. He knew it was a bad break straight away.

'I remember him saying to me, "You're going to be in trouble with that". It was the index finger on my left hand, and it was broken in two places, down and across the knuckle.

'I put olive oil on it and tried everything I knew to get it right, but there was a very slow healing process. Because it was my catching hand again, I'd get a jolt of pain when I was cupping it to close in on the ball.

'Funnily enough, I discovered the best cure for it was at home in the farmyard. By milking the cows with that left hand, I found that the movement and the natural bend of the finger gradually returned.

'When I could see it improving, I stuck to that plan, but it was a long time before I could play with any freedom again.'

Wexford and Oulart-The Ballagh both suffered in the interim.

IT WAS THE first time since 1968 for Mick not to feature on the field of play with the county in a championship campaign.

Seamus O'Connor from Faythe Harriers, the under-21 centre-back, was thrown in at the deep end for his first-ever senior game in the Leinster semi-final against Dublin, and an unconvincing 5-16 to 4-13 win.

Christy Keogh was given the No.6 slot for the Leinster final against Kilkenny, and Mick rallied the players with a few well-chosen words in the dressing-room before battle commenced.

And while the versatile Enniscorthy man had a storming game, the quest for three successive titles ended with a 2-16 to 1-16 defeat.

The clubs of Wexford decided to run the senior championship on a league system in 1978, and the new format wasn't to Oulart-The Ballagh's liking.

Mick featured in late-April when they were held to a draw by St Martin's, the intermediate titleholders, but he was in serious trouble with that injury by the time they were pitted against Cloughbawn in Wexford Park on June 24.

It took all of his willpower to line out, and it was only because the club meant so much to him, but their qualification hopes faded with a 1-9 to 0-9 loss after what seemed like a legitimate late goal from Brendan O'Connor was disallowed.

Mick Jacob hurled one-handed because of a finger injury, The People noted. *He got in some nice touches but even to a player of his ability, the handicap of an injured left hand was too great.*

Fully fit, he would have made an immense difference.

To make matters even worse, he also dislocated his right thumb and split it in two places, although that injury healed a lot quicker.

The third round game, a seven-point win against Naomh Eanna, was the first championship outing for the club that Mick had missed since 1971.

A victory was still required against Buffers Alley in Gorey on July 30 in order to advance, and it never looked like coming. Not alone was Mick absent, the club was also minus the services of its other inter-county stalwart Jimmy Prendergast, who had broken ribs against Cloughbawn. The 1-17 to 0-9 loss meant that, for the first time since 1973, Oulart-The Ballagh were out of contention before August.

'It's hard on a club when they have to replace one central man, let alone two, so there was a bit of a downer on everybody before we played the Alley. I remember thinking after the injury that I wouldn't get to play in any game for the rest of the year.

'That was a crushing blow.

'The finger was straight, and I couldn't get it to bend naturally. If I'm honest, it was never the same again, but eventually I was able to adjust to it. The minute I got that belt in San Francisco, it was sore. It didn't help that I hurled on with it for another half-hour after that either.

'With a broken finger, with every strike of the ball you would feel the sting of pain going up your arm. I didn't get back to hurl properly again until April of 1979, and I really missed it.

'We had moved in to the new house after getting married, and I hurled up and down the living room with Breda. It's only when you get a long-term injury that you realise just how much you miss the whole thing.'

If there was a silver lining to his long-term absence, it was the chance it afforded Mick and Breda to settle into married life without the usual distractions caused by the sport they both loved.

'We moved into our new home in Oulartwick from day one, and we've been here ever since.

'Monavullen was two miles away, and it was about three and a half miles across the fields to Breda's homeplace in Knocknaskeaugh.'

'It was almost a direct line, in fact,' Breda confirms. 'My late father used to go up to the field at the back of our homeplace, and he could see all the way over to the lights at our new house.'

BREDA HAILS FROM a big family of 13 children, one of whom – as in the

Jacobs' case – died as an infant.

Everyone from her side of the parish in Boolavogue gravitated towards Buffers Alley in their youth, and several McCleans attended national school with the Dorans.

'My brother Jim was on the team that beat Oulart-The Ballagh in the county final of 1975, while Tony was in the subs. John Stamp played with them and he would have come from the same Monageer-Boolavogue background.'

It was no surprise that Mick should choose a kindred spirit for his partner in life.

Breda first played an organised game of adult camogie in 1962, the same year as her husband-to-be's hurling debut.

St Ibar's from Castlebridge travelled up to Boolavogue for a challenge match, and she was an enthusiastic participant. However, it transpired that her own parish couldn't muster enough players to enter a championship team, so the few that remained interested threw in their lot with the Ibar's instead.

Breda played with them from 1962 to '68, featuring in three of the county senior finals they won in the four-in-a-row of 1964 to '67. She picked up Leinster intermediate and junior medals along the way with Wexford, before a newly-formed club attracted her interest in 1969.

After transferring to Buffers Alley, she captained them to the county junior title at their first attempt.

Bridie Jacob developed her love for camogie at a later stage, having attended boarding school in Arklow where hockey was the favoured sport.

She played in one county final with St Ibar's – their 1969 loss to St Abban's – before linking up with Breda and the rest of the Buffers Alley crew in 1970.

And with the hurlers and camogie players of the adjoining parishes moving in the same sporting and social circles, it was only natural that some lasting relationships should develop.

'I can't remember the exact date when we started going out, but I do know that the first big function we attended together as a couple was the All Stars in 1972,' Breda says.

Some people bond in a crowded room, but for Mick and Breda the setting was a farmer's field.

'We were very conscientious about our training when I played camogie with

Wexford,' Breda explains.

'I often travelled in to St Patrick's Park with Bridie, and Elsie Walsh, who would go on to marry Brian Cody. Elsie would come on her bike to Boolavogue to my house, and then I'd drive over for Bridie.

'One particular night, we felt we hadn't done enough at training, so we decided that when we got back to Bridie's house in Monavullen, we would run a few extra laps around a field beside the farmyard.

'Up to that I would have just known Michael vaguely as being one of Bridie's brothers.

'As we were going around the field, I could see a figure looking across at us. At some point, I got myself tangled up in a loose piece of barbed wire, but the other two women avoided it and ran ahead.

'I was slower coming around as a result, and when I got back Michael was there and I guess a bit of a spark developed between us that evening. It took him ages to wake up and ask me out, though. He finally invited me to a dance in Gorey, and we never looked back from that night.'

When Robbie Jacob hears that story, it prompts a playful joke on his part. 'Barbed wire? He definitely set a trap for her, no doubt about it! Mick was never the same once Breda came on the scene.'

The man himself is the picture of innocence and denies all knowledge, but he had eyes for nobody other than Breda after that fateful summer's evening in Monavullen.

'We got engaged on the day after the All Stars do in 1977… December 10,' Breda says.

'I remember getting the ring when we were up there in Dublin. Between hurling and farming it was a very busy time, so that's why we agreed to work our honeymoon around the All Stars tour.

'I was teaching in the national school in my native Boolavogue at the time. They delayed their Easter holidays to coincide with my honeymoon, ensuring the days were available for me to travel.'

Later that year, a vacancy arose in the four-teacher Oulart NS, in a building comprising a prefab and three classrooms. The following year, Breda Flood, who had been teaching there for several years, became principal.

The game of hurling was equally precious to her, as her uncle Mick Morrissey adorned those all-conquering Wexford sides of the mid-50s before hosting Mick on his first New York trip in 1971.

One of the most successful backroom teams in the history of under-age GAA was about to be formed.

Breda says: 'All three of us were mad about hurling, and we were all qualified GAA coaches. I had done residential courses in Gormanston College, in Meath, organised by the Camogie Association, soon after I graduated as a primary teacher, while Breda Flood and I also attended summer courses organised by Wexford GAA.

'In 1985, at Eastertime, Mick and his fellow Wexford selectors travelled to Galway for a week-long coaching course for inter-county mentors. I accompanied them, and attended all of the sessions as well. It was wonderful to see so many former star players willing to increase their knowledge of how to pass on the skills of hurling.'

With Mick Jacob in the role of coach-trainer, assisted by the organisational and coaching qualities brought to the table by the two Bredas, Oulart-The Ballagh would experience sporting riches like never before.

Those first steps taken in 1978 would prove the catalyst for the club's complete dominance of hurling in Wexford many years later.

The Jacob family on Mick and Breda's wedding day – May 11, 1978 – with Robbie (left) sporting a war wound from the hurling fields; love blossomed for the happy couple (left) in the early-70s, and they made their home in Oulartwick.

The second successive All-Ireland final loss to Cork in 1977 (above) marked a low point in Mick's long career. He describes it as 'the toughest defeat of all'.

« CHAPTER 8 »

THE WEXFORD HURLING landscape altered significantly in the late-70s and early-80s.

It was a gradual process, but the team that came up short to Cork in those three All-Ireland bids would disassemble bit by bit.

Teddy O'Connor and Dave Bernie moved on after 1978, while '79 was Christy Keogh's last year.

Willie Murphy and Jimmy Prendergast departed in 1980, with Ned Buggy and Colm Doran leaving the inter-county scene in '82.

Retirement never entered Mick Jacob's head, though. He vowed to keep going for as long as he possibly could, a forerunner in the leadership and experience stakes along with Tony Doran and Martin Quigley.

'I never thought my chance was gone, even when I wasn't far off 40. It was always about the next game for me, and preparing even harder again.'

Eager players like George O'Connor, Paudge Courtney, John Conran and Seánie Kinsella were starting to step up and make an impact, and Mick was still full of vigour and enthusiasm at the age of 33.

The early indicators in his comeback games were all bright. It was just eight days shy of a full year away from the inter-county scene when he returned for a 1-10 to 1-9 defeat to Kilkenny in the last round of the National League in Nowlan Park on April 8, 1979.

Brendan Furlong wrote: *Though a little short of match practice, [he] was still able to display his artistry and, despite his long absence, he has lost none of his positional play, and had a steadying effect on the defence right through the game.*

A fortnight before the Leinster Championship began, Wexford accepted an invitation from future GAA president Dr Mick Loftus to promote hurling in his home club Crossmolina in Co Mayo.

It was Mick's one and only time to play a game in that part of the country, and he gave a *classy performance* in a five-point challenge win over Galway.

The tight confines of Geraldine Park in Athy could never be rated a happy hunting ground for Wexford teams and – in a portent of things to come – they were steeped to get out of there with a 0-17 to 2-10 win over Offaly on June 24.

With Tony Doran out injured, and the midlanders two points up, it looked like the county's record of contesting every Leinster final in the 70s along with Kilkenny would be shattered.

That was until Mick stepped forward with trademark defiance to show that long lay-off hadn't adversely affected his ability to influence a game.

The respect he always showed to the opposition stood to him in that encounter.

'I was on Paddy Kirwan and Offaly were expecting big things from him. I had seen him playing on an under-21 team that beat Wexford and I studied him closely.

'He was a very useful player but I was ready for him. That was a close, tight game; it was obvious Offaly were coming with a really strong team.'

MICK'S SIXTH AND last Leinster final defeat at the hands of Kilkenny would follow. While Tony Doran was fit again and contributed 1-1, the loss of Jimmy Prendergast was immense.

Christy was no longer a selector in 1979, as the county board had moved away from the one per District plus one from the county champion format. Instead it was a three-man backroom comprising Tom Neville, Jim Dillon of Adamstown, and Ned Power.

'Tom Breen was a very promising young lad, and he was playing well at the time with Monageer-Boolavogue and UCD.

'It was clear to everyone that full-back was his best place, but they brought him in and played him in the left corner on 'Cloney' Brennan who had a very good day.

'I have always maintained that every position on the hurling field demands special attributes. There's a huge difference between playing at full-back to corner-back, for example… or centre-back to wing-back as I found myself on many occasions. Tom was put in a position he wasn't comfortable in, and it was a pity because he had ability and could have offered us something going forward. He drifted off the scene after that.'

Some tangible recognition for the hard work involved in making it back to the big stage came in the form of another All Star nomination in September.

Mick was one of seven Wexfordmen shortlisted, along with Willie Murphy, Eddie Walsh, Colm Doran, Martin Quigley, Seánie Kinsella, and the sole Wexford man to make the grade, sharpshooter Ned Buggy.

Late 1979 also brought his first Oireachtas medal after wins over Galway and Offaly respectively, and that title was retained the following year against the latter opponents in Birr.

Mick was bestowed with the added distinction of captaining the team to that second victory. Breda remembers the trophy being on proud display around the house afterwards, with callers to Oulartwick to see baby Michael also treated to the sight of a gleaming piece of silverware.

'That was a nice honour, and it was good for us to go up there and come home with a win.'

A less pressurised National League would be experienced in 1979-80, given that Wexford had dropped out of the top flight for the first time in Mick's career.

That campaign began with his first-ever game against Kerry, with colleague Fr Martin Casey relishing the chance to face his native county in a 2-7 to 0-2 win in Ardfert. The only real test in the group stage came in a draw with Waterford, and Wexford were underprepared for a knockout duel after also defeating Laois, Dublin and Antrim respectively.

That was reflected in a 3-10 to 1-13 quarter-final loss to Limerick in Nowlan Park, with Mick at right half-back while the selectors experimented with Rathnure's Jim Higgins in the centre.

OULART-THE BALLAGH'S second experience of the league championship structure in 1979 was more favourable than their first, with star man Mick now fully back on board.

A draw with Faythe Harriers plus wins over St Martin's and Naomh Eanna saw them safely through to the quarter-final against Cloughbawn, but they advanced without striking a ball in anger.

Four days before the game, the opposition's Ger Flood was ruled out by a foot injury sustained in the Leinster under-21 final, and they weren't prepared to play without him.

The irony of the situation wasn't lost on observers because, only three years before, Cloughbawn were up in arms when Oulart-The Ballagh were granted a postponement against them as a result of Mick being injured on Wexford duty.

The rule introduced as a result ensured they wouldn't be afforded the same leniency in 1979; by that stage the fixtures committee had plenary powers, and clubs had to play when they were told.

Oulart-The Ballagh would have much preferred the game, particularly as it resulted in a full three months without a competitive outing before they faced off against Rathnure yet again in Bellefield on August 26.

And although Christy scored three goals off no less an opponent than Dan Quigley, the overall performance wasn't up to scratch and a 1-16 to 3-5 defeat ensued.

One thing Oulart-The Ballagh never did was throw in the towel, and they had another go in an oddly-structured 1980 championship.

They were one of four teams in a seeded group, all of whom were guaranteed a quarter-final game regardless of results. It meant that a poor record of a draw with Faythe Harriers, followed by losses to Naomh Eanna by one point and Rathnure (by nine), counted for nothing in the overall scheme of things.

The real action would start with a quarter-final against Duffry Rovers in early August, and that hurdle was comfortably cleared by 3-14 to 2-4, thanks largely to the devastating defensive form of Mick, Jimmy Prendergast and star man Paddy Kehoe.

Three weeks later, that crushing déjà vu feeling returned. *The immaculate Mick Jacob seemed to be forever clearing his lines,* one reporter wrote of an afternoon when Rathnure qualified for a fourth final on the trot with a 2-13 to 2-7 success. They had paid their rivals back in spades for the outcome of their 1975 meeting by that stage.

EARLIER THAT SUMMER the county hurling scene was agog with Offaly's achievement in winning the Leinster title.

The decision to introduce an open draw in the province served as a catalyst, particularly when Wexford and Kilkenny – finalists every year from 1970 to '79 – were pitted together in the penultimate round.

The game took place on June 15, and Mick had a major scare just a fortnight earlier. In his capacity as club chairman, Robbie would put in tireless work from 1976 with the target of developing a new pitch in the heart of Oulart village.

It was on a parcel of land directly behind the school Mick attended in the late-50s, and a supreme community effort raised the necessary funds over the years.

The day an entire parish longed for arrived on June 1, 1980. The official opening was marked by a challenge between Wexford and Dublin, with Mick playing at centre-back in a seven-point win.

'I got a belt in the eye and I had to go off. I had to go down to Waterford to get it treated. The right eyelid was dropping down but it wasn't coming back up again.

'I could have done without that type of hassle, because Michael was due to be born around the same time.'

Thankfully, the problem was resolved and, five days before becoming a father, Mick faced up to Kilkenny yet again, only on this occasion in the Leinster semi-final. His participation remained in doubt, though, right up to the morning of the game.

The People explained how *Mick Jacob only decided to line out three hours before after a light training session in the Phoenix Park*, and he agrees he was, 'lucky enough to make that game'.

And after a third successive championship exit, by 4-18 to 3-16, a local journalist wondered if Mick's days might be numbered.

Mervyn Moore felt: *This must have been the last chance for glory for the likes of Willie Murphy, Tony Doran, Jimmy Prendergast and Mick Jacob.* It was the first time Mick was subjected to this type of speculation.

The writer was only partially correct, because while Murphy and Prendergast did indeed depart, neither Mick nor Tony had any intention of calling it a day.

Murphy did stay involved in 1981, but as team trainer rather than key player. Christy Keogh was also a selector, along with Joe Doran, Jim Dillon and Tony Dempsey, with Ned Power still on board as coach.

And Mick was a target of their early experimentation, as he juggled a short-lived new role in the full-back line with the sleepless nights that went hand-in-hand with being the father of a new-born.

Michael was due to arrive on June 6, 1980, but he must have had a sixth sense about his daddy's eye injury as he delayed his entrance into the world for another 14 days. Mick quickly embraced the joys of fatherhood, doing his fair share at home while his understanding wife actively encouraged his ongoing involvement with Wexford.

For the first game of 1981, a challenge away to Westmeath, he was even tried at full-back for the one and only time, before four National League outings followed in the right corner.

It wasn't a happy experience for the man himself, and he ruefully looks back on the day when Eamonn Cregan took him for two goals in a drawn game in the Gaelic Grounds.

'I couldn't see myself either as a full-back or a corner-back, if I'm honest. Centre-back and midfield were the two places on the field I could really feel happy and safe in.

'I always felt on edge at corner-back, it was a completely different game. The ball was available a lot more in the half-back line, and you could sweep across from right to left and always stay involved. At corner-back it was all about covering off the forward and making sure he didn't give you the slip.

'It made a huge difference to be in a position where you knew exactly what you were doing. Even wing-back isn't the same as centre-back. I had played a lot of games in the centre, so I had a good knowledge of where the ball was going, and an understanding with the lads beside me.

'It's never good to break up an established line on a team in order to make one change. The centre-back is the mainstay of any hurling team. If he's playing well, the rest of them will respond.

'It was like a tonic for me when they moved me out to the centre again. I remember thinking... *I'm where I want to be... I'll show these lads now.*

For all his discomfort as a No.2, he must have done a fine job in hiding it, because his combined corner-back displays against Tipperary, Limerick and Galway still earned him the national B&I Line GAA Personality of the Month award for March 1981.

He was only the third Wexford player to be honoured, nearly five years after Tony Doran and Willie Murphy were selected for July and August 1976 respectively.

THE CHOPPING AND changing did end for the 1981 championship, with Mick delighted to be returned to centre-back, flanked by John Conran and Colm Doran on either side.

Journalist Seán Nolan forcibly argued the point after a play-off loss to Galway in Thurles led to another relegation. *There are a number of things that the league campaign has clearly illustrated. The most glaring is that Mick Jacob must line out at centre-back or not at all.*

Nothing of benefit was learned in a 2-20 to 0-8 dismissal of Dublin in Wexford Park, but the acid test would come. At 35 years of age, Mick met Kilkenny in the Leinster semi-final for the second year running and shone in a first championship win over them since 1977.

'That happened a lot in my career; Kilkenny would win a few and then, just when they thought Wexford might be slipping, we'd come back and beat them. We could always rise our performance for Kilkenny, no matter what game it was.'

The 4-12 to 1-18 win set up the first Leinster final of Mick's career against Offaly. By now the midlanders were very much part of the game's elite, and Wexford would suffer in the exact same way that Oulart-The Ballagh had done for so long.

Just like beating Rathnure and Buffers Alley in the same year was beyond their reach, the county team in the latter part of Mick's career couldn't do likewise against Kilkenny and Offaly.

Wexford supporters will always point to the blow that ended Tony Doran's involvement in the 1981 Leinster final after just 15 minutes as the game's key moment. They were already 2-1 to 0-3 in arrears, and in all the circumstances it was a serious achievement to run the holders to two points by the end (3-12 to 2-13).

Performing against the midlanders was never a comfortable task. 'They were so good at opening teams up, playing the ball wide and firing it into the corners. It was the sort of delivery a forward like Johnny Flaherty loved. He'd be deadly; it was never a 50-50 situation from a back's point of view.

'Liam Currams brought great pace to Offaly at midfield, and Joachim Kelly covered every blade of grass. Pat Delaney was a rock at centre-back, and Ger Coughlan beside him was a great hurler for a small lad.

'Losing that Leinster final was a huge disappointment after such a good win over Kilkenny. The loss of Tony Doran so early in the game had a major influence on the outcome, because he was the main man in the forwards. But, to be fair, other lads stepped up well that day and, even though we were defeated, it gave me great hope that Wexford were on the up-and-up again with some very promising newcomers emerging.

'George O'Connor was exceptional that year, bringing great energy to our attack, while our inside line was greatly boosted by Seánie Kinsella, who was a wizard of a hurler. John Conran was another who shone brightly, as did Cloughbawn's John Fleming and Rapparees' Paudge Courtney.'

Further All Star nominations followed, both for right corner-back and centre-back. George O'Connor was the only one of the nine Wexford players in contention to gain selection, at centre-forward.

Nonetheless, it was further vindication of Mick's efforts, at the end of a year when he also had the unusual distinction of playing a hurling game in Holland. That occurred on September 12, when Wexford beat Clare by 2-17 to 3-11 in an exhibition hosted by the Hockey Club of Amsterdam.

There was a pressing matter on Mick's mind on that short break – Oulart-The Ballagh had another county semi-final to play on the following weekend, and for the very first time they had dodged a bullet by avoiding both Buffers Alley and Rathnure.

Now the big question was: could they make the most of it?

BOTH THOSE TEAMS beat them earlier in the seeded league group, before Rapparees were overcome by six points, but once again all four were destined for the knockouts regardless.

And luck was on their side in the quarter-final against Duffry Rovers, coming from behind twice to draw (2-11 each) after a rousing half-time team talk from new trainer Tony Dempsey and a haul of 2-8 from Brendan O'Connor.

The big full-forward was in the form of his life, scoring an incredible four goals in just two minutes at the start of the second-half of the replay as Oulart-

The Ballagh romped home by 6-9 to 0-6.

It set up the club's first-ever knockout championship clash with Faythe Harriers, themselves chasing the county title after a 16-year gap.

A tense tie in Bellefield remained in the balance until the bitter end, with Mick one of the central figures. After scoring an impressive six points, including two '65s' and one free, he sustained an injury that resulted in referee Tommy Rowe adding four minutes.

And with the sides deadlocked on 1-12 apiece, Oulart-The Ballagh had three chances of winning it, from a 50-yard free, a 70-yard free, and a '65'. The knock sustained must have left its mark, because Mick shot narrowly wide on each occasion. Tomás Dunne, who was later to captain Oulart-The Ballagh to their first senior title in 1994, got his first taste of senior championship hurling in those matches.

The Harriers had taken the game to their rivals after trailing by 1-6 to 0-4 at half-time, but they still knew they were lucky to get a second crack. Two weeks later, a strong finish masterminded by dangerous attacker John 'Stella' Walker powered the town team home by 3-10 to 1-11.

Another year, and more crushing disappointment; and it didn't ease the pain in the slightest when the Harriers went on to stun the Alley in the final with a last-gasp winning goal direct from a Ned Buggy '65'.

'The Harriers had a very strong team and deserved their win in the replay,' Mick admits. 'But for us there was big disappointment after that year as a good few of the older players realised that they had missed another opportunity to get to play in a county final.'

ROBBIE CAME ON board as a Wexford senior selector in 1982, along with outgoing pair Christy Keogh and Joe Doran, as well as Rathnure's Tom Mooney and Bernie Radford of St Martin's, while Mick Kinsella from Buffers Alley was the coach/trainer.

Mick played in six of the seven National League group games, including a couple of outings back in the corner against Kerry and Kilkenny respectively.

'Some of the selectors didn't understand at all how Mick could be still hurling at the highest level at the age of 36. Of course, they didn't know him as well as I did,' Robbie says.

'They had no idea of the training he put in himself behind the scenes. Some of them felt that once a man passed the early-thirties mark, it was time to go. In their minds, they were gone themselves as players at that age, so they thought he should be too.

'Picking him in the corner was their way of giving him a hint, and setting him up to hang up his boots. They were trying to put him out to grass.

'I had to be careful that I didn't go overboard with my loyalty, but I knew deep down that when it came to the crunch games, they would need Mick at centre-back and they would realise that for themselves.'

Sure enough, that's how it panned out, and he wouldn't be moved from the No.6 role for the rest of that selection committee's tenure after delivering a stunning showing while directly opposed by Bobby Ryan in a National League quarter-final win over Tipperary in Waterford. *There was an outstanding performance from Mick Jacob – back in his best position of centre-back – and from John Conran and Barry Murphy*, Mervyn Moore enthused in *The People*.

There was a great cheer when Mick Jacob capped a huge contribution by sending over a free from seventy yards in the last minute.

That score topped off the 0-16 to 0-11 win and, with Tony Doran returning for the first time since the previous November, Cork were beaten by 2-17 to 1-16 in the semi-final in Thurles.

'Any time you beat Cork it's a good day, and that was a great boost especially after our negative experiences against them in the 70s.'

Kilkenny lay in wait in the county's first National League final since the victory over Limerick nine years earlier. And they lasted the pace better, with two goals in a three-minute spell in the last quarter consigning Wexford to a 2-14 to 1-11 defeat before a 23,125 attendance.

That game was played on April 18, and the squad witnessed wholesale changes by the time the Leinster Championship opener against All-Ireland holders Offaly arrived on May 30. Robbie explains the rationale of the backroom team:

'We felt we had made good progress, even if we didn't hit the same level of performance against Kilkenny as we did against Cork. We were looking for something more after the league, and we felt we needed to bring a cutting edge to the team. We learned a lot from the league final, and we tested various players in challenge matches.

'We were trying to find anything that would improve it in any way. We were willing to hunt down fellas from anywhere.'

Three challenge matches were played, against Limerick for the Seamus Quaid Memorial Cup in Castlemahon, and versus Clare and Waterford for pitch openings by the Horeswood and Cloughbawn clubs respectively.

By the time that championship clash with Offaly came around, six members of the league squad had lost their places. 'There was a serious desire there to win, especially after what happened to Tony Doran in 1981,' Robbie recalls. 'We went for goals too much near the end, but we came very close.'

That 2-16 to 3-12 defeat on the last Sunday in May was described as, *ANOTHER IN A LONG LINE OF HARD LUCK STORIES*, in one newspaper headline.

The People reported that *Wexford's men of the match were Tony Doran and Mick Jacob, outstanding players who deserve much more success than they have achieved in over a decade of service.*

Unusually for the time, Robbie and his fellow mentors had been appointed for a two-year term, and this prompted them to keep the momentum going over the summer of 1982. Every opportunity to participate in a challenge was taken, with Mick continuing to impress in games against Waterford, Tipperary (twice), Cork and Offaly from late June through to August.

IT HAD BEEN seven years since Oulart-The Ballagh's last county final appearance and, while they were widely accepted as being the third-best team of the 70s, now it was time to make another serious push.

'With Wexford going out at the end of May, that was a big addition to the club because it meant we had everyone together for the whole summer,' Mick points out. 'That would never have happened before, certainly not with me anyway because I was often still with the county through to August and September.

'Getting to the All-Ireland finals in 1976 and '77 didn't help a club like ours because we didn't have a big panel. When Jimmy Prendergast and myself were away with Wexford, the lads struggled to get challenge games.

'And when the county was going well, it would have taken a lot out of the players too by the time they got back to the club. Wexford going out in May helped Oulart-The Ballagh, because we had everyone together for the whole summer and went here, there and everywhere for practice matches.'

Jimmy Kennedy, Tom Dunne and Christy Jacob were the men in charge in 1982, and the opening group game provided an immediate boost as Rathnure were pipped by 2-7 to 0-12.

It was the first win over the black and ambers since the 1975 semi-final, although Buffers Alley dampened some of the initial enthusiasm in round two when they romped home in Gorey with 12 points to spare.

With a knockout place guaranteed, Oulart-The Ballagh's policy of blooding as many young players as possible looked to be paying off when they gained revenge on holders Faythe Harriers for that 1981 replay loss by a five-point margin.

On all known form, they were expected to have too much ability for Geraldine O'Hanrahans to cope with in the quarter-final. And so it proved, as the New Ross men lost by 0-13 to 0-9, only for a replay to be ordered.

'Human error' was cited as the reason for the inadvertent omission of Jimmy Prendergast's name from the official teamlist, and the county board decided on a re-fixture.

This game produced an almighty scare for Oulart-The Ballagh. The GOH scored three goals on their first three attacks when playing into a strong wind, and in the end it required a driving run by Mick to force the free that led to Brendan O'Connor's equaliser (0-15 to 3-6).

Oulart-The Ballagh also trailed by 2-6 to 0-11 with eight minutes left in the third meeting, but they hit the last four points of a tight game to finally edge through.

Three games against Rapparees in 1974 had improved Oulart-The Ballagh no end, and the same held true eight years later after that saga with the Barrowsiders. When they met Rathnure in yet another semi-final in Wexford Park on September 26, they were hell-bent on making up for losing to the same opponents at that stage in 1977, '79 and '80.

It simply couldn't go on like that; enough was enough, and all neutral followers were delighted to see the tables turned as Oulart-The Ballagh bridged a seven-year gap since their last final appearance with a commanding 1-13 to 0-10 win.

A GENERAL FEELING abounded that this might finally be their year, even though Buffers Alley lay in wait once more after dethroning Faythe Harriers.

Four prominent hurlers were asked for a verdict on the game beforehand, and only Rathnure's Jimmy Holohan tipped the Alley; 'Stella' Walker, Paudge Courtney and Johnny Murphy all fancied the underdogs.

'That was Tom Dempsey's first final for the Alley,' Mick recalls. 'He was only a chap at the time. The backs on both sides were on top, and it was hanging in the balance for long enough. We had our chances, but a few bad misses cost us.'

One save by Henry Butler from a 'Butch' O'Connor handpass stood out in the after-match analysis after Oulart-The Ballagh shipped another tough defeat, this time by 1-9 to 1-6. It was like 1974 all over again, with his team beaten but Mick giving a performance for the ages. He received an ovation from the crowd at the presentation and left the stand grasping two trophies: the overall Man of the Match, and the award for the best player on the losing team.

CROWD SALUTE BRILLIANT JACOB AS ALLEY TAKE TITLE, was the headline in *The Echo*, and that says it all; the achievement of the victors was almost overshadowed by the majesty of the losing team's centre-back.

Tom Dempsey has a vivid recollection of that county final. 'Seventeen years of age and suddenly I found myself in the parade before the 1982 Wexford hurling final in what was probably the most bitter of all rivalries.

'Two parishes separated by a thread geographically and yet with more connections by marriage than any other. O'Connors married to Butlers... Jacobs married to Dorans... yet all forgotten in this arena of fanaticism with a pairing that always packed Wexford Park.

'My mind was racing: how had I found myself here at such a young age and would I live to tell the tale? But, despite my anxiety, nerves and downright panic, my gaze – almost as if mesmerised – was drawn to one figure in the opposing line.

'Though slight in stature, the steely look of the red and black No.6 Mick Jacob... and the awe in which I held him – fuelled by his majesty in the 70s – made me feel somewhat unworthy of actually being on the field with him. He was always so distinctive looking (all greats are).

'You see, where I come from you weren't supposed to admire anything about our fiercest rivals and vice versa, but anyone that has any love or feel for hurling couldn't help but have the Oulartwick man as a hero.

'My first memory was the poster of the 1972 Carroll's All Stars after Mick had the audacity to collect an award despite Wexford's lack of success in that period.

'My real idolatry arrived, however, in the years of 1976 and '77 when he marshalled a team that stole my heart. Consistently amongst legends in those two years, he was the top performer.

'No opponent unnerved or matched him and, in the era of ferocious Pat Delaney-type centre-forwards, he used the most skilful way of out-thinking and out-hurling his opponents.

'He did everything so effortlessly with a reading of the game that in my opinion has been surpassed by few. I know by now that Mick was a fitness fanatic, but his delivery of the ball and ability to be almost omnipresent was amazing.

'When regaling everyone on the merits of Tony Doran, we were always reminded by the men across the parish border not to forget who was hitting the ball into Tony, and we could not deny Mick's perfect delivery.

'He could deal with any challenge and had an amazing ability whether in the air or on the ground. To this day, he remains one of the most complete hurlers I have ever had the pleasure to watch or, I am happy to say, share a field with.

'A non-drinker and non-smoker, he was a player that my father consistently put forward as a role model for myself in terms of how to prepare and how to play the game.

'So, as I gazed across at what I can only say was elegance in motion… you may be getting some feeling of why this legend was the focus of my attention.

'Standing in close enough proximity to Mick during the game, it soon became apparent that my admiration wasn't without foundation as the legend came to life and gave one of the most outstanding county final performances in living memory.

'He almost appeared as if wearing slippers (despite the heavy conditions) such was his balance and poise. I made sure to shake his hand after.

'He smiled, and for him to know my name was an incredible feeling for a teenager.'

THAT SUBLIME PERFORMANCE saw Mick chosen one week later as the Sealink GAA Personality of the Month. It was a new scheme introduced in Wexford 11 months earlier, and GAA president Paddy Buggy travelled down from Kilkenny to attend the presentation ceremony in Hotel Rosslare.

Mick vowed to keep going, of course, but that was another defeat that seriously tested his resolve.

'After that loss I don't think I was able to talk or nearly walk for a week. But then I settled down and said to myself that I'd give it a go again. The main thing about our team was that we never gave up.

'Those lads kept the whole thing going in the club. They got a lot of hard knocks but that only made them go even harder.

'Our team was relatively new to senior in 1974 and '75, and to get so close to winning encouraged the youth of the parish to think that anything was possible. To get back to the finals in 1982 and '89, even though it was disheartening to lose, was further proof that we were there or thereabouts.

'The unquenchable spirit and brave efforts of the men from the 60s, 70s and 80s laid a strong foundation for the teams that finally reached The Promised Land in the 90s.'

Another National League campaign beckoned, with Wexford back in Division 1. And Mick proved the main man once more in Wexford Park on November 28, when he shot five points from frees in a 1-10 to 0-6 win over Cork. It was his joint-highest scoring haul in a competitive game in a county jersey, matching the tally he recorded against Kilkenny in the Kehoe Cup final of 1977.

MICK CELEBRATED HIS 37th birthday in early 1983, with absolutely no intention of calling it a day.

If anything, he was improving with age, and the first three months of the year brought two more notable personal accolades, along with a losing National League semi-final appearance against Limerick.

First up he was named as a replacement All Star for Kilkenny's Ger Henderson – the only Wexford hurler called up for another trip to the States, his sixth in all. Along with his three awards, it was the third time for him to make the journey as a stand-in for an All-Ireland medal winner.

He didn't just travel to complete the numbers either, scoring two points and playing well as the All Stars lost the first of two games to Kilkenny by 1-16 to 1-13 in Gaelic Park, New York. It was back to his favourite haunt in San Francisco one week later, with the All-Ireland champions winning that one in the Balboa Stadium by 5-10 to 1-15.

After four super showings in the National League against Tipperary, Offaly and Clare (twice), Mick added another Sealink GAA Personality of the Month – the first person in the history of the scheme to be honoured twice.

That award was presented to him on the day before leaving for the All Stars tour, and he returned to play his part in a routine 7-18 to 1-13 Leinster Championship victory over Westmeath.

John Quigley came out of retirement to play his first game at that level since 1978 but, despite his subsequent haul of 1-5 in the semi-final, All-Ireland holders Kilkenny would deny Wexford by 5-13 to 3-15.

Mick, flanked in the half-back line by Rathnure's John Conran and James O'Connor of Duffry Rovers, remembers the recently-deceased Harry Ryan posing a lot of problems after appearing as a substitute in that game.

'Harry seemed to get plenty of room on the wing and linked up well with Liam Fennelly inside. He was quick, and a very good forward for a small lad. He was a difficult opponent to play on, and he was going all out to keep his place because it was hard enough to get on that Kilkenny team.'

THE YEAR ENDED on a farcical note, with Mick an unwitting victim of his own versatility. A well-intentioned competition was organised to raise funds for the Rehabilitation Institute, with supporters invited to pick their best Wexford hurling team from 1940 to '83.

It transpired that Mick got more votes than anybody else, and yet he didn't make the final selection!

It was Wexford's embarrassing equivalent of what happened to Brian Whelahan in 1994, when the Offaly great was named Hurler of the Year, but was omitted from the All Stars team.

In Mick's case, he was nominated for all three half-back positions, as well as midfield, with the spread of votes working against him.

The team chosen was – Pat Nolan; Bobbie Rackard, Nick O'Donnell, Tom Neville; Jim English, Billy Rackard, Willie Murphy; Ned Wheeler, Jim Morrissey; Padge Kehoe, Tony Doran, Paddy Kehoe; Oliver 'Hopper' McGrath, Nickey Rackard, Tim Flood.

Dan Quigley was quick to rush to Mick's defence. 'In Mick Jacob, Wexford had a player of style and real class,' he told Enniscorthy journalist Seán Whelan.

'He had been, unfairly and incorrectly in my opinion, compared with Billy Rackard from the earlier Wexford team in a recent "Best all-time Wexford team" poll in the local papers, and while I wouldn't agree with that, I certainly would put him on that team ahead of some of those voted on it.

'Mick's style is the kind I admire, and he would rank with any of the top players from any part of Ireland.'

THE CLUB SCENE in 1983 commenced with a hard-earned win over newcomers, Half Way House-Bunclody, followed by a one-point loss to Cloughbawn on the Sunday after that Leinster Championship exit.

And then, for just the second time, after a gap of nine years, Oulart-The Ballagh managed to beat Buffers Alley and exorcise some of the demons from 1982. It was only a group game, but it still meant a great deal to the players who had suffered so much at the hands of their neighbours.

The final score was 2-8 to 1-9, with the holders flummoxed by the unexpected decision to play the 40-plus Robbie at full-forward.

Another boost came when Glen Rovers travelled up from Cork for the Buffers Alley tournament final in August, and Oulart-The Ballagh beat them by four points.

'I always loved playing on that pitch in Monamolin,' Mick says. 'We hardly ever lost down there.'

Rathnure lay in wait again one week later, only this time in the quarter-final, and they were without the services of Dan and Martin Quigley, Jimmy Holohan and Jim Higgins owing to injury.

The odds seemed to favour Oulart-The Ballagh to repeat their 1982 semi-final win, but two lucky goals saw their hopes crushed on a 4-5 to 1-12 scoreline.

That would be Tom Byrne's last game in the club jersey, after a decade and a half of outstanding service. The All-Ireland winning Wexford minor captain of 1968 played with the county seniors from 1970 to '76, and finally in 1979, combining a stellar hurling career with the demands of being a prominent local government official.

He was Town Clerk in Wicklow in 1983, and after that defeat he decided to join his local St Patrick's club.

'Tom was a great player, and he did very well on 'Fan' Larkin a few times with the county team. His aunt was married to an uncle of ours. He was born in

Blackwater and came to live in Ballincash, so he went to school in Oulart.

'Tom was a big, solid man and a gentleman out and out... very intelligent. And a great stick-man. He could do anything with a hurl and ball.'

Six years later, Tom recalled his youth and his connection to the Jacobs in an article for the county final programme. 'I remember fondly carefree days spent around Ballincash and Scollough in the shadow of Oulart Hill where the Insurgents had one of their early victories to come when I would fleetingly cross the fields along the old Mass path to the House of Jacob (I mean, of course, the home of the illustrious Jacob hurling and camogie family) to catch a lift to John Doran's field at Mountdaniel.

'Those long balmy summer evenings were spent with the camán and sliotar, learning and practicing the art and skill of our ancient national game under the expert guidance and direction of Fr Frank Staples.'

The defeat to Rathnure arrived on August 21, 1983. Quite incredibly, Oulart-The Ballagh wouldn't play another senior club game until 1986, while it would be 1988 before Mick featured again in the grade.

The centenary year of 1984 was supposed to be one of joy and celebration for GAA folk, but it brought some dark days to the Jacob household in Oulartwick.

MICK'S FOCUS NEVER wavered as he diligently prepared for the GAA's big year of 1984.

'I started training away on my own in September 1983, the day of the All-Ireland final between Kilkenny and Cork. I said to myself that I will be really ready, and nothing would upset me.

'After work I'd put on my wellington boots in the evening and head off. There was about five or six fields I went to regularly. I went up hills and down hills, and sprinted on the flatter ground.

'I did that three nights per week, along with some training with Wexford as well. Murphys of Ballyboy are heavily involved with horses, and they had this sand-based gallop that I frequented.

'When I got to the top of the hill over there, I'd look down at night and see all the lights shining in The Ballagh. It was really tough getting up to the top through the sand, but then you could free-wheel down.'

It was a savage schedule, and even one of his fittest colleagues on the Wexford squad at the time baulked at the severity of the challenge.

Johnny Murphy had soldiered with Mick every year since 1974, as well as giving that one club season to Oulart-The Ballagh in '75. He was quite similar in build, lacking in height but a tough, athletic competitor with speed to burn.

'Johnny came with me alright one evening,' Mick recalls with a laugh. 'He said he'd never forget how tough it was. He told me he wouldn't come again and he stayed true to his word!

'I was supremely motivated to be in the top condition for championship hurling. To tell you the truth, I was never as fit in my life as I was going in to 1984 at 38 years of age.

'I had never put myself through such a tough regime like that before, even though I was always very dedicated to my personal fitness.

'The main thing in hurling is to keep yourself ticking over, and not to be putting on a stone or two either and then rushing to get fit again over a short period. I never drank or smoked, and of course that helped. And I'm glad to say I didn't need to either. I was still able to enjoy myself immensely and have the craic.'

Christy Keogh had the managerial reins for 1984, with Harry O'Connor coaching the team. Bernie Radford of St Martin's was a selector, along with a newcomer in Mick Kinsella from Marshalstown, and they used Mick sparingly through most of the National League campaign.

In fact, he was brought on five times, and his one and only start arrived at left half-back in a heavy final defeat to Limerick in Thurles. 'I finished that game at centre-back on Liam O'Donoghue and I got on well. You can't beat playing in the place you're used to more than anywhere else.

'At centre-back I knew exactly where I was supposed to be, whereas wing-back is a different job entirely. We were well beaten that day and could have no complaints; Joe McKenna got a couple of goals and we were never really in contention.'

At least Mick had been vindicated, holding his own when finally given the chance. He certainly hadn't let the side down.

'That would be Mick all over,' Robbie stresses. 'To be fair to the new selectors, they believed this lad probably still shouldn't be around at his age.

'It looked like the selectors were only picking him on the panel so as not to insult him, but the more he was kept out, the more willing he was to do whatever it took to get his place back.'

THE GAA INTRODUCED a new open draw Centenary Cup competition to give the year some added gloss, with Wexford pitted against Roscommon in Athleague on the Sunday after the loss to Limerick.

What should have been a routine opportunity to get that defeat out of the system will instead be forever remembered as one of the darkest weekends in the county's storied history. While most of the team made the long journey on the Saturday, Mick was busy on the farm, as well as dealing with the pitter-patter of tiny feet at home in Oulartwick.

The Jacobs had three young children at that stage. Michael was still a couple of months shy of his fourth birthday, while Helena and Rory ensured Breda needed all the help she could get from her husband.

'It didn't suit me to travel on the Saturday, so I went up in the car with Mick Kinsella and a few others instead on the morning of the game.'

'I was never as ashamed in my entire life. Everything went wrong that day.'

The final score was Roscommon 3-5, Wexford 2-7. Nobody could believe it back home, and the knives were quickly sharpened.

It soon transpired that several of the players had over-indulged on the previous night in a local nightclub. Christy Keogh was in the firing line and, with national journalists looking for an explanation, he inadvertently tarred everyone with the same brush.

A man of honour, Mick wrote a letter and sent it to both local newspapers in order to clear his name.

'As one of the Wexford hurlers who played against Roscommon on Sunday last, I would like to set the record straight by stating the following:

(1) I, along with some other players, travelled on Sunday morning, so we could not have been involved in Saturday night revelling in Roscommon.

(2) In a blanket condemnation of the team (Evening Press, April 16) Christy Keogh says that he couldn't pick out one player who seemed to be trying. They didn't show any degree of commitment or interest in the proceedings, he said.

I would like to refute that statement most emphatically. I have always been proud to wear the Wexford jersey and this is the first time in my career that someone has questioned my commitment to Wexford hurling.'

Supporters demanded a positive response to the debacle, and in fairness the players delivered against Kilkenny two months later.

'We had a really good meeting among ourselves after that and cleared everything up. If we didn't produce something after losing to Roscommon like that, I don't think we would have been able to stay in Wexford.

'The only way we could go was up. That left everybody fully focused for the championship.

'And maybe Kilkenny were saying to themselves that these fellas mustn't be up to much this year. It turned out we had a great win over them.

'I was playing right half-back that day, with James O'Connor in the centre and George O'Connor on the left. And Kilkenny played the type of game that really suited James. They kept putting high balls down on top of him and sure he mopped them up, he was a very strong man in the air.

'Martin Fitzhenry scored two great goals that day. Tony (Doran) slipped him in a lovely pass for one and got the other himself… having Tony back for the championship was a great boost.'

And his goal at the end will be remembered forever.

The 3-10 to 1-13 result marked the fourth and last time Mick contributed on the field of play to a championship win over Kilkenny, adding to the successes in 1976, '77 and '81 respectively.

'That was the day when all Mick's hard work over the winter shone through,' Robbie says. 'The man he was marking, Richie Power, was an All Star in 1982 and he was taken off.

'Mick had a training regime that nobody only a crazy man would follow. You'd have to witness it for yourself to believe it.'

JULY 8, 1984.

Croke Park.

Leinster hurling final day.

And Offaly!

It would be Mick's 158th and last senior appearance with Wexford, not that he could possibly predict that at the time.

It was the eighth provincial final loss of a career that yielded three Leinster medals won in 1968 (as a substitute), '76 and '77. While many publications credit him with one from 1970 as well, he wasn't part of that year's panel until the All-Ireland semi-final against Galway.

Offaly had the type of start in 1984 that most teams dream about, yet rarely if ever set in motion.

They posted the first eight points, with Pat Carroll absolutely flying at wing-forward just two years before his premature death at the age of 30.

'Pat was on song from the word go, and he must have got three or four points before John Conran went back on him and tightened the thing up.

'I was on Paddy Corrigan on the opposite side, and Robbie was after telling me how he didn't like a lad playing tight and close on him. His brother Mark came out on to my wing in the second-half.

'Diarmuid Healy was in charge of Offaly, and he had seen how Kilkenny operated against us, so he deployed the tactic of playing the ball wide and fast.'

It was an incredibly frustrating outcome, with Wexford battling back but coming up short by the minimum margin of 1-15 to 2-11 amid strong claims of a premature final whistle from Kilkenny referee Paschal Long.

'I knew I was in great fettle that year.

'I'm convinced we would have beaten them if we were quicker in making a few moves. It comes back to what I said earlier about specialised positions.

'John Conran was an out-and-out wing-back and Georgie was a born midfielder, and yet they started the other way around. The way Wexford placed their team that day really suited Offaly.'

That year, no different to any other, there was a club championship to concentrate on afterwards, although this one was somewhat different.

WITH EXTRA EVENTS on the schedule to celebrate the centenary, the county board reverted to a straight knockout championship for the first time since 1977 to ward off fears of a cluttered schedule potentially posing fixtures problems.

Oulart-The Ballagh knew from bitter past experience that they should never expect to get an easy draw. And when they were picked out of the hat to meet the winners from Buffers Alley and Cloughbawn in the quarter-final, they must have wondered if their luck would ever change.

The three-in-a-row seeking Alley duly cleared their first hurdle by 2-17 to 3-4. Three nights later, Mick and Breda loaded up the car with the three children and headed to the local field in Oulart for a challenge game against Naomh Eanna.

It was two and a half weeks after losing to Offaly, and Mick was looking forward to a good run-out with his clubmates as the latest test against the Alley was pencilled in for early August.

A summer's evening that started out brimming with promise is one he will never forget.

A freak accident on his favourite playing field in all of Ireland would keep him out of the game he loves for three frustrating years.

THE MATCH WITH Gorey was midway through the first-half when Mickey Sheil, one of the visitors' best-ever servants, threw up the sliotar and prepared to strike. Mick was close to the action but slightly behind an Oulart-The Ballagh colleague, who wasn't as quick to react.

Instead it was Mick who stretched out and made a partial block, but that meant he was fully exposed when the sliotar spun back towards Sheil. And when the Naomh Eanna man instinctively lashed on it again, it hit Mick full force in the right eye from no more than three yards.

Wearing a helmet always came naturally to him, as he was one of the first Wexford players to invest in some headgear when they became popular in 1970.

'It was something new and I tried it at training and quickly adjusted to it. Most lads put on a helmet that time and would take it off again after 10 minutes, but I felt comfortable wearing one.'

As well as being one of the classiest hurlers of his generation, Mick was always immaculately attired… Cooper helmet, jersey tucked inside his shorts… socks up to the knees, and shinguards in place.

'Robbie got a really bad belt on his shinbone one time, and the cut was very deep. I couldn't afford for the same thing to happen to me with all the farmwork, so I wore shinguards from that point on.

'They worked for me whereas they mightn't suit others. It just felt like the natural thing to do.'

Sadly, his helmet couldn't save him on that night in 1984, two years before someone had the bright idea of attaching protective bars to reduce the likelihood of facial injuries.

'It felt like someone had picked up a hammer and hit me as hard as they could with it.

'I got an unmerciful smack… a brand new ball, at full force… straight in the eye from three yards.

'My natural fitness stood to me when it happened. I stayed down for a few minutes with the shock.

'Eventually I managed to get up, but my cheekbone was shattered too. I didn't realise that at the time, of course. Somebody brought me by car to hospital in Wexford, and then I was transferred by ambulance to Waterford. I spent a fortnight down there, and had a couple of operations… one to repair the cheekbone.

'They told me the optic nerve was damaged in the back of the eye. It was eighty percent gone. If I close my good eye, even today, someone could be only three or four yards away from me and they'd be blurred.'

Breda notes her husband, 'had brilliant eyesight before it', and that was a saving grace.

'Yes, thankfully my left eye is very good, but there's a fog over the other one the whole time,' Mick adds. 'The pupil was dilated for a long time after it happened too.

'It was a big shock and a huge disappointment, but at the same time I felt lucky that I didn't lose the eye altogether.

'I was in unnatural pain, but the amazing thing was that it never drew even a trickle of blood and my face wasn't cut. I didn't have to get stitches, the ball just hit me straight in the eye itself.'

'Mickey Sheil met us later and he was so apologetic,' Breda says. 'It was totally accidental and everybody knew that.'

Robbie remembers Mick actually playing on in the seconds immediately after being hit, before the shock set in. 'He cleared the ball straight away, and only then did he go down.

'I would have rather seen blood, but he had got it full belt in the socket itself. I knew it was serious.'

Breda was immediately concerned too, and it wasn't easy dealing with the commotion that followed as she had three toddlers also demanding her attention.

Thankfully, a lifetime of watching games ensured she was able to keep some perspective. 'Michael already had the incident with the dropped eyelid at the Oulart pitch opening in 1980 but, like Robbie, I could quickly tell that this time it was worse.

'I went to Ardkeen with Michael's mother every single day when he was down there. Two specialists worked on him. One rebuilt the shattered cheekbone, while Mr Conlon, the top eye surgeon in Ireland, was very good to him.'

In a horrible quirk of fate, Ellen Jacob had two of her sons to visit in the hospital at the same time.

Christy had picked up a serious infection earlier in the year. And when the problem returned, he was readmitted to Ardkeen and ended up losing his left eye completely.

Sixteen years of working as a building contractor had taken a heavy toll. In an era when health and safety on sites wasn't prioritised like today, constant exposure to dust particles led Christy inadvertently down this dark path.

It seems the Oulart-The Ballagh club was jinxed when it came to eye problems. First Mylie Ryan, then this double whammy of Mick and Christy, while PJ Harris later lost an eye too in a car accident.

'Pat Hartigan of Limerick had to give the game up as well,' Mick says. 'It was planned to send him out of the country for an operation, but then it emerged that nothing could be done because the damage was to his optic nerve.

'The way Mylie suffered wasn't really in my mind after my own injury, because I didn't know how bad it was until a week or two later down in Waterford. The eye had closed up and swelled up so much by the time I got there, it was going to take a while to fully assess the damage.

'My teeth were damaged too, and I lost a good few after that. They spent a long time building up the cheekbone again.'

Breda recalls the anaesthetic having a long-lasting impact. 'He was very tired when he came home and that was unusual for him.

'They were after explaining to me fully about the damage by the time I came home,' Mick says. 'I used to sit there, shutting my good eye and seeing how far I could see with the other one. I was hoping it would come good again.'

The sad fact that this incredible servant didn't get to bow out of inter-county hurling on his own terms hit him hard.

'That part wasn't easy to deal with. I thought I'd have a couple more years at least with the county team, even though I was 38. It took a while to adjust to the idea that it was all gone.

'I had to adapt when driving and working too, and generally to get back into the real nitty-gritty of everything. For a while on the farm I was inclined to hit into things while I was going about my business, so I was hindered in that way.'

The prospect of a return to hurling wasn't even entertained in the immediate aftermath.

'It looked like playing ever again wasn't even a distant hope,' Breda says. 'With eighty percent plus of the sight lost, there seemed to be no way back.'

'It's a pity helmets didn't have safety guards that time, because it would have saved me,' Mick says. 'I firmly believe that no young lad should go out without a helmet, and never attempt to cut the bars out if it's affecting your vision.

'That even applies to a harmless puckaround, everyone should have their helmets on. Nowadays I see the children running out on to Wexford Park for a few strokes at half-time.

'I'm always fearful of an accident when I look at that, a stray ball could come out of anywhere. It will be too late to talk about it after a child's eye is gone.'

AS IF HIS enforced retirement wasn't enough to be dealing with, insult was quite literally added to injury by the county board in 1984.

With the Oulart-The Ballagh club left reeling by the loss of two of their star players, Mick and Christy, they sought a postponement of the game against Buffers Alley. They knew both wouldn't be back, but it was such an upsetting event for everyone in the parish that they needed a little time to come to terms with it.

When the club's request was turned down, they decided to concede a walkover as a means of protest.

'If that game was called off, it would have been a gesture that we would have appreciated,' Robbie says. 'It was like we were doubly penalised. Our players had given a lot to hurling, but we didn't get any sympathy.'

Mick notes Buffers Alley were willing to play the match another day. 'What happened was a fierce disappointment to me as a county player, and a terrible injustice to our club. They could have made a bit of an effort to help us.'

It got worse before it got better. As a result of conceding the walkover, the county board decided that Oulart-The Ballagh would be regraded to intermediate for 1985. And despite fighting that ruling to the bitter end in the boardroom all the way to Leinster Council level, the controversial decision stood.

'To lose our senior status in such a way was an unreal thing to happen,' Mick says. 'After fighting tooth and nail to reach the senior grade, to be put down again to intermediate in those circumstances was shocking.

'It would have done me and the club the world of good if they showed a bit of compassion. I really couldn't believe it.'

A CHANCE TO stay involved on the inter-county hurling scene came out of the blue. John Doyle of Buffers Alley won a vote to succeed Christy Keogh as manager in early September, and he turned to Mick for assistance.

A product of the hurling nurseries of Kilmore/Rathangan and St Peter's College in the late-50s and early-60s, John joined the priesthood and was a teak-tough corner-back on four senior title-winning Buffers Alley teams from 1968 to '76. He played with Wexford on just one occasion – in the National League quarter-final loss of 1971 to Clare, when Mick was at midfield.

In 1984, the by-then former clergyman sought out three giants of Wexford hurling to assist him as selectors. Mick didn't need to be asked twice when the opportunity arose to work alongside Padge Kehoe and Martin Codd, becoming the third Jacob brother to serve in this demanding role.

'The whole thing came out of the blue for me. John Doyle contacted me, and sure I was delighted to be asked. I went in to Padge's house one night for our first meeting, and we took it from there.

'There was no hope of me ever playing inter-county hurling again. In fact, there wasn't even the chance of any club hurling at that stage, so this was the next best thing. I said I'd go in and give it my best shot.

'I had hurled with a lot of the players of course, but that was never an issue and it didn't create problems for any of them or for me. I tried to do my best for the team and for Wexford, and I treated everyone the very same. I was just out to pick the best possible team.'

The gesture on John Doyle's part was much appreciated by Mick's closest confidantes.

'John thought outside the box a little bit in order to keep him involved. It was good for Mick, because he would have been in a complete vacuum other than that,' Robbie says. Breda is in full agreement. 'That was typical of John Doyle. It was very thoughtful and considerate on his part.'

Mick quickly learned that the sideline can be a lonely place. After Offaly romped home by 2-17 to 0-13 in the National League opener in Birr, reporter Mervyn Moore sought him out for a comment.

'We just couldn't match their fitness and it showed out there,' he lamented.

That was the first of four pre-Christmas defeats, with the only respite coming in the form of an 11-point home win over Cork.

A surprising bogey team emerged, with Wexford unable to respond despite being forewarned. Mick only met Laois three times in his own playing career, boasting a one hundred percent record from one championship and two league games.

The O'Moore men's vintage of 1984 and '85 was probably the county's best since their run to the All-Ireland final of 1949. It was the team of John Taylor, Pat Critchley and the Cuddys, and they had made it to the Centenary Cup decider against Cork.

A new-look Wexford first encountered them in Rathdowney on November 18, 1984, and the nine-point loss wasn't a pleasant experience. Although the team briefly rallied in the new year with wins over Limerick and Tipperary, the points gained were only good enough to force a relegation play-off, with Laois again providing the opposition.

The game was played on a quagmire of a pitch in Athy, directly after the Wexford footballers lost to Roscommon in a battle for promotion to Division 1. The scoreline of 1-8 to 1-4 in favour of Laois says it all. Already some knives were out and being waved menacingly in the direction of the new selection committee.

The salvation that a decent championship run would have guaranteed also eluded them. For the first time since 1941, Wexford made their exit to Laois, bowing out by 1-18 to 2-13 in Croke Park on June 23.

'I found it frustrating at times when I was a selector. At least you can do something about it when you're a player, but it's not as simple on the sideline.'

After stewing on the matter until November, the selectors came under fire when the county board debated 'The state of Wexford hurling'. John Doyle said, 'As far as I am concerned, I did my best and if that is not good enough, now is the time to change'.

Padge Kehoe reminded delegates: 'We are nowhere near as good as we think we are', adding that it was impossible to replace players like Tony Doran (who retired after the 1984 Leinster final), Michael Jacob and John Quigley in a day.

The selectors survived, when a notice of motion asking the county board to have their record re-examined was defeated by 28 votes to 6.

Being in Division 2 gave them an opportunity, 'To try a few different things, and to build up confidence by winning again', as Mick says.

Along the way they made up in spades for that Roscommon nightmare, putting eight goals past their Connacht visitors in Enniscorthy on a day when Martin Storey made his senior county debut.

Tipperary, the strongest opposition in Division 2, were hammered by 14 points in early 1986, and 'It was a good day's work' as Mick recalls, when Limerick were knocked out in the quarter-final in Portlaoise on a 2-12 to 1-10 scoreline.

Two meetings followed against Galway in Thurles, with Wexford well beaten by nine points in the replay. Overall, the signs were more encouraging than in 1985, but Kilkenny lay in wait in the Leinster semi-final and ensured the summer was over before it really started with a 1-21 to 0-18 win on June 1.

Martin Quigley, then 35, was recalled to the panel by the mentors after the league campaign and came on in that defeat. They also tried to entice another stalwart back, persuading 40-year-old Tony Doran to tog out for a May challenge game against Waterford in the Bannow-Ballymitty club grounds.

'We asked Tony in alright, because we thought he still might have something to offer,' Mick confirms. 'But after playing that day he felt himself he wasn't up to it any more, so he asked us not to consider him for the Kilkenny game.'

'If a player is hurling well enough, I think age doesn't matter. I used to always think in my own head that I was still only a young fella… I certainly never let it be a barrier to me.'

That 1986 campaign would be Mick's last as a Wexford senior selector. The county board moved fast on this occasion, and by mid-July the appointment of Wexford CBS principal Brother Michael O'Grady as manager, with assistance from Tom Neville and Tom Mooney, was ratified.

While it didn't go as he would have liked, it is worth noting that the 18 new faces given their first chance at senior level during his tenure included two All-Ireland heroes of 1996 in Martin Storey and Tom Dempsey.

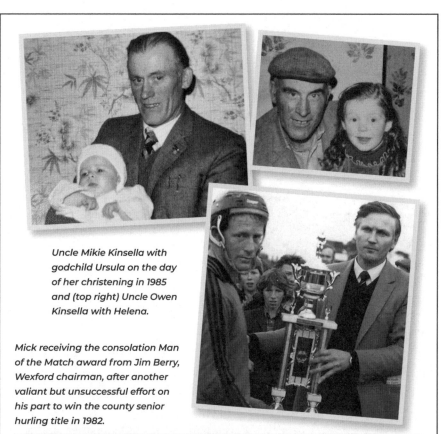

Uncle Mikie Kinsella with godchild Ursula on the day of her christening in 1985 and (top right) Uncle Owen Kinsella with Helena.

Mick receiving the consolation Man of the Match award from Jim Berry, Wexford chairman, after another valiant but unsuccessful effort on his part to win the county senior hurling title in 1982.

The Oulart-The Ballagh team on county final day in 1982. Mick won the overall Man of the Match, plus a second trophy for best player on the losing side, but that precious medal still eluded him.

« CHAPTER 9 »

A COUPLE OF purely random events, in late 1987, led to Mick Jacob's hurling comeback at the age of 41.

Big brother Robbie, four years his senior, was still enjoying his games in a less pressurised environment with the Oulart-The Ballagh junior team.

The club's second string hadn't won a title of any description since 1969, and there was no expectation that they would bridge that gap.

And then, like a bolt from the blue, they pipped Duffry Rovers in the Enniscorthy District final in mid-September, with the scoreline of 0-6 to 1-2 indicating a dour struggle. Not long afterwards, Robbie was out for a stroll in town one day and spotted something of interest.

'A company called Mycro had a new helmet on the market. It was blocky in shape and different to the Cooper design, but the big thing was that it had a faceguard,' Robbie explains.

'Straight away I thought of Mick, sitting at home and going mad to hurl again. He had accepted fairly well in 1984 that he couldn't play, but I felt this might give him a chance.

'I bought this blue helmet on the spot and arrived in Oulart with it. I put it on the table in front of him and said, "See what you think of that!".

'We had won the District title, and that convinced him to play the county semi-final against Shelmaliers a few weeks later. He got nearly another 15 years' hurling out of it after that.'

This new piece of equipment offered a lifeline that Mick was only too pleased to grasp. 'It was hard to watch when I couldn't play. I was itching to get back out on the field.

'That has never left me. Whether I was 50 or 60, I'd always think I could change the game if I was out there myself.'

Any visitor to Oulartwick popping their head around the living room door in late 1987 would have wondered if the man of the house had lost his marbles.

'He used to wear this new helmet with the faceguard for hours on end,' Breda explains. 'He wanted to get used to it and forget about having to look through the bars, so he had it on constantly at home.'

ED ROWSOME FROM Monageer-Boolavogue was a 13-year-old schoolboy in 1987, and strolled in to St Patrick's Park out of curiosity on October 4 to watch Oulart-The Ballagh playing Shelmaliers in the county junior hurling semi-final.

A couple of things caught his eye about one particular player wearing red and black.

'This fella had a Wexford shorts with the purple and gold stripes down the side,' Ed recalls. 'They're freely available to buy nowadays, but at that time you would rarely see them worn by anyone apart from a Wexford player.

'That grabbed my attention, but at first I couldn't make out who it was because he was wearing one of the new helmets, a blue Mycro. Soon enough I realised, though.

'Mick was back. What a wonderful sight. Every hurling follower was thrilled for him.'

Oddly enough, neither of the local newspapers picked up on the significance of his return. It was merely reported without any fanfare that Oulart-The Ballagh pipped the Shels by 0-7 to 0-6.

Mick wouldn't have wanted any fuss one way or the other. Just being able to swing that hurl again on a field for the first time in over three years meant the world to him.

'I didn't take much persuading when Robbie asked me. I wasn't after doing anything at all training-wise, but when I got the helmet I started pucking around at home.

'I was back where I started in 1962, playing junior again 25 years later after one hell of a hurling journey. It was a great privilege for me to be able to put on that Oulart-The Ballagh jersey once more in a county semi-final.

'The helmet made a huge difference, although it did take a while to adjust to playing again. I was relying a lot on just one eye, and I might not see a lad if he came towards me on my right side.

'But I wasn't nervous at all. Once I got back on the pitch I had no qualms about it, it was the very same as if I was never hurt. It was a great thrill to be able to get out there again and forget about all those things.'

Robbie says: 'It only took him 15 minutes to get his bearings'. Starting at centre-forward, he moved to midfield and met a real tartar in John Harding. The Shels man, son of Jack from the All-Ireland winning Wexford team of 1960, had won a Leinster junior medal earlier in the year and was an eager speed merchant.

After keeping tabs on the opposition dangerman, Mick never looked back, although another county medal would elude him. The drawn final with Taghmon-Camross in Wexford Park was a high-scoring classic, with Mick contributing 1-2 from midfield to Oulart-The Ballagh's tally of 5-10 that was matched by 3-16 from their O'Gorman-powered rivals.

The replay a fortnight later proved a bridge too far, as the opposition romped home by 5-11 to 2-3 to claim the title for the first time since 1949.

THE FIRST TEAM in the club had coped as well as they possibly could in Mick's enforced absence. After the shock of relegation, they bounced back at the first attempt with a win over Rathgarogue-Cushinstown in the intermediate final of 1985.

The next campaign was all about consolidation back in the top flight, and then in 1987 – with Mick part of the selection committee – they reached the semi-final but shipped a heavy defeat to Cloughbawn.

The last act of that year made the world of difference. A fortnight after the junior final loss to Taghmon-Camross, the under-21 team beat Buffers Alley by two points to capture a county title.

It was an emotional time, because two of the club's most promising young players – Anthony Stamp and Richard Ormonde – had lost their lives in separate accidents.

Mick, Christy, Aidan Moran and PJ Harris started their second term as senior mentors in 1988, buoyed by the promise shown by the young guns.

And after holding his own with the juniors, he was ready to step up to the big stage again. Reinventing himself as a corner-forward, Mick was a regular in a five-game campaign that ended in a two-point play-off loss to Cloughbawn after a disputed late goal.

It seemed like a natural progression to him, playing with the seniors again for the first time since 1983, now 42 years old. In fact, his fitness was so good that he started the third match in that championship at midfield, partnered by a 20-year-old Liam Dunne.

Mick's comeback story veered in a different direction in 1989. After his appointment as team trainer, he decided to step away from the playing side of things. 'I didn't want to put myself under pressure by doing the two. I'd rather be on the sideline looking at everything in that situation.

'And I didn't want people saying I was putting myself forward to the selectors to play just because I was the trainer, and maybe holding up the progress of a younger lad.'

After the seven-year gap between the club's county final appearances in 1975 and '82, history would repeat itself. The first sign that something was stirring again came when, in the space of two and a half months, an 11-point group game loss to Rathnure was transformed into a seven-point quarter-final win over the same opponents.

Oulart-The Ballagh owed Cloughbawn one after being knocked out by them in 1987 and '88, and they did the business at the third attempt with a 2-14 to 1-12 win.

Veteran Jimmy Prendergast was still going strong at full-back, with the three Dunne brothers and Martin Storey to the fore along with fresh new faces like Martin and Bartle Redmond, and Martin Dempsey. Another key figure was the late goalkeeper Dave Sinnott, a native of neighbouring Oylegate-Glenbrien who had represented Mayo and Connacht before arriving in the parish.

Mick was joined on the backroom team by his brother Christy, Pat 'Boiler' Dempsey and Peadar Mythen. All four had played in that previous county final against Buffers Alley in 1982, but something seemed different to Mick before this latest showdown.

'The lads were fairly relaxed, and there was less pressure on them maybe than in other years. The Alley had won the All-Ireland title on the previous St Patrick's Day, so that meant people weren't talking us up.'

Some club stalwarts were consumed by an unedifying thought – after all his years' service, wouldn't it be terrible if this most elusive of titles was finally won and Mick wasn't part of the squad?

MEDAL FOR MICK? ran one newspaper headline, with the story elaborating that plans were being hatched in the Oulart-The Ballagh camp to list him as a substitute.

Of all the county final disappointments in Mick's era, this was the one that Oulart-The Ballagh came closest of all to winning. When 'Butch' O'Connor scored a late goal to secure a one-point lead, the breakthrough was closer than ever.

However, an immediate pointed free from Mick Butler tied the final again. 'That game should have been won, the Alley looked beaten that day. We got a free right at the end and I'm sure Brendan O'Connor would have sent it over the bar.

'But a row started before it could be taken and referee Dickie Murphy blew for full-time. We had a chance to win, but our lack of discipline cost us dearly.'

And after Mick's name appeared again in the match programme for the replay, many neutrals were surprised that his services weren't deployed. It was another tight and very tense game, with extra-time required before Buffers Alley inflicted further misery on their neighbours with a 3-16 to 2-13 win.

'When Mick was asked to become trainer in 1989, it was a challenge he found difficult to resist,' Robbie says. 'He brought the lads to a high level of fitness, but I think it was a mistake not to bring him on.

'I'd have tried him in the full-forward line and I think he would have made a difference. Mick wouldn't have put his boots on just to get a medal, he would have done it to try to play his part in winning the match.

'Tony Doran played for the Alley in those finals and he was around the same age. And Mick's physical fitness was at a serious level for a man in his forties, but that factor wasn't taken seriously enough.'

The issue was ironed out over the winter, because Mick was both trainer and player in 1990, with the same trio of selectors still on board.

After starting the two group games at corner-forward, he was given a new role at left corner-back for the quarter-final against Cloughbawn.

The game ended in a draw, but the unthinkable happened for the replay in Bellefield six days later. Mick didn't make the team for a five-point loss, and his senior club career was finally over at the age of 44.

ED ROWSOME MARVELS at his idol's reaction to a call that raised many eyebrows at the time. 'Some lads would have sulked and stayed away altogether. Others would have stood up on the grass bank with their friends and given out about the selectors.

'But Mick wasn't like that. I'll never forget him that day, he was up and down the sideline urging the players on and trying to get the best out of them. He was still their trainer and that was all that mattered to him.'

Looking back more than 30 years later, Mick bemoans the fact he was shifted from attack to defence during that campaign. 'They wouldn't leave me in the one spot, and I think that's vital so you can settle in a particular position.

'I also felt that because I set my standards so high, they were all expecting that I should be super-human in every game, even at the age of 44. They were still judging me on what I was capable of before, but in fairness that wasn't going to happen again.

'That cost me dearly when lads were picking teams… they were looking for an unreal performance out of me every day.'

He may have been down, but most certainly not out. In fact, an entire decade still lay ahead in which he contributed immensely to the club's cause in the junior grade. Another dimension was added in 1991 when the GAA introduced a Masters competition for the over-40 brigade. Wexford immediately warmed to an event that combined the social and sporting aspects of hurling, and Mick partnered Jim Higgins at midfield when they beat Kildare to win the first-ever All-Ireland final in Carlow.

'I really enjoyed that competition. I had played with many of the lads with Wexford before, but we were joined by others who hadn't been county hurlers in their prime. It was a great kick for those lads to be in with us.

'I remember, on our way home that evening, Johnny and Mickey Connors marching down the road into their home town of Bunclody and carrying the cup. That All-Ireland meant the same to them as any one that was ever played in Croke Park in September.'

The following two years brought successive wins over Kilkenny in the Masters shield final, with Mick captaining the side from centre-back in 1992 when Robbie was on his right while Christy was a selector. In 1993, he hit three points from midfield in the decider when his partner was Dickie Nolan of Ferns St Aidan's.

He missed out on the next few years, simply because he was too busy with the club, but he did come on in the All-Ireland final of 1997 at the age of 51, when Kilkenny won by five points.

His second coming as a junior player yielded another Enniscorthy District medal in 1992. Thirty years after winning in that grade for the first time, he was joined at centrefield by Brendan Flood, one of six under-21 players on board for a seven-point success against the Rapparees in Farmleigh.

'I was playing on "Hacksaw" Murphy that night. It was a nice game to win, and good to see more young lads coming through.

'The seniors got to the final again in 1992 and lost to the Alley. They didn't score from play in that game, but we were building all the time. Fethard beat us afterwards in the county junior semi-final, and they had made it to senior with that team by 1995.

'The Rapps turned the tables on us in the junior District final in 1993, but we got on very well in '94. That year featured a fundamental change in how Wexford GAA went about its business. The tried and trusted formula of playing all junior competitions within the four Districts in order to produce semi-finalists was scrapped in favour of a countywide league-style championship.

And Oulart-The Ballagh warmed to the new system, emerging unbeaten from their group with wins over Blackwater, Clongeen, Tara Rocks, Craanford and St Fintan's.

Mick contributed 1-8 in the latter game, before posting 10 points from frees in a repeat victory over Blackwater in the quarter-final. He had reinvented himself as a centre-forward by this stage, and Oulart-The Ballagh went on to beat St Anne's before St Patrick's (Ballyoughter) halted their great run in the final by 0-13 to 1-5.

'I hardly had a night at home in '94. I was a senior selector and over the chaps, but the juniors were going well and I had to be there too. There was no such thing as missing training. We had a very good run and we weren't too far off it in the end.'

Ed Rowsome experienced, 'One of the greatest honours of my life,' when he marked Mick at midfield in a league game, fully 30 years after his father had put four goals past him. 'Mick and Tony Doran were my two idols growing up, so it was a privilege to be sharing the pitch with him.

'And he was such a gentleman on the field. The stakes weren't too high in that game, so he talked away to me during it and gave me tips on how to improve. I'll never forget it.'

In 1995, with the competition on a straight knockout, Oulart-The Ballagh fell to eventual champions Geraldine O'Hanrahans by four points, despite Mick's contribution of 1-1.

BY THE TIME the 1996 campaign came around, he was 50 years old but more enthusiastic than ever after watching Wexford light up the summer en route to that first All-Ireland since his maiden year of 1968. The sight of inspiring captain Martin Storey raising the Bob O'Keeffe and Liam MacCarthy Cups, and Liam Dunne adorning the No.6 jersey he had graced himself for so long, filled him with immense pride, while Paul Finn also featured in the campaign and came on in the final.

All local championships were delayed until late September as the county went wild. And the Oulart-The Ballagh juniors got off to a flying start when corner-forward Mick pointed four frees after whipping an early shot to the net to guide them to a 1-12 to 2-4 victory over Clongeen.

On October 12 in Hollymount, another family milestone put some gloss on a quarter-final exit to St Mary's (Rosslare). 'Here, you take that'... those four words marked 16-year-old Michael Jacob's introduction to adult championship hurling. The command came from his father and colleague in the full-forward line, so he duly obliged.

'We were against a gale wind and the free was at midfield. He wouldn't have let me take it if it was a handy one he could have tapped over the bar himself,' Michael jokes.

Mick is having none of it. 'Not at all, sure I had to give it to him to make sure he'd get at least one stroke!' Michael, one of the club's brightest young prospects, was only briefly passing through the junior ranks on the way to senior, although father and son did team up once more in 1997.

They manned the corner-forward berths in a replay win over Ballyfad and a quarter-final exit to Ballygarrett, with veteran Brendan O'Connor between them.

'We went out of it completely in the second-half that day,' Michael recalls. 'They brought daddy outfield near the end to try to rescue it, but it was too late.'

By 1998, Michael was with the seniors while Mick was ever-present up front in a junior campaign that featured wins over Tara Rocks, St Martin's and Blackwater, before a semi-final exit to Ballyfad.

The wheel turned full circle in quite remarkable fashion in 1999.

At the age of 53, and 37 years after his adult debut, Mick played his last junior championship game against the very same opponents.

Neighbours Blackwater always tended to rise to the occasion against Oulart-The Ballagh, and the identity of their trainer lent an even keener edge to proceedings.

'Mike Carroll asked me to come down and give Blackwater a hand that year,' Robbie recalls. 'We had a bye in the first round, and then Oulart beat Clongeen by a couple of points to set up the derby meeting.

'It was played in Monamolin, and Mick was corner-forward on John Whelan. He got a goal early on at the top end of the field from an opportunist one-handed flick.

'I think John was a bit over-awed playing on him, but eventually Blackwater settled and squeezed through by a point. That was a huge win for them, and they got great encouragement from it. They would go all the way to the junior title two years later.

'Mick was a competitor to the last, though. I remember him being thick with me coming off the field for being involved with Blackwater!'

NOBODY CAN SAY with any degree of certainty when exactly Mick called it a day because, true to form, he didn't make any song or dance about it. There was no formal announcement, and no fuss of any description.

Rory never played alongside his father, but he has a clear memory of the pair togging out as substitutes for a game played in St Patrick's Park in 2000.

He also recalls a goal Mick scored in Bree that stayed in his memory. 'A ball broke off Brendan O'Connor at full-forward, and he struck it first-time off his right hand-side… low into the left-hand corner. He was always on to me to do the very same any time I got into a similar position.'

When Blackwater repeated the previous year's championship outcome against

Oulart-The Ballagh in the summer of 2000, Mick wasn't involved. The curtain was finally drawn on a quite magnificent playing career at the age of 54, although there is a suggestion that he did briefly mount a comeback at 56!

'I could have played on for another few years but I decided enough was enough,' Mick says. 'I wanted to concentrate on the under-age and I had been involved a lot as a senior mentor too, so there was an overload of things going on.

'I suppose I never really gave up hurling as such, because I was always down in the field with the young lads. I got great enjoyment out of it. I loved every minute of it and had unbelievable craic.

'I would have loved to go on forever, I enjoyed the game so much. But I didn't make any major announcement or anything when I finished up, I just went off in my own quiet way.

'I never made a big deal about it, and I wouldn't want anyone else making a big deal about it either.'

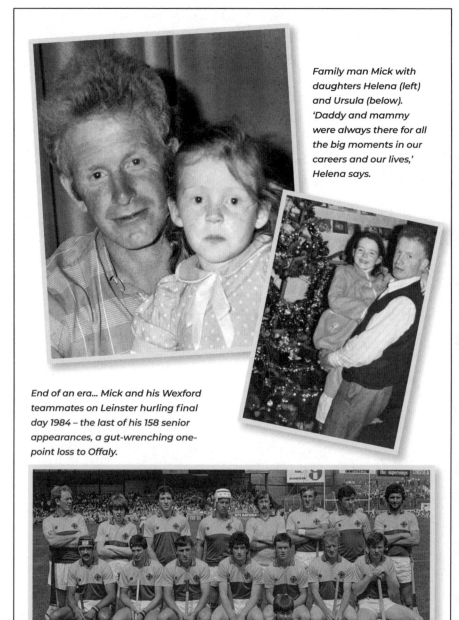

Family man Mick with daughters Helena (left) and Ursula (below). 'Daddy and mammy were always there for all the big moments in our careers and our lives,' Helena says.

End of an era... Mick and his Wexford teammates on Leinster hurling final day 1984 – the last of his 158 senior appearances, a gut-wrenching one-point loss to Offaly.

« CHAPTER 10 »

THAT LONGED-FOR first senior hurling title seemed as far away as ever on the evening of October 25, 1992. Confronted yet again by Buffers Alley on county final day, there would be no repeat of the close-run two-game saga from three years before. Oulart-The Ballagh lost by 1-11 to 1-5.

Their entire tally came from placed balls, courtesy of centre-forward Brendan O'Connor (1-3) and centre-back Liam Dunne (0-2). With 19 minutes left they trailed by 0-10 to 0-1, and it was one of the more forgettable encounters between these keenest of neighbours.

They usually produced sparks of some description, but not this time.

For Mick, it was his last chance to win a senior medal as a player. Wearing the No.19 jersey, in all truth the panel's most decorated veteran was never likely to feature. He was 46 years of age at the time, and it made more sense for Oulart-The Ballagh to bring on the younger duo of Pierce Redmond and James Ormonde for some county final experience.

Given the Alley's clear superiority from an early stage, there was more value in keeping Mick in reserve so he could remain eligible for the following month's junior county semi-final – lost to Fethard by four points.

Robbie would manage that 1992 side, assisted by three of the Jacobs' staunch teammates of the 60s in Mylie Ryan, Tony Byrne and Johnny Murray. And although the final was a complete write-off, he still picked out some positives from the inevitable post-mortem in the parish.

'In 1991 the seniors ended in a relegation play-off and only got out of it after beating Crossabeg-Ballymurn in a replay,' Robbie remembers. 'From that point of view, getting to the final the next year was a big achievement.

'I also felt it was a serious help to get back to that stage just three years after our last appearance. We had waited seven years from 1975 to '82, and another seven years then until 1989. That junior team of Mick's was going to produce a few new players too, so it wasn't all doom and gloom.'

In 1993, the veteran netminder Henry Butler turned a late shot from Martin Storey over the bar, and Buffers Alley duly survived to win a quarter-final clash by 2-11 to 2-9. It would prove the last sting from a dying wasp.

Oulart-The Ballagh weren't involved in the semi-finals, but the outcome from that double-header in Wexford Park on the last Sunday in September suggested change was afoot.

Rathnure and Buffers Alley, the traditional big two and persistent barriers to outright success, were dumped by Cloughbawn (the eventual champions) and Rapparees respectively. All other contenders took immense heart from those results, although the riches that would follow were still frankly unimaginable.

That 1992 county final brought title number 12 to Buffers Alley, but it would also be their last thus far.

IN 2016, WHEN Oulart-The Ballagh retained their crown against Cloughbawn, they climbed above their arch-rivals – second now only to Rathnure (with 20) on the roll of honour.

Thirteen senior championships between 1994 and 2016 – it exceeded Mick Jacob's wildest dreams, and it included a history-making five-in-a-row from 2009 to '13, never achieved before in the annals of Wexford hurling.

Ask anyone from Oulart-The Ballagh and they will respond in kind – the first win was the most important, finally exorcising those nagging demons of the past and unleashing the torrent of success that would follow.

And not surprisingly, Mick's handiwork was all over that breakthrough title in 1994. The appointment as senior manager of Tom Neville, his former Wexford colleague, at that year's AGM would prove one of the best decisions ever made by the Oulart-The Ballagh club.

'I had no involvement in Tom being approached, even though I knew him so well from playing with him and against him, and also playing under him when he was a Wexford mentor,' Mick says. 'After he got the job, he asked the three of us – myself, Jimmy Prendergast and Willie Sunderland – to join him as selectors.

'Players realised straight away that he meant business. He had won the All-Ireland club with St Martin's of Kilkenny in 1985 so that got them on board pretty quickly. He was big on discipline, and we needed that. Tom was coming from Carlow every night, and Willie was travelling from Newbridge, so their commitment rubbed off on everyone.'

Tom set up a system whereby players had to attend a specific doctor and physio, enabling him to keep a direct handle on everything happening on the injury front.

'That needed tightening up, there was no such thing as a lad faking anything after that. Tom knew the entire story then, and nobody could hide.'

Players quickly realised that special treatment would be a non-runner. Fifteen places were up for grabs from game to game, and every man stood a fair chance of selection. Three or four different faces were introduced, with John Cleary and John Rossiter forming a new and effective midfield partnership.

'Lads knew they had to train seriously and be fully fit to be picked. The team was freshened up, it was quite young but there was a good blend of experience there too.'

Ever the optimist, Mick started with the same positive outlook he had deployed since Oulart-The Ballagh's very first senior campaign 25 years earlier. 'I'd always be thinking this is going to be our big breakthrough. There was very little in a lot of the games we lost, so I'd take every match as it comes.

'I did feel we were gelling well and putting in a lot of good work. The improved discipline was noticeable, there was no more retaliation and fellas were a bit smarter. It was clear that the players were out to impress Tom and the selectors.'

The 1994 senior championship would start as it finished, with Oulart-The Ballagh meeting St Martin's. A draw was secured after Martin Storey equalised with the second-last puck. The record was unblemished for the rest of the five-game group, with wins recorded over holders Cloughbawn by three points, Half Way House-Bunclody by nine and Rapparees by seven, before Rathnure were pipped (1-17 to 0-19) in mid-August.

Momentum was building steadily, and the quarter-final gave Storey another chance to showcase the speed and accuracy that made him virtually unmarkable in club hurling at the time. His exhibition in Gorey, securing seven points from play, resulted in a repeat win over the Rapps (2-11 to 2-7).

Huge interest surrounded the semi-finals, with Rathnure the only team left with senior titles to their name, but they were dismissed by St Martin's.

Earlier that afternoon, Oulart-The Ballagh came up against a Crossabeg-Ballymurn side appearing at that stage for the first time. And in what *The People* described as a *rousing tussle*, a calmly-taken individual goal by 17-year-old Jonathan Mythen with 13 minutes left proved the key score in securing a 3-12 to 2-9 success.

'That tight game was a big help to us for the final. We had to win it under a lot of pressure, and it proved one thing to the lads… if we stuck at it again in the same circumstances, we'd get through.'

A POIGNANT SCENE unfolded after that match, one that is still repeated to this very day after any Oulart-The Ballagh success. Mick could tell he had a willing participant and a child full of enthusiasm when Stephen Hayden – son of his good friend Johnny – attended training for the first time.

By 1992, Stephen was full-forward on the club's under-21 team in a Premier county final loss, but it only took a traumatic few seconds for his life to veer sadly and tragically off course.

In December 1993, a tyre he was working on exploded, causing a permanent brain injury. His prospects of a long career in the red and black of Oulart-The Ballagh were cruelly taken away, now confined to a wheelchair for the rest of his life and in need of constant care.

That semi-final of 1994 was the first game Stephen was able to attend after his accident, watching from a car parked on the old grass bank behind the Clonard end goal in Wexford Park. And once the action was over, the players hightailed it to Stephen and made him feel part of this special day.

It established a pattern that neutrals have come to admire over the years, a sure sign of a parish looking out for one of its own.

'Stephen always had a very good attitude and great drive when I trained him. He played a lot of games at corner-back and there was no drawing back in him.

'If anyone around Oulart is ever feeling a bit sorry for themselves, they should have a think about Stephen to put it all in perspective. He had his whole life in front of him when the accident happened, and yet he never shows any bitterness. His attitude inspires a lot of people.'

The Jacobs and the Haydens go back a long way, and there's a special bond between Mick and Johnny, Stephen's father, who makes sure his son never misses a club match. That connection was strengthened in 1967, after the entirely innocent Mick was struck for his troubles following the county semi-final win over Craanford. Johnny wasn't having it when he saw his old schoolmate and Rackard League colleague from 1958 – the most sporting player in the parish – subjected to such an unwarranted attack.

He was the first spectator in to defend him, putting the boxing skills he had acquired in his youth to practical use with a neat left hook.

'Johnny has always been a great clubman,' Mick says. 'He's at every match with Stephen, and he's kept the sod on the pitch in super nick since it opened in 1980. He takes huge pride in that, either doing the job himself or supervising someone else. The Haydens give generous sponsorship every year and are great fund-raisers as well.

'The Haydens are all special people, Johnny and Irene, and Stephen and his sister Janette. They are an example to everyone in the way they face and overcome adversity.'

Johnny continued to soldier on in spite of being immobilised somewhat by a stroke, and Mick was delighted in 2020 when the club selected him to be their award winner at the first Enniscorthy District presentation night.

Happily, those joyous scenes with the Haydens and the players would be repeated over and over in the years after 1994.

COUNTY FINAL OPPOSITION wasn't provided by either Buffers Alley or Rathnure, but that didn't have a major bearing on the players' attitude in the build-up as Mick recalls.

'We were thinking more in terms of our drawn game with St Martin's in the first round. Two teams with no experience of winning a final were meeting, so it all boiled down to who would take their chances better on the day. We had a fair idea it would be close again.

'The goal Martin Redmond got in the first-half was a huge boost. Rory McCarthy did a lot of hurling for them and it was nip and tuck for the whole game.'

An estimated crowd of 10,000 thronged Wexford Park to witness the crowning of a new champion.

And the game dished out drama in spades, with the sides level no fewer than 10 times before centre-back Liam Dunne landed a mighty point from an 80-yard free via the fingertips of rival goalkeeper Terry O'Dowd with one minute left.

St Martin's had two late chances from frees, but both were sent wide to leave them trailing by 1-14 to 0-16 on the scoreboard.

And at precisely 4.36pm on October 16, 1994, one last toot of referee Brian White's whistle and the spreading of his arms set off some of the most ecstatic celebratory scenes ever witnessed at the venue.

TEARS, CHEERS AND raw emotion.

Oulart-The Ballagh people swarmed on to that field as if freed from a lifetime of oppression. It was, without question, the greatest moment in the club's history, a breakthrough that would transform club hurling in Wexford for ever more.

'It was an unreal feeling,' Mick says. 'After all the struggles, we finally made it. I felt huge relief, because if the Martin's had scored a few more frees we mightn't have been champions. I thought to myself... *Thank God we had the luck today.* You'll never win a tight final without it.'

'Our crowd and players went absolutely crazy out on that field. It was 25 years of frustration all unleashed in the space of a few minutes,' Robbie says.

Breda made her way down from the stand to join that joyous sea of red and black. 'I remember meeting himself on the pitch and it was just wonderful. It was the fulfilment of a dream, an ambition realised... something they had worked so hard for.

'There was relief mixed with elation. I remember thinking... *So this is what it feels like to win a senior county final.* We were one big, happy family out there, and it was great to be able to share it with the older people. Men like Bobby Walsh, Lar Dempsey, Mikie Murphy, Paddy Doran, John Storey, Paddy Pender, Phil Redmond, Martin Leacy, Mike Nolan, Tony Sutton, Fintan Cooney and so many others who had given their lives to the club.

Robbie reminisced on the early days when Mick and the remainder from their era longed to be like the title-winning clubs such as St Aidan's, Rathnure, Buffers Alley, Shamrocks, Faythe Harriers and Geraldine O'Hanrahans.

'We came from very humble beginnings, out of a farmer's field in Mountdaniel. Finally getting to join those great clubs on the roll of honour was a fantastic feeling to be fair. We had come through a lot of tragedy too. Stephen Hayden's accident was devastating. Pat Reddy, who won the intermediate title with us in 1985, had died since of motor neurone disease. And then there was Robbie Sinnott – the one man above all others that I was so disappointed wasn't still around to witness it.'

Robbie died in August 1992, but the presence of his daughter Catherine Dunne-Hendley as club chairperson lent a suitably poignant air to those 1994 celebrations.

'It was lovely that Catherine was in the chair at such an auspicious time, a nice connection between herself and her father,' Breda says. 'She expended every ounce of energy to make sure things were done right. It was a very onerous task.'

Catherine was MC when the hordes made it back to Oulart village after a celebratory meal in the Talbot Hotel. And when she handed Mick the mic, he was already thinking of the future: 'Let's have more success. Don't just stop at this,' he declared to roars of approval.

The Jacobs were delighted when Tom Neville selected corner-back John 'Rocker' Stamp, one of the unsung heroes of the team and a very honest hurler, as his Player of the Year. 'John was a real driving force,' Mick says.

'He was playing junior with me at one stage, and it was like an All-Ireland between the two of us at training. There was great heart in him, he was driving on the whole time.'

TOM NEVILLE'S PAST experience with St Martin's in Kilkenny ensured a serious approach was taken to the club's first Leinster campaign.

'Tom let them celebrate for a while, but then he was all set on playing the next game,' Mick says. 'We prepared well for Camross of Laois, we knew it was going to be tough. We had met them before in a good few challenge games and they were hardy men.'

A Pierce Redmond goal sealed a 10-point victory on a very wet day in Wexford Park, before Kilkenny champions Tullaroan were brushed aside in what Neville regarded as the team's most complete performance of his tenure.

In a tight, low-scoring final against Birr, it required a rather fortuitous Martin Storey goal to earn Oulart-The Ballagh a draw against the All-Ireland runners-up of two years earlier.

'Our chance was maybe gone after the first day,' Mick laments. 'They might have taken us a bit for granted, but they were better prepared in the replay. Experience alone stood to them in a big way… they had Brian Whelahan, Daithí Regan and the Pilkingtons, all in peak form.

'Offaly were All-Ireland champions too. The biggest problem the second day was that we conceded three goals to leave us a good bit down. John Cleary got a goal back early in the second-half but we couldn't get any closer than three or four points; Birr weathered the storm.' As first ventures go, it was a decent showing overall. And, as Mick had always believed, after finally discovering what it's like to win, Oulart-The Ballagh proved difficult to stop.

'When we finally won the title, we all got greedy like Buffers Alley and Rathnure.'

A key date in the journey was January 8, 1995. The delayed league final of the previous year took place in Gorey, and Oulart-The Ballagh were men on a mission.

They were always likely to prove too strong for Buffers Alley after that extended run in Leinster had carried them through to early December. Still, the 3-15 to 0-3 demolition came from a team intent on showing who was the new boss in this never-ending battle for bragging rights.

Indeed, the landscape has altered to such an extent that the Alley have only beaten Oulart-The Ballagh once in championship hurling since. That occurred in a group game in 2009, and even then the tables were clinically turned on county final day with a five-point victory for Michael, Rory and their teammates.

That came two years after one of the most pleasing outcomes of all – when Buffers Alley were beaten by 4-14 to 2-6 in the decider of 2007, Rory collected the Man of the Match award 25 years after Mick got the same accolade for his heroics in defeat. Oulart-The Ballagh have taken on all-comers and proven their worth, with the spread of final victims a source of pride. Of their 13 county titles, four were won against St Martin's, along with two apiece versus Buffers Alley, Rathnure and Glynn-Barntown, with Faythe Harriers, Ferns St Aidan's and Cloughbawn completing the list.

That's seven of the leading lights of Wexford club hurling defeated in other words, with just four final defeats along the way, to St Martin's (twice), St Anne's and Rathnure. And while Mick's direct involvement as a selector was confined to the first three wins, his fingerprints were all over the others too as every player had come through his under-age training regime.

There was no margin for error in 1995 as the championship reverted to knockout format, especially when the first round threw up a repeat of the previous year's final pairing.

'The Martin's were all out after losing, but it was easy enough to motivate our lads,' Mick recalls. 'That draw got us switched on immediately, and there was a fierce ambition to do it again after getting a taste for winning.'

Having recorded a two-point victory, the holders beat Duffry Rovers by three in the quarter-final before setting any lingering Oulart/Alley arguments aside once and for all. With Paul Finn contributing seven points from play, a 0-19 to 1-10 win sealed a clash with first-time finalists Glynn-Barntown.

'We were more relaxed and confident, whereas they were in the same position we had been in during my playing days. It's just so hard to get over the line and win the first, but when it happens it's such a huge weight off the shoulders on the bigger occasions.

'It took 25 years of hardship before we got our first, so the two-in-a-row was special for everyone.'

The one big regret from 1995 is that the Leinster title eluded the club for the second year running. After coasting past Castletown of Laois and Kiltegan from Wicklow, a Glenmore team packed with Heffernans, O'Connors and Phelans got the job done by three points in Carlow on the last Sunday in November.

'We didn't play well in the first half-hour and were seven points down,' Mick recalls. 'We made a couple of changes at half-time, bringing Brendan O'Connor on and moving Paul Finn to midfield, but we couldn't make up the difference. The two easy games beforehand didn't help us at all.'

The young Jacobs switched vantage points and witnessed an Oulart-The Ballagh onslaught, but sadly it wasn't enough. 'Myself and Rory went up behind the goal we were attacking,' Michael says. 'We had all the play, and if the game had gone on five minutes longer I think we would have got something out of it.'

That year did end on another high, with Seán Dunne scoring what is still regarded as one of the best goals ever seen in Wexford Park. He finished a flowing team move that started deep in defence as the club defeated Rathnure to complete another league and championship double.

It was a reward for Tom Neville's 'silent hurling' drill in training, whereby players would be tasked with passing to a colleague who wasn't allowed to shout for the ball. It honed instinct, awareness and positional sense, and it bore rich fruit in that game.

WHILE RATHNURE WOULD end their three-in-a-row bid in the championship semi-final of 1996, the club scene was almost an after-thought in a county revelling in All-Ireland glory.

The involvement of captain Martin Storey, Liam Dunne and Paul Finn ensured Oulart-The Ballagh were in the thick of the celebrations.

'It was hard to get going after the All-Ireland,' Robbie says. 'Maybe they took their eye off the ball, but I think there was going to be a natural dip anyway. That group had put in such a huge effort to win two titles, so I don't believe it was in them to win another one in '96.'

Stung by the loss of their crown, Mick and his fellow mentors demanded an even bigger effort from the squad in 1997. Comfortable wins over Half Way House-Bunclody and Oylegate-Glenbrien were followed by the first big test in the semi-final, when a miraculous Martin Storey point 'with three lads hanging out of him on the sideline' secured a draw with Faythe Harriers.

By now Michael was 17 and a substitute in his first year with the seniors. 'Larry O'Gorman scored an unbelievable point from a free to level it up, but we made it through in extra-time,' he recalls of a game featuring the performance of a lifetime from Bartle Redmond at midfield. 'We prepared very well that year, real old-school type training.'

Those two clashes with the Harriers were the stand-out matches in that campaign. A second final victory over Glynn-Barntown in the space of three years followed, with the key score arriving two minutes from the end when a fluffed point-scoring attempt from a Paul Finn free ended up in the net (2-11 to 0-14).

'Mick and the boys made a shrewd move that day in Bellefield,' Robbie recalls. 'Willie Carley was playing wing-back on Martin Storey and doing a good job. Our selectors brought Storey to midfield and Carley followed. Martin got a run on him near the end, and Seán Dunne also finished the game well.'

Preparation was always essential for Mick on the sideline. 'I'd be a fierce thinker about the game and would have worked out possible changes in my head beforehand. I'd consider things while working on the farm, and even in bed I'd be lying there plotting and planning.

'That move certainly worked out in the 1997 final. If a decision had to be made, that would be it, no going back. There would be no point in lads arguing about it... that didn't happen with us. You must be decisive on the sideline.'

The Castletown team Mick and company would prepare for in the Leinster first round of 1997 had improved beyond all measure since the one-way traffic of two years earlier.

A drawn game in Rathdowney brought the sides back to Bellefield, on an afternoon that will be remembered for the misfortune that befell Liam Dunne, his team's star centre-back.

The Man of the Match winner from the county final was in the form of his life, but he broke his leg in an accidental collision during the first-half. Oulart-The Ballagh, leading by 0-5 to 0-3 at the time, ended up losing by 1-8 to 0-10.

'It gets to players when that happens to one of the best men on the team, a great leader. It was a dog of a game, but nobody had much stomach for hurling after that incident. Even after the match, there was concern for Liam more so than disappointment at losing.'

THE STRICKEN CENTRE-BACK grew up idolising the parish's most favourite son. 'On a Sunday morning, people went to Mass in Oulart to pray to God. I went to Mass to meet my God, and that was Mick Jacob,' Dunne says.

He modelled his own game on his hero, and in time he would follow in his footsteps by winning an All-Ireland senior medal and three All Star awards.

One of the biggest thrills of Liam's life arrived in 1980 when he jumped at a personal request made to him by Mick, who was training his under-14 team at the time.

When he was asked to accompany him to the field in Oulart, and hit the sliotar back as he practised his free-taking, it was like a dream come true. 'This was the big time now. I was Mick's Mini-Me and delighted to be, thank you very much,' he wrote in *I Crossed The Line – The Liam Dunne Story*.

'Although I was only 13 at the time, the truth is I idolised the man and was thrilled to be asked to bang a few balls with him.'

The pair would go on to play together on the club senior team in 1988, before filling instrumental roles on and off the field during the breakthrough years.

However, the tale would take an unexpected twist at the next club AGM, when Tom Neville and his successful backroom team were voted out for 1998 after winning three senior titles in four years.

Bitterness isn't part of Mick's nature, and he accepted it and moved on. He had more than enough to occupy himself anyway, given his ongoing massive commitment to the Bord na nOg teams.

'They broke up the winning package we had, and it took a good while to get it back. We got everyone pulling in the one direction, but things were a little bit disorganised after that.

'We had moved Oulart-The Ballagh ahead of the rest of the county in terms of preparation. Hours were spent on video analysis, and then we'd go up to Carlow to pick the team with Tom Neville.'

Mick's last involvement with the club as a senior mentor arrived in 2003. After losing out to Pat Herbert for the manager's role at the AGM, he agreed to work with him as a selector.

However, the ex-Limerick defender vacated his position three weeks before the championship started, and the club would exit to Rathnure in the quarter-final.

With Rory and Michael heavily involved by that stage, Mick felt it was more prudent to step away and leave them to it.

He did spend two years mentoring Helena and Ursula as manager of the camogie team. After winning the county final of 2007 with a spectacular showing versus Rathnure in Wexford Park that yielded 4-23, the title was relinquished in a repeat meeting 12 months later.

In between there was a three-year stint as a Wexford under-21 selector from 2004 to '06, with Kilkenny inflicting three successive defeats. The first (with Rory as captain) and the last were by clear margins, but the 2005 semi-final produced a superb effort that deserved greater reward.

A star-studded Kilkenny team, powered by Eoin Larkin, Michael Fennelly, John Tennyson, Richie Power, Michael Rice and 'Cha' Fitzpatrick, were extremely lucky to emerge from Wexford Park with a 2-13 to 0-15 win.

Near the end, and with the outcome hanging in the balance, Stephen Nolan – who was reared on Noreside – took a penalty and hit it with such force that it broke goalkeeper Damien Fogarty's collarbone on its journey over the bar.

'We completely underperformed in the 2004 Leinster final,' Rory says of his last year in the grade. 'The big factor was that the game was played three days after Wexford won the senior title. We weren't as focused as we should have been.'

Mick remembers a good display in a challenge against Tipperary set the team up for that brave bid to surprise Kilkenny in 2005. 'Andrew Kavanagh from our own club outplayed 'Cha' that evening, it was an awful shame he didn't stay at it because he was a senior-class player.'

His period on the sidelines with Davy Morris, Cormac Quinn and Len Hall ended after an early exit to Kilkenny in Callan in 2006. 'I enjoyed it very well, we put in a lot of work over the three years.'

Rory harbours one big regret from his father's lifetime involvement in the game. 'It's a pity that over the years he hasn't got an opportunity with some county team to put his own complete stamp on it as manager.

'When you're a selector, everything is still at the behest of the main man. Daddy went for the manager's role in 2004, and he was asked to go in with Davy Morris then when he didn't get it.'

Michael adds that 'when Seamus Murphy got the under-21 job in 2001, daddy went for it as well'.

A very enjoyable three-year stint as an inter-provincial selector with Leinster yielded a couple of titles. Nickey Brennan of Kilkenny, a long-time opponent, chaired the provincial council from 2002 to '04 and appointed Mick to serve along with goalkeeping great Noel Skehan and ex-Offaly defender Aidan Fogarty.

Their reign started on a bright note, with a Leinster team including Wexford pair David 'Doc' O'Connor and Colm Kehoe pipping Munster by 4-15 to 3-17 in the 2002 final in Nowlan Park.

The big highlight arrived one year later when the title was successfully defended against Connacht in the Giulio Onesti Sports Complex in Rome, with Rory featuring at corner-forward.

It was the first overseas trip as officials tried something different to boost an ailing competition. And if he hadn't retained those sharp reflexes from his playing days, Mick could have been stripped of his spending money!

'We were with the other officials on the train when it was attacked by pickpockets,' Breda explains. '"Rackard" Cody from Kilkenny was looking after the gear on the trip, and his wallet was robbed. Some locals saw what happened and the police recovered the wallet, but he lost some stuff.'

As for Mick, he had a narrow escape. 'I felt a hand going into my pocket so I drew out with an elbow. That was the end of that!' Rory, who would add a second inter-provincial medal to his collection in 2012, has fond memories of 'an unbelievable trip', flying out on a Thursday and returning on Sunday after a Saturday final that also featured Liam Dunne and 'Doc' O'Connor.

'There was great spirit in the Leinster camp and we had a very strong team. Henry Shefflin was playing, Brian Whelahan, Liam Dunne, Tommy Walsh, Brian Carroll, Rory and Gary Hanniffy. The game was played on some class of a rugby pitch and it was as rough as could be, but there was big competitiveness in it. Both teams took it very seriously.'

Mick's last involvement with Leinster arrived in 2004, when their semi-final loss to Munster was a curtain-raiser to the International rules contest between Ireland and Australia in Croke Park.

Michael, who played that day, would go on to feature on the title-winning teams of 2006 and '09, with the latter final played in Abu Dhabi.

'After winning six Railway Cups myself – three on the field and three as a substitute – it was nice that Michael and Rory won two each. And that trip to Rome was the highlight.

'To me, the inter-provincial series is a fantastic competition and it was one of my greatest honours to win it as a player and a selector. I got to play with and against some of the greats of the game from different counties.

'Being a selector for three years with Noel Skehan and Aidan Fogarty was very enjoyable and a huge learning experience. To select the winning team in 2003 from the cream of the crop in Leinster and to win the competition in Rome – the first time that it was played abroad – was extra special. I hope that the GAA will consider reinstating the competition, because it is still loved by all of the players.'

In another fitting gesture from the provincial council, Mick's service on and off the field would be acknowledged in 2016 with his induction into the Leinster GAA Hall of Fame, just a few months after his appointment as Oulart-The Ballagh club president.

With Rory, Seán and Michael after the twelfth of Oulart-The Ballagh's 13 county senior title wins in 2015 (left); selector Mick and manager Rory with the spoils of success following the club's under-21 victory in 2013 (below).

Mick, Stephen Hayden, Peadar Murphy and Johnny Hayden (below) – four happy Oulart-The Ballagh men after the club won that elusive provincial title in 2015; receiving his Leinster Hall of Fame award from John Horan (Leinster chairman) in Croke Park in 2016 (right).

« CHAPTER 11 »

THERE'S NOTHING UNUSUAL about a prominent GAA player giving something back to his club in a coaching capacity. In most cases, it's par for the course, a natural progression.

However, some people go above and beyond what is expected of them, and Mick Jacob stands tall in that regard.

A couple of aspects of his coaching journey merit particular praise.

First of all, he didn't wait until his playing career was over before lending a hand. Instead, at the height of his fame with Wexford in the 70s, he was combining a busy schedule of games and training with looking after the under-12 hurlers in the parish.

Success didn't come easily at the outset, but an outstanding structure was put in place by Mick, his wife Breda, and Oulart national school principal Breda Flood.

The Rackard League's role in improving the young hurlers in the parish was nurtured by Fr Frank Staples from 1959 until his departure in 1974, and all three were conscious of carrying on that proud tradition.

Mick's growing passion for this aspect of hurling was reflected in the profile of QUIET MAN MICK in *The People* before the All-Ireland senior final of 1977.

Though it's nice to get a break, Mick is never happy too far away from the game and just recently he has branched out into coaching, the piece noted. *He has taken an exceptional interest in the young boys of the area and is anxious to impart some of his knowledge to them.*

On two evenings a week and also on Sunday mornings he is to be found surrounded by over thirty boys, all listening intently to his every word. One day they may backbone Oulart's and perhaps even Wexford's challenge for further honours.

IN MAY OF 1978, prior to his wedding, the under-12 boys were pictured in the newspaper making a presentation of a tea set to their diligent trainer.

And he returned from his honeymoon in time to watch with pride as the Rackard League team won a replayed county final against Ferns in early June. After getting a taste for coaching, Mick never looked back.

'I nearly got more pleasure out of it than playing myself or winning those All Stars,' he admits. 'I got a great kick out of working with all those young lads down through the years… they gave so much in terms of commitment.'

The Rackard League title in 1976 would mark his first big achievement as a coach, with a team including Martin Storey, Seán Dunne and John Rossiter bridging a 13-year gap since Jimmy Prendergast had captained the parish's first-ever winners. The dedication displayed by the hundreds of players that came under his wing was replicated in spades by Mick himself, and that's the second aspect of his coaching career that merits special credit.

The amount of time he gave to the cause was on another level entirely. And this reached a peak in the period from 1992 to '97 when – still assisted by the two Bredas – he trained every single club team in both hurling and football, from under-12 up to and including minor.

'Luckily, with Michael being a farmer he wasn't tied to specific times for work,' his wife says. 'He could be in the pitch to take one team from 4pm to 5pm, and then do another one at 6.30pm… and a third at 8pm. There was a hell of a lot of commitment, but the three of us made sure any overlapping was kept to a minimum.'

The successes enjoyed were off the charts, with Oulart-The Ballagh winning All-Ireland under-14 Féile titles in 1994 (with Michael as captain) and 1997 (when Rory was a star attacker) on teams that included future Wexford stars Darren Stamp, Anthony O'Leary, Paul Roche, Keith Rossiter, Des Mythen, Stephen Doyle, Dennis Morton, Lar Prendergast and Andrew Kavanagh.

After securing the under-12 hurling Roinn 1 crown in 1992, the club stepped up to Premier ranks and gathered an incredible six championships on the trot – the first five with Mick as trainer.

Ursula got in on the act in 1997, scoring one of the goals in a dramatic one-point win over Half Way House-Bunclody, when her teammates included future All-Ireland winning camogie colleague Mary Leacy.

Bear in mind that during that timescale, Mick was also a selector with the seniors and playing with the juniors. And when he moved away from the lowest grades in 1998 – with Martin Storey, Brendan O'Connor and Tom Whelan capably taking up the reins – he continued to work with the juveniles and minors.

A new selection team of three was formed along with Sgt Brendan Moore and Fr John Jordan, and the results were every bit as impressive from the off, with a first-ever juvenile Premier title plus a minor Roinn 1 win in 1998.

That juvenile crown was retained one year later, while Oulart-The Ballagh made further history in late November with a replay victory over St Martin's in Bellefield. The club had never won a Premier minor crown as a single parish unit prior to that contest, so it was a sensational breakthrough.

A QUICK GLANCE at that teamsheet from 1999 reads like a who's who of some of the most skilful and talented hurlers to represent club and county.

Rory was centre-forward on a side that also featured his next-door neighbour Keith Rossiter, Darren Stamp, Des Mythen, Paul Roche and Stephen Doyle. All of them – and hundreds of others – were moulded into hurlers of renown by the special coaching talent of Mick Jacob.

'Daddy's tactics were always spot on,' Rory says. 'In 1998 we played New Ross in the juvenile final and we were lucky enough to get a draw. Their centre-back Mark "Bull" Rellis was very strong, so The Three Wise Men devised a puck-out strategy – before there ever was a puck-out strategy!

'Before the replay, our midfielders were instructed to pull out wide. Kevin Stamp was moved to centre-forward and Paul Roche, our full-back, was told to drill every puck-out low and directly in front of him. It worked a treat.

'The following year, we drew with Faythe Harriers in another juvenile final. The plan they came up with for that replay was to put myself, Des Mythen and Colin Sunderland – three of the stronger players – across the half-forward line to counter-act their tactic of double-marking Des.

'And then in 1999, 'Gizzy' Lyng did a lot of damage for St Martin's in the drawn minor final in New Ross. Daddy decided to put an unheralded player Brian Martin on him to follow him everywhere for the replay, and he did a great job.

'That was always a big strength of daddy's, when he'd get a second chance he'd generally get over the line in the replay. He'd always learn a lot from game to game.

'Nobody would be allowed to drop their standards, and daddy wouldn't be afraid to lay it on the line to players either. For example, at half-time in the replayed juvenile final of 1999 in New Ross, myself and Kevin Stamp were told in no uncertain terms that we had to take over in midfield. None of us got any favouritism from him over the years.

'But lads responded to it, because they had so much time for daddy. He'd be tough on you when it was needed, but it was all underlined by a massive respect that cut both ways.

'From the time we were eight years old, training would start on time... there would be no messing, and everything would be done right. That created a great camaraderie.

'We were all the one, and every young lad had a great pride in playing for the club. When you look back on the videos from that time, you can see the reaction of players towards daddy after finals. The bond was always very strong.'

Mick adds: 'That year in 1999 was very special. To win the top grade of juvenile and minor was something the club had never done before. Those lads were a great group to train and they had a huge will to win.

'We had strong players right throughout, not just the big names. That under-16 final in '99 was of the highest standard. The Harriers pushed us all the way and it took huge commitment, desire and great belief and skill to get over the line.

'Six of those juveniles went on to play a prominent part in us securing the very first Premier minor title for Oulart-The Ballagh. Those victories in 1998 and '99 gave the club a great platform to build a very strong senior team again, and on the 2004 senior championship winning team 10 of them were starters and seven were amongst the substitutes.

'That began the most successful period in Oulart-The Ballagh's history which featured the unique Wexford five-in-a-row (2009-'13) and the Leinster Club Championship in 2015.'

'THE FIRST YEAR I got involved, Michael Bracken was school principal in Oulart,' Mick says. 'He moved back to his native Clare, and it really took off then when Breda starting teaching there, and Breda Flood was appointed principal.

'It had started before that with Joe Hyland getting me on board to help with class leagues after school. Breda Flood put me in charge of some coaching then when she replaced Mr Bracken.

'And my involvement grew more intense as the years moved on, especially with Breda teaching there. And of course when our own young lads started playing, there was an added dimension.'

The children of the parish moved from the building Mick frequented himself in the late-50s to the newly-built Scoil Mochua in September 1985.

And when the Rackard League titles started to flow, and the club grew dominant on the Bord na nÓg scene, it was cherished all the more because it didn't happen overnight. 'We won again with the school in 1981, but it took a while to make an impact with the club,' Mick says.

Breda remembers 1983, when a team that included Martin Redmond, Declan Stamp and Stephen Hayden beat Rathgarogue-Cushinstown in an under-12 final.

'We didn't get to any Bord na nÓg final then until 1991, and the parents made a huge fuss because it was so long since the last one. We lost that game, in under-12 football, but in 1992 we beat Our Lady's Island in the under-12 hurling final and that was the start of an exceptional era.'

On one particularly busy and memorable county final day in October 1993, a double-header in Hollymount saw 10-year-old Rory winning an under-12 football medal before 13-year-old Michael played in goal on a successful minor hurling team.

'We didn't really spend time playing hurling in school, it was always after hours when Mick could schedule his farmwork around it and come with us,' Breda says. 'Breda Flood was club secretary as well as being principal, and we formed a great partnership. It evolved from the school teams, and we began doing the club sides as well.

'We were well organised and always knew what was coming up next. All three of us did a certain amount of coaching, but Michael did the real donkey work.

'And we were lucky in the calibre of people we were able to attract to Oulart for our medal presentations. DJ Carey came down at the height of his career which was lovely to see, and Mick O'Dwyer had a captive audience of young lads sitting around him one night while he gave out advice. We had another memorable night when the late, great Joe McDonagh, president of the GAA, attended.'

ONE PARTICULAR VISIT by an outside team left a lasting impression on the man himself. 'Sixmilebridge from Clare came to Oulart for the national Féile in 1984 and it was a real eye-opener. Davy Fitzgerald was in goal, and they gave us an awful hiding.

'I said to myself... *This is the standard we have to get up to.* From that day on I really worked hard on the lads, hurling off both sides and doing things at speed. After watching Sixmilebridge blow us away, I knew we needed to push hard and really get down to business.'

When it came to coaching, Mick possessed a thirst for learning. Just because he was a star hurler, there was never an assumption on his part that he knew it all.

In 1978, Breda attended a coaching course in St Peter's College organised by Mick Kinsella, her husband's fellow All-Ireland medal winner from 1968.

The guest speakers included Fr Bertie Troy from Cork and Limerick's Michael O'Grady, who was a Christian Brother at the time and would later manage Wexford. Mick took great interest in the course content and determined to put some new ideas into practice.

Mick's own views on how to approach the game were always eagerly sought, and he wrote a compelling article on 'The role of the defender' for *Coaching News* in 1985.

The closing paragraph contained advice he swore by himself throughout his career: 'A player should learn something from every game. If an opponent outplays you or out-wits you in any particular situation, think about it calmly after the match, and plan how to counteract that particular move when next confronted with it.

'This will undoubtedly improve your game as well as keeping you looking forward to the games ahead.' Every eager youngster coached in the field in Oulart became well versed in the art of what Mick refers to as 'line hurling'.

'That was always my starting point. I'd spread the players out in lines right up the field, and then do a good bit of ball work. I tried to sharpen them up for a game situation, so the first lad would hit it to the next in his line.

'He'd have to control it then, and move it on at speed. I'd get them to do it off their right side and left side, and all the basic skills would be covered. I would get them to use the ball, and to concentrate. And if a mistake was made, I'd blow the whistle and show them how it should be done.'

That's where Mick really came into his own, given his playing background. It also guaranteed him a captive audience. If some of the children hadn't seen Mick play, their parents would at least have told them about this three-time All Star in their midst.

And if a young lad didn't want to take wise advice on board from their club's own hurling hero, then it was clear that the game simply wasn't for him.

That didn't happen very often to be fair, with Mick marvelling at the dedication shown by his troops over the years. He was relentless in getting the very best out of the more limited players, because Oulart-The Ballagh rarely had the luxury of large numbers.

'We only had seven boys in Rory and Keith Rossiter's class, for example,' Breda says. 'And when we won the first Féile in Limerick in 1994, Des Mythen was only 11 and starred at corner-forward.'

'Winning that was a huge boost for the club,' Mick notes. 'It was Division 2 but we would have probably beaten most of the Division 1 teams. We stayed in Bruff and beat Na Piarsaigh of Limerick in the final.'

'We were only allowed 20 on the panel but it was a fantastic weekend,' Breda adds. 'We had Willie Harris driving us around in the mini-bus. We were on a shoestring budget, but we made sure every player had three or four hurls tied together. That created a big impression on the opposition when they saw our lads getting off the mini-bus.'

RORY HAS FOND memories of his father putting him through his paces from a very young age. 'The first thing about going to the field with daddy was that it wasn't acceptable for anyone to be late. And when we were there, everyone was trained properly.

'He'd have four lads spread out the length of the field doing his line hurling, and the two in the middle would be going flat out. They were learning all the skills and developing their fitness too without realising.

'And if some lads were struggling, daddy would slow the drill down and work through it with them. He was very good at developing a weaker player, and he was prepared to spend time with them because he knew the club hadn't the luxury of numbers. Some lads who took a while to get the hang of it ended up playing with me in senior finals.'

The pair would combine off the field with very impressive results in 2013, with Rory the manager and his father a selector on the under-21 team that won the county title with 24 points to spare over St Martin's.

Mick believes the opening of the new pitch in 1980 worked wonders for the overall development of the club. 'We were grateful to John and Kathleen Doran for the use of the field in Mountdaniel for so long, and it served us well, but the location wasn't ideal.

'But now we had our own place in the village of Oulart, so it was easier to get to and there was always plenty of supervision around. Parents were happy when they dropped their children off to train or let them travel down on their bikes.

'It took up a lot of my time, but I got a great kick out of it. I'd leave things on the farm for a few hours most nights, and go back then afterwards to finish the work after training a few teams. I was fully committed, so I made sure they gave the same commitment too.

'There's something magical about heading away from everything and going down to the field for some hurling. I used to love it myself even before an All-Ireland final or a county final... getting a few pucks in before I'd go to Croke Park or in to Bellefield. In the early days I used to do that puck-around with my sister Bridie.

'I'd nearly be able to know from that if I was going to play well in the game itself, I could judge my form and my mood. I used to encourage the young lads to do that as well.

'I was always preaching to them to never give up; even if you're 10 or 15 yards off your opponent... keep going because he could drop it. I wanted them to compete for everything, and I was determined that there should be no fear factor.

'Instilling the winning mentality was essential.'

HURLING HAS TAKEN up a large chunk of Mick's life, but it's not his only pastime.

As an avid Manchester United fan, it means he usually has the bragging rights in any discussions with Michael and Rory, who both support Aston Villa. Mick has travelled to Old Trafford with his good friend Peter Keane, although he had neither the time nor the inclination in his playing days to line out with The Ballagh United FC, the current tenants of the old hurling field at Doran's in Mountdaniel.

Before lockdown he was a regular with Breda and friends every Wednesday night at the bingo and dancing sessions in *The Porter House* in Castlebridge. With their good friend Joan Doyle working behind the bar, and John Kenny supplying the music, he was usually one of the last to leave, although future visits will never be the same after Joan's sudden death in January 2021.

The loss of such a popular and much-loved figure – mother of Stephen, the ex-Wexford hurler and one of Mick's protégés – rocked the Oulart-The Ballagh club to its foundations.

'Michael would mix with everyone. He can be the life and soul of the place and he never seems to get tired,' Breda says. 'He'll talk to everyone and dance with everyone too, the quick-step and old-time waltz are his favourites.

'Michael has a very good way with people. Covid in 2020 and '21 sadly put a stop to his visits for the time being, but he was always very caring if someone asked him to call to a person living on their own.'

His love of dancing saw him team up as one of 12 couples with Catherine, mother of current Wexford hurler Shaun Murphy, for the club's 'Strictly' fundraiser some time ago.

'He still jeers me about that,' Ursula says. 'I was dancing with Dean O'Connor, and he loves reminding me that himself and Catherine got to the final but we didn't.'

'He hurled all his life for the club, and then he danced for them,' Breda adds. 'The club would use him a lot in other areas to raise funds, and Michael would always sell plenty of tickets. He loves dancing anyway, so it was no trouble to him to take part.'

'There was a lot of work in it but it was very enjoyable,' Mick says. 'We had three dances to perform so there was practice every night for a long time. Going down to Castlebridge every week when we're allowed keeps me young. And if there's no hurling or football on the TV then I love sitting here on the sofa listening to country music; Mike Denver, Patrick Feeney and Derek Ryan especially.'

For the most part, though, it's the great outdoors rather than the comforts of home that continue to hold the most appeal.

A DOG-LOVER since his earliest days on the farm with his uncles, Mick has also traversed every nook and cranny around the parish he knows so well through his lifelong passion for hunting and shooting.

'We always had a very good sheepdog on the farm to bring the sheep and cattle along the road, it was essential. You wouldn't need four or five of them if you could train one to do a really top-class job. I'd take him with me to bring in the cows for milking.

'I became good friends with men like Tim Flood, Norman Deacon and Toddy Lambe, who were all very big into the dogs. They would come around and do their trialling with my sheep in the fields.

'I had that same interest from the time I went to work on the farm with my uncles at the age of 14. I used to train sheepdogs and then sell them on to people. I picked up a lot of tips from Tim and the lads on how to go about it in the right way.

'It was something completely different from hurling and I always loved it. It was good for the mind when you weren't thinking about the game non-stop, and of course there was great exercise in it too.

'I always had a few terriers on the go as well. I'd go out hunting rabbits when I was a young fella with Peter Murphy, who was an uncle of Martin Storey. Money was scarce at the time, so we used to head out at night to catch a few and sell them to a man named Dobbs in Enniscorthy.

'It was a great pastime to have, out in the dead of night with only a searchlight and a dog. It was like being in another world, and it also meant I had a bit of money in my pocket. Peter was a neighbour, and he used to travel around on a motorbike with me on the back. He'd be revving her up going around corners, and then he'd burst her down the hill in The Ballagh.

'If anything happened the two of us would have ended up in the ditch. We always had a spade, and thank God it never got into the spokes. It was great craic.

'A lot of hurlers were into their hunting that time. Men like Tom Ryan and Padge Kehoe from the 50s team used to come out to me and we'd head off into the fields.

'I was out one night with Paudge Courtney on top of Hurlers' Hill and this rabbit appeared. I turned the light off and poor Paudge ended up in the briars and bushes beside me.

'Martin Codd was a big man for hunting after rabbits too; Lar Rigley of the Shamrocks and the Rapparees was another, he was one of the fittest lads around.

'I loved the relaxation it gave me away from hurling and all those I've mentioned felt the very same way, it was great to have an outlet like that. You wouldn't be thinking about hurling when you were out hunting – you wouldn't be thinking about anything really.

'Other times I would go off hunting foxes with Batt Earle. We'd often walk four or five miles before we'd come across them.'

One such journey – after his dog was attacked – got Mick and a neighbour into strife, leading to a court prosecution that made the national newspapers in June 1991 and resulted in a £100 fine for an incident involving the death of a badger.

'Going after rabbits was a big thing for us in the winter,' Rory says. 'Nearly every Saturday and Sunday a crowd would leave the house with daddy and Robbie – the four of us, Robbie's three lads (George, Jim and Bob) and Keith and Mark Rossiter from next door.

'You could be gone for three or four hours every night, and there was no such thing as daddy waiting for you. He'd head on with the lamp, and the rest of us had to keep up with him.

'A group of lads from Bunclody would come down… Johnny Connors along with his band of brothers. They'd all set off with the dogs around Oulart Hill, so delighted to be going out hunting with Mick Jacob.'

'I used to head away with Tom Dunne also,' Mick remembers. 'His two biggest chaps Tomás and Seán loved it. They still talk about it… the nights out lamping. It was good for young lads to get out there and develop their fitness, you could easily walk six or seven miles on any given night.

'Myself and William O'Connor would go beyond Blackwater village… down by Ballyconnigar. Poor William had no sense of direction at all, but I had a fair idea where I was going all the time. It was full of rabbits on the sandy land near the sea. The two of us would go after foxes as well whenever they threatened the lambs.

'I always had a pointer or a setter for pheasant shooting season, and sure I knew the whole area like the back of my hand. One day I was after walking a good bit with Mick Ryan, who would die at a young age, God be good to him.

One of us shot this big cock pheasant and it was in very swampy land, but Mick didn't know that of course.

'I said to him, "Go in there Mick and get that". In he goes anyway, and he must have sunk down four or five feet into the ground before I ran in to pull him out. I laughed my heart out that day, with poor Mick walking beside me and the sound of the water squidging in his wellingtons.

'Peter Keane is another big shooting friend of mine and a great character, he's still a fierce Buffers Alley man. We can't get it out of him, even though he's living in Oulart a long time now and his wife Anne is a daughter of Batt Earle and from the parish.'

Mick seldom misses a Thursday night in Peter and Anne's house, where they have fierce craic. 'Uncle Owen was a great friend of Anne's parents Batt and Lil, and was there every night. I'd go over on Thursday night and there'd be all sorts of characters there – lads like the late Patrick Flynn, Jim O'Connor and Teddy Sinnott, along with Matt Flynn, John Quigley, Garry Morton, Dean O'Connor and Robbie.

'It's always a very welcoming house, with copious supplies of tea, cakes and tarts, and lots of slagging and winding-up by Peter. Lil was the heart and soul of the place and she loved all of the people calling, even though she was unmercifully teased by Peter and his cronies.

'WE WERE OUT one Sunday shortly before he was due to have a cataract operation. After a few minutes this cock pheasant appeared, but Peter never budged.

'I said to him, "Did you not see that? There must be something seriously wrong with your eyesight". "Wait until I get this job done, I'll miss nothing after that," he replied.

'I'm fortunate that I still have good sight in my strong eye, although I do have reading glasses and distance glasses now. I only got them a few years ago... the distance ones are a bit of help when looking at matches alright.

'There's great relaxation in getting out there with two good dogs, and then watching them working together and backing each other up,' Mick says. 'I had two really good hunters one time that I got as pups from Tommy Foxton and Tom Martin, one terrier was whole white and the other was black and white.

'Silver and Jock were two of the best sheepdogs I ever had, they were unreal around the farm. It takes a good bit of training to get the dogs attuned to minding the sheep, but the best ones have a great brain for work.

'They'd be able to go to the top of the field and bring the sheep down to me. Their lifespan is usually around 15 years.'

Rory reckons no more than four main dogs have been used on the farm in his lifetime... Jock, Silver, Brandy, and Fly, the current incumbent.

'A lot of the working dogs only react to daddy's voice. They're trained on that, and they know who's boss,' he says.

The dogs are always kept over at the main farm buildings and never at the family home in Oulartwick, with one exception, Belle, a miniature Jack Russell that was given to Breda nine years ago. Belle is spoiled rotten by everyone in the house, and is given free rein indoors. Even Mick does not expect her to earn her keep, or know her place. She repays them all with her affection, devotion and absolute cuteness.

Some evenings, Belle and Mick can often be found asleep together on the sofa.

Mick with his dear friend Joan Doyle – post-Covid trips to The Porter House for bingo and dancing will never be the same after her sudden death in January 2021; despite his best efforts, Mick has been unable to convert Buffers Alley stalwart Peter Keane (below) into an Oulart-The Ballagh man.

Mick at the top of his beloved Oulart Hill.

« CHAPTER 12 »

MICK AND BREDA added a fourth bundle of joy to the household with the birth of Ursula, and with Michael, Helena and Rory already clamouring for their parents' attention, it made for a hectic home life in Oulartwick.

And there was a remarkable symmetry with the previous generation of Jacobs, given that Mick and his three siblings also arrived in a five-year timespan from 1942 to '47.

The only difference was the even split between boys and girls this time, in contrast to Bridie's childhood in Coolnahinch when she had three older brothers looking out for her.

There's nobody better placed than Breda to turn to for an appraisal of Mick's qualities as a father and as a person.

'He was always a really good daddy, very hands-on. He was proud of the way he could comfort them when they were upset, or how he could get them to fall asleep in his arms. And the children loved the rough and tumble of his play with them. His bedside stories were noisy, and full of adventure, involving rabbits, foxes and birds.

'Mick lives his life the way he hurled, with total honesty. What you see is what you get. He's very humble and unassuming; he'd never boast about anything. He's also big on loyalty, to his family, his friends, his club… his teammates.

'There's not a negative bone in his body and he has no time for bitterness, begrudgery or jealousy towards others. He's got a great love for his native place and takes immense pride in the achievements of its people, sporting or otherwise.

'Mick also has a boyish sense of fun. He's always up for the craic. His energy is boundless, and he still thrives on physical work. He might be known for his grit and determination but, at heart, he's a big softie, especially when it comes to those he loves.'

As soon as the children could stand, they were up and down to the fields with him.

'We have a fairly long living room, a sort of indoor pitch. When he was trying to recover from that serious finger injury, I'd hit balls down the room to him so that he could improve his grip.'

And after the children took their first steps, that was where their natural ability with stick and ball was nurtured too.

'Michael took to hurling very early, from the time he could stand up. He had the grip, the eye and the stance… you could tell he had a firm grasp of the basics,' Breda explains.

'Rory was more into football at the start and loved watching Mikey Sheehy of Kerry, his favourite player. He cried when he heard Mikey had retired, and asked me to write a letter to him and plead with him not to stop.

'I did as I was instructed and Mikey sent back a lovely reply. We met him many years afterwards at an event hosted by President Mary McAleese, and he remembered that letter from Rory.'

Although hurling would quickly take over, Rory did have the distinction of being the Oulart-The Ballagh club's only dual county minor since Tom Royce in 1966 when he was selected for both Wexford teams in 2000 and '01.

'From the time they were toddlers, the four of them couldn't wait for daddy to come home for a few strokes as we called it,' Breda says.

'And when we travelled anywhere, the youngsters always brought the hurls with them. If we passed by a pitch on the way home and the gates were open, then we had to go in. Their daddy was the biggest child of all in the car. Getting him away from a pitch was the hardest part.'

FOUR YOUNGSTERS HAVING fun and learning in the company of their father – Mick had direct experience of this simple pleasure from a child's viewpoint himself prior to George's untimely demise in 1956.

It made him all the more determined to cherish every second he could muster with his children. And amidst all the fun, he was delivering important messages about the game along the way.

'Getting the skills right is one of the hallmarks of Oulart-The Ballagh hurling,' Breda stresses. 'The concentration on skills training was always close to Michael's heart. We're firm believers in the old saying that, "Perfect practice makes perfect".'

'The four lads were exactly like us when we were small, out on the lawn,' Mick adds. 'That was the place to pick up all the tricks and the movements, and to learn about the game and how to fight for your own ball in tight situations.'

'Daddy had a great way of developing your instinct completely for the game,' Rory says. 'Think of all the outstanding hurlers that he brought through the system. Liam Dunne was a product of daddy's… Michael here was a very skilful hurler, then you had Darren Stamp, Keith Rossiter… Martin Storey.

'And I have to add in Des Mythen and Stephen Doyle, probably the two most naturally skilful players to come from Oulart-The Ballagh. The talent all those lads had didn't just fall out of the sky.'

Ask any Wexford supporter to produce a highlights reel from the past 20 years, and two contributions from the Jacob clan are guaranteed to feature prominently.

First of all, the Leinster senior hurling semi-final of 2004, when Michael blocked Peter Barry's attempted clearance at the Canal End, turned and buried the sliotar in the Kilkenny net in one swift movement, bringing a crest-fallen Brian Cody to his knees.

And then eight years later, at the same spot in Croke Park, Ursula scored one of the best goals ever seen at the venue, a stunning first-time pull into the top left corner of the net against Cork that powered Wexford to a third All-Ireland senior camogie title on the trot.

The instinct and natural ability required to perform such feats may have been nurtured over many years by various mentors, but the starting point was on the lawn in Oulartwick with the man they all refer to with an endearing warmth as 'daddy'.

The children were fortunate to share in some wonderful experiences in their formative years. With Mick so heavily involved, they had ringside seats for the club's breakthrough in 1994 and picked up lots of worthwhile lessons along the way.

'When Tom Neville came in, the four of them used to go down every night to the pitch,' Breda says. 'They knew their place, they wouldn't interfere. They were just watching and learning along with lots of other children.

'Tom would then stop here for tea on his way back to Carlow, so there was always lots of discussion. It didn't affect their academic performance. They spent a lot of time looking at the seniors in training, but they didn't neglect their schoolwork either.'

'We didn't miss a session that year, and we loved it,' Helena confirms. 'Liz and Caroline Murphy would always be there with us… and Des and Marie Mythen.'

THE FAMILY WERE out in force for Wexford's All-Ireland victory in 1996, with Rory having the added thrill of playing in the mini-sevens exhibition at half-time.

'That ensured we got two tickets from Cumann na mBunscoil, and then Mick managed to get two more as an All-Ireland medal holder,' Breda says. 'Helena and Ursula used them and sat beside the heroes of the 50s and 60s. The likes of Billy Rackard and Ned Wheeler looked after them very well when they realised who they were.

'Michael was on his own in the Cusack Stand. We were all scattered but we didn't worry about them because they were used to going to Croke Park. We always had an agreement that everyone would meet after the game at the Railway End.

'We promised them we would stay overnight in Dublin for the final. Michael and I were lucky enough to be invited to the hotel in Malahide for the banquet, and the children were in a nice B&B nearby.

'We brought them out to The Burlington Hotel the next day. The team attended another function there before heading home, and we wanted them to experience everything.'

The children quickly learned one thing when they started attending the big games: their daddy was public property.

While most journeys were made in the family car, sometimes they would take the train for an alternative experience and hop off for a bite to eat in Bray.

'We'd get on in Gorey, and the whole way up daddy would be in big demand. "Well Mick, what do you think today?"

'We'd hear that question over and over, and sure daddy would talk away to everyone,' Rory says.

'And then the team might lose, and there would be a cloud of depression on the train going home. The question would change then. "Well Mick, what will we do now?"'

AS THE YEARS progressed, and his children all made their mark with club and county, they amassed an array of medals and trophies that almost filled the house in Oulartwick from top to bottom.

Consider this, for starters: of the 36 senior championships played in Wexford since 2003, combining hurling and camogie, Oulart-The Ballagh have won a staggering 24, or two-thirds to be exact.

The camogie team has contested every final bar one since 2001, collecting 13 titles in the process. Helena, who captained the first-ever winners in 2003 from corner-back, won another two medals from that position before adding seven more after carrying on the family goalkeeping tradition.

Along the way she won four All-Ireland senior medals as Wexford's reserve netminder, along with one on the field with the intermediates in 2011. And she bowed out on the best possible note, as her last senior game with the club was in the All-Ireland final of 2015 when they beat Mullagh from Galway in Croke Park by 15 points.

Three years before, Oulart-The Ballagh were equally impressive in demolishing Drom-Inch of Tipperary by 3-13 to 0-5 to win that coveted title for the first time.

Helena would go on to manage the Wexford senior camogie team. In 2014 they won the Leinster title and only lost the All-Ireland semi-final after a replay to eventual winners Cork. She also managed the WIT Ashbourne camogie team that won an historic five-in-a-row (2009-'13). At the moment, she is a mentor with the Wexford under-16 hurling development squad of which Michael is manager.

Her parents agree, she is the most 'determined' of their children.

'She is probably more like her daddy from a temperamental point of view than any of the others,' Breda says. Mick concurs: 'She had to work harder at her game than the rest but she succeeded.'

Help was always readily at hand whenever it was needed. 'I was lucky enough to captain Oulart to win our first senior camogie title in 2003, but I didn't play well in the semi-final against Rathnure,' Helena says.

'In fact, I was never as poor and I was really disappointed in myself, I should have been taken off if truth be told and it upset me. I was probably quite harsh on myself too because I was captain. Between the semi-final and final daddy and Robbie spent three or four nights in the house going through what I needed to do in order to improve.

'All that was done to help me, and it worked. It typified the close-knit nature of the family. Whenever you were disappointed in sport, they would be there to remind you that life can be like that too. But there would always be someone to step up and offer to dig you out.'

Ursula has played in every single one of the club's county finals since 2001 – a staggering 20 games including one replay – with her Leinster semi-final versus St Jude's of Dublin put on hold at the start of 2021 as Covid-19's tentacles refused to let go.

Along with 13 county medals, five Leinsters and those two All-Irelands with the club, she won four All-Ireland senior titles with Wexford between 2007 and '12, captaining the team for the second leg of their three-in-a-row in 2011. Her senior inter-county debut came at the tender age of 14 between the posts, retiring 16 years later after a glittering career as one of the leading forwards in the history of the game.

She scored a combined 3-20 in those four All-Ireland final victories, and is a multiple Ashbourne Cup medalist as well as a four-time All Star award winner from 2010, '11, '12 and '14.

In a house filled with fun and banter, she likes to remind her daddy every now and again that he only has three!

'She fancies herself as a free-taker too, but when she says that I have to tell her about the day I put 10 of them over the bar against Blackwater when I was nearly 50 years old,' Mick laughs.

'When I was younger and started taking frees, daddy said he'd show me how to do it properly,' Ursula says. 'He brought us down to the field and put Helena standing behind the goal.

'Daddy was getting me to align myself in the right way, and he was frustrated because I wasn't doing it like he wanted. I have an unusual free-taking style even now... I'll only straighten up to face the posts at the last second.

'I kept putting the ball over the bar, but he was still cross because of my stance. We're going to have a free-taking competition some day, and that will settle it once and for all.

'If I do well in a game, he'll say, "I might give you that alright". But if the frees go over for me, I'll remind him it couldn't possibly be from anything he ever taught me!'

Remarkably, the four siblings have won a combined total of 44 county senior medals: 13 for Ursula, 11 for Michael, and 10 apiece for Helena and Rory. And they regard each and every one of them as precious, acutely aware that their father would have given anything 'To Win Just Once' as The Saw Doctors so memorably sang.

'Daddy and mammy instilled a love for sport in all of us, and gave us lots of opportunities,' Helena says. 'We all would have done gymnastics up to the age of 10, and it would have been my main sport. And from the time we started playing hurling with daddy in the living room, he would always emphasise the fun aspect.'

MICHAEL AND RORY would join Mick on the list of Leinster senior medalists from Wexford in 2004, and they were also on board when that elusive provincial title finally came to the club with a two-goal win over Cuala 11 years later.

The brothers have secured All-Ireland Féile na nGael, Leinster under-21 and Fitzgibbon Cup honours amongst a host of other accolades, simply too numerous to mention. Both were honoured for being centurions with Wexford, as Rory played 138 times between 2002 and '15, while Michael featured on 106 occasions from 2001 to '11.

Individual records weren't kept during Mick's era, but research undertaken for this book can confirm that he outlasted the two boys with 158 appearances – that's one up for daddy!

MICK JACOB CAN do no wrong in his children's eyes, although there was one occasion when his bond with Ursula was tested to the limits.

'Rory was on the under-14 Wexford team that won the Tony Forristal final in 1997, and the game was in Dungarvan,' she recalls. 'I travelled down with daddy, and Mary Leacy was with us. The traffic was heavy, so we were in a rush when we finally pulled in somewhere.

'Daddy's walk was more like a fast jog, and we struggled to keep up with him, we would have been 11 or 12 at the time. At one point I fell and cut my knee, and that increased the distance between us.

'By the time we got to the turnstiles, daddy had already gone in. We were shouting in at him, but he didn't hear us.

'The man on the stile wouldn't let us in, and we had no money between us. It was 1997 so neither of us had a phone either, and we didn't recognise any of the other people in the queue outside.

'We had to figure out some way of getting in. Eventually we went around to the far side of the pitch, and we were able to climb a wall and scramble over a wire fence.

'It was half-time before we made it over to the stand and eventually found daddy. And you know what? He was so engrossed in the game that he hadn't even noticed we were missing!

'I remember looking at him and thinking to myself... *Are you for real?* But he's made amends for that a hundred times over. We had a pretty brilliant childhood and adulthood, and we're very lucky with our two parents. They've always been there for us.'

After leaving Scoil Mochua in Oulart, the girls went to Coláiste Bríde while the boys attended the CBS on the opposite side of Enniscorthy town. All four won numerous schools medals before taking the same path down to Waterford IT for their third level education.

Helena and Rory are secondary school teachers in Gorey Community School and St Peter's College (Wexford) respectively. Michael has farmed the land at Ballinerode with his father for more than 15 years now, while Ursula is an administrator with Tusla, the child and family agency, when she's not appearing regularly on our TV screens as a hurling analyst with RTE. She holds a business degree in Sport and Recreation, and a masters in Sports Psychology.

When Mick finally called it a day as a player in 2000, one of the immediate bonuses came in his ability to attend more of the girls' camogie matches than ever before. However, neither felt neglected by their father in that regard beforehand.

'He's being too hard on himself if he thinks he wasn't around enough for us before he retired,' Helena says. 'Daddy and mammy were always there for all the big moments in our careers and our lives.'

'I'd be fairly anxious now as a spectator,' Mick admits. 'I'd nearly be the same as if I was playing the game myself.'

Breda says her husband 'would always be concentrating on our team, and wouldn't get involved with anyone else'.

She has a clear, if somewhat painful, memory of his reaction after Michael scored that wonder goal against Kilkenny in 2004. 'He can be animated enough at times. That day when we won, he turned to me and hugged me so tight that I thought my ribs were crushed. I wasn't able to breathe properly for a long time afterwards!'

THE JACOB FAMILY suffered a double blow in a short period in 2011. Ellen, Mick's inspiring mother, passed away on August 8 at the age of 92, while his uncle Owen followed just six weeks later.

Given the hardship Ellen endured in her younger years, Bridie and her brothers bow to nobody in their love and admiration for this wonderful woman. She remained strong and defiant to the last, taking her final breath in the arms of Christy and Robbie in the same house in Monavullen she had moved into under that cloak of unimaginable grief in 1956.

As if the pain of losing her beloved husband George wasn't enough, it was compounded by the death of her father Michael Kinsella in 1957.

By the time her mother Elizabeth would depart nine years later, Ellen had guided her four children into young adulthood and helped them over the numerous obstacles that can strike from all directions after the sudden loss of a parent.

'Bridie was particularly close to our mother in the years after we lost our father,' Robbie says. 'She might be giving a positive outlook to the three of us, but if she had any stresses she would always confide in Bridie.'

Breda remembers her as 'a fiercely determined woman' who could turn her hand to anything. 'She was a wonderful cook and homemaker, with a great flair for interior decoration. She was quite adept at home maintenance, and excelled at gardening and furniture restoration. She always looked for the best quality in things for the house, and in clothes. She really enjoyed shopping for fashionable outfits. That interest was turned to good account in organising fashion shows that raised huge funds for the GAA club when the main pitch was being purchased and developed.

'She also took charge of the catering for the 'Oulart Festivals of Marquee Dancing' that were held in the 70s.' Oulart-The Ballagh provided a guard of honour at her funeral and among the gifts brought to the altar were reminders of her long association with hurling.

Christy never left the family home, and the others are grateful to him for his devotion to her care.

'She wasn't too alert in the last four or five years, her memory was starting to fade,' Mick says. 'She was at the Leinster final in 2004 with Bridie, and she might have gone to the county final in 2007.'

'She wasn't that mobile near the end and would have spent most of her time in the house,' Robbie adds. 'She would go into Wexford with Christy once a week, but she didn't go to matches in the last few years.

'She made the dinner for us on the farm every day until near the end of her time,' Mick adds. 'She had hens over there too, and turkeys, she'd be selling them before Christmas.'

Rory remembers a special woman who always looked out for her grandchildren. 'Nanny was happy enough once you were doing something you enjoyed. She had a huge interest in hurling and loved talking about our matches.

'She was a massive figure on the farm when we were young. Herself and Owen got on fierce well, but she would go mad all the same if he wasn't keeping the place tidy. They could fight like cats and dogs.

'Owen died six weeks after nanny, and I'm convinced he said to himself... *I'm not going to go before her, I want to be the last one in the family.* About a week after nanny died, he said, "I can go now".'

Owen lived to the age of 86, and Ursula was one of his last visitors to show him the O'Duffy Cup after she captained Wexford to All-Ireland glory.

Mick's bond with his uncle was unbreakable after more than 50 years of working side by side, so it was fitting that he was with him in the final hours.

'Owen could be very sick but wouldn't want to go to the doctor... you had to read between the lines with him always. On the night he died I was there along with Bridie and Bill, and Anne and Peter Keane were visiting too.

'He was sitting on the chair and got up, saying, "I'll go down to bed now". I stayed there that night and heard a bit of noise from his room at about 1.30 or 2am. He died very peacefully and quickly.'

THE CHILD IN Mick Jacob has acquired a new focus in recent years.

'We have three grandchildren and he's absolutely besotted with them, he can't get enough of them,' Breda says. 'He's the softest-hearted man in the world and he adores those beautiful children.'

Seán – Michael and Joanne's lad – was 11 this May, while Rory and Judy have two tearaways in MJ, who turned four on the day before Christmas Eve, and Ella (2), who shares her September 7 birthday with aunt Ursula.

The days before Covid-19 were carefree and full of laughter whenever grandad and granny were paid a visit in Oulartwick. 'Daddy has such a fun-loving side, there's so much more to him than hurling,' Ursula says. 'He absolutely loves dancing, and you can always judge how good a wedding is by the length of time he'll spend on the dance floor.

'Before Covid he wouldn't miss the Wednesday night visits down to see poor Joan, God rest her, for bingo and dancing in *The Porter House.*

'He's very outgoing and is always in the thick of it, only stopping to sip his glass of water. Mammy would be happy to sit in the corner, but he'll dance with every woman in the place.

'And then he'd be visiting friends all over the parish. He has a way of connecting with people regardless of their age, it doesn't matter if they're young or old... he'll see the person behind that and will find something in common to talk about.

'For the last few years before Covid, the three women of the house would go on holiday and leave daddy behind. At first we were thinking... *How's Mick going to survive without us?* Sure half the parish would be feeling sorry for him and queueing up to look after him.'

URSULA RECALLS A question she was asked over and over during the Ashbourne Cup days with WIT. 'Katie Power, Collette Dormer, Trish Jackman, Sarah-Anne Fitzgerald... they'd all be wondering... *Will Mick be at the match today?* He'd always have a kind word for them, as well as lots of praise and encouragement.

'But the one thing, above all others, that gives him joy is spending time with his grandchildren,' Ursula adds. 'He's the biggest child himself, and they bring that out in him.' Mick's competitive instinct will never leave him, with Helena offering a prime example. 'On Christmas Day two years ago, we decided to have a few games in the evening, so we said we'd have a Fittest Family competition.

'Daddy was against Seán, and the two of them were down in the plank position. Daddy wasn't giving in, and this must have gone on for about three minutes until mammy leaned down and had a quiet word in his ear.

'Another time he learned how to bake bread. He's very proud of his porridge bread, and nothing would do him but to enter it in the "Best Bread" category at Killag Show. He was really put out when he didn't win!'

'It's great when the three youngsters are around us,' Mick says. 'Having grandchildren means so much to me, especially after my own father died so young. I missed out on plenty of that fun stuff myself, it was a lot to deal with from the age of 10. I'll make sure to get these three out and about with me as much as I can… doing whatever it is they enjoy.'

There's plenty of time for them to acquire a real taste for hurling. They will all grow and develop at their own pace and whatever it is they are interested in, Mick and Breda will encourage and support them. All that really matters is that 'they are healthy and happy, leading useful lives'.

Naturally, the doting grandparents would love for them to experience the joys of hurling and, if any of the next generation happen to don the famous red and black, they will have their two greatest supporters behind them all the way.

'We are a very close-knit family and we never miss an opportunity to celebrate all special occasions together. In December 2021, Ursula will marry Brendan Cruise, a very sound, likeable and sociable Westmeathman, who is already well integrated into our local community,' Mick says.

'They intend building close to the family home. Michael lives in a new house on the farm, under Oulart Hill, with his wife Joanne and Seán, and they are due their second child in August of 2021. Joanne is a highly qualified nurse, and she's fun-loving, and warm-hearted.

'Rory lives on the other side of the parish, in The Ballagh area, with his wife Judy, and MJ and Ella. Judy is a hard-working, progressive dairy-farmer, and she's got a kind and generous nature.'

'BREDA AND I are very fortunate to be blessed with good health, happy dispositions, great memories and… an attitude of gratitude.

'We count our blessings often.

'We have family and friends whom we love and care for, and we know that we can depend on them in good times and bad.

'What more can you ask for in life?'

All the Jacob men – Mick, Michael, Seán, MJ and Rory – on Michael's wedding day.

Michael and Joanne on their wedding day with Judy, Rory, MJ, Breda, Seán, Mick, Helena and Ursula.

« EPILOGUE »

IT'S A BIG birthday for Mick Jacob today, but only his nearest and dearest are able to congratulate him in person.

Covid-19 has seen to that, with Level 5 lockdown restrictions in full force as he turns 75.

And yet, for a man whose glass is always half-full, he is very happy with his lot. Blessed with good health and a positive outlook, he's constantly looking forward to the brighter days that will inevitably return.

The brief window when club games resumed from mid-July to early October 2020 produced one notable highlight.

Oulart-The Ballagh beat St Martin's by 3-17 to 2-12 in the senior camogie championship final, with Ursula contributing nine points on the way to her thirteenth county title, and first since 2016.

Unfortunately, Mick wasn't there in the flesh, but he was willing her on every step of the way, watching a live stream of the game in the company of Breda, Brendan, Christy and Michael's family.

'From the time we were young, I'd say to him, "Give me your energy" before a match, and he'd give me a big squeeze,' Ursula explains. 'I'm 35 years of age now, and that hasn't changed, I got another squeeze before leaving for the final.

'It was unusual not to hear him in Bellefield that day. The three people whose voices would stand out at our games are daddy, Margaret Leacy and Martin Storey... three legends.'

With restrictions in place, Ursula was lucky enough to win one admission ticket before the final.

'We decided to have a draw for it, and my name came out of the hat,' Helena says. 'Daddy was raging when he heard that, he's still convinced the draw was rigged!

'And he got on to me afterwards, because he said he couldn't hear me shouting on the live stream.'

Mick also watched the two lads in action with the club's second string in the intermediate A grade, while a promising young senior team exceeded many expectations by running Naomh Eanna to a point in the county semi-final.

Michael and Rory are 40 and 37 now, so they still have a long way to go before they can match their father's remarkable longevity of service in the red and black.

AND WHILE MICK is a sprightly 75, he'd happily play another game in the morning if his limbs would allow it.

'He'd still think he's good enough to be on the Wexford team,' Ursula confirms. 'We were watching a documentary on the Olympics lately, and he was saying he'd loved to have run at that level. He has always kept himself in such great shape.'

It's mainly sheep now on the 200 acres, along with a bit of tillage after a gradual easing away from cattle. And it's a father and son duo running the show, as Michael has been Mick's constant companion for more than 15 years at this stage.

Uncles Mikie and Owen passed away in 1998 and 2011 respectively and, at some point in between, Michael decided on a career change from banking and insurance to pursue his passion for the land.

Those fields under Oulart Hill continue to shape Mick's life, more than 60 years after he finished his schooling and joined the Kinsellas full-time.

However, he was home 'a little earlier than normal' on his 75th birthday, according to Helena, who was on baking duties earlier in the day. After the savouries, he sat down to eat a selection of his favourite desserts, made with extra care by his daughter to keep her daddy's high blood sugar levels in check.

'Mammy sent him to a support group after he was diagnosed with diabetes, and he was so proud to go back after six months and learn he had controlled it by changing his diet.'

After indulging his sweet tooth, an extra surprise lay in store. 'The others recorded happy birthday videos for him, and he got quite emotional looking at the children on screen,' Ursula says.

'MJ was on his new guitar imitating Bruce Springsteen, with Ella on the drums, and Seán had Molly the dog with him. It finished off with a short compilation of his hurling career that Ed Rowsome put together for us, and it was lovely.

'It was actually one of the nicest birthdays he ever had, and he really appreciated the good wishes from everyone.'

IN 1982, AT the age of 36 and preparing for a National League final against Kilkenny, Mick was warmly referred to as 'The prince of centre-backs' in a local newspaper preview.

And of all the words written about him, few encapsulate his hurling qualities in such a succinct, accurate manner.

His ability to inspire respect was a natural by-product of his own heroic displays. Leading by example came as second nature to a man whose grace under pressure and supreme style marked him out as one of Wexford's all-time hurling heroes.

It is generally accepted that Mick's three best-ever displays arrived in the All-Ireland senior final of 1976, and the county finals of 1974 and '82 respectively.

The unfortunate common denominator saw him on the losing side on all three occasions and that, in itself, is a true reflection of his greatness. After all, it's a lot easier to be the star on a winning team.

Despite various setbacks, Mick's career was characterised by sportsmanship, a humble acceptance of the outcome whether in victory or defeat, and a burning desire to improve for the next game.

His 158 senior appearances with Wexford featured 31 championship outings, 99 in the league, and 28 in various official secondary competitions.

The top five counties he faced were Kilkenny (33), Offaly (23), Cork (17), Tipperary (16) and Galway (15). His three most frequented venues were Croke Park (35), Nowlan Park (14) and Semple Stadium (14), with 43 appearances on home soil shared between Wexford Park (13), New Ross (13), Bellefield (8), Gorey (6) and St Patrick's Park (3).

Building on those Leinster and All-Ireland senior medals as a substitute in 1968, he featured on the field for two more provincial titles in 1976 and '77 along with National League (1973), Oireachtas, Walsh Cup, Kehoe Cup and Grounds tournament successes.

He was a runner-up in three All-Ireland senior finals along with three National Leagues, eight Leinster finals, and three county finals. At the outset of his career, he won an All-Ireland under-21 and three provincial medals along with a Leinster intermediate title.

On the individual awards front, those three All Stars plus six tours of the USA (three as a replacement) were undoubted highlights, along with six Railway Cup medals (three as a substitute).

His outstanding ability saw him line out in Wembley, New York, San Francisco, Los Angeles, Amsterdam, Inverness and Coventry – not bad going for an unassuming son of Oulart Hill!

In truth, a true warrior of Oulart Hill.

AND IN ALL that time, he never lost sight of his chief goal.

'I always wanted to be the star, whether I was having a puck-around in the school yard or playing in an All-Ireland final.'

That he succeeded so admirably isn't open to debate.

Mick Jacob, the prince of centre-backs and a class act, filled hurling hearts with joy wherever he went. The people of Oulart-The Ballagh and Wexford will be forever in his debt.

Clockwise (top left): Ella and MJ with Breda and Mick after Covid restrictions were lifted in summer 2020; Ella and MJ helping their grandad on the farm; Mick and Seán at Ella's Christening in December 2019; with Helena at the wedding of Bob, Robbie's son; Breda and Mick with Ursula and her fiancé Brendan Cruise; Mick and Breda at home before leaving to watch Wexford win the Leinster hurling final in 2019.

One of the greatest achievements in Oulart-The Ballagh's history was becoming the only Wexford hurling team to win five-in-a-row of senior championship titles between 2009 and '13. Oulart schoolteacher Hamish Stuart, a native of New Zealand, composed this music in honour of the magnificent occasion. It is now a regular part of the school band's repertoire.